D0380613

THE CALCULUS

*the text of this book is printed
on 100% recycled paper*

ABOUT THE AUTHOR

C. O. Oakley received the degrees of B.S. in engineering at the University of Texas, M.S. in mathematics at Brown University, and Ph.D. in mathematics at the University of Illinois. He has taught in all these institutions as well as in Bryn Mawr College and the University of Delaware. He has recently retired as head of the mathematics department at Haverford College, and is at present in Australia on a Fulbright Fellowship. Professor Oakley is a Governor of the Mathematical Association of America, and has served as general mathematics editor of *Colliers Encyclopedia*. His publications include more than twenty mathematical papers in American and foreign learned journals, *Principles of Mathematics* (with C. B. Allendoerfer), *Analytic Geometry* (a companion Barnes & Noble Outline), and *Calculus: A Modern Approach*.

THE CALCULUS

C. O. OAKLEY

Professor Emeritus
Department of Mathematics
Haverford College

BARNES & NOBLE BOOKS
A DIVISION OF HARPER & ROW, PUBLISHERS
New York, Hagerstown, San Francisco, London

©
Copyright, 1944, 1957

by Harper & Row, Publishers, Inc.

All rights reserved. No part of this book may be reproduced or utilized in any form or by any means, electronic or mechanical, including photocopying or recording, or by any information storage and retrieval system, without permission in writing from the publisher.

L. C. catalogue card number : 57–12290

ISBN: 0-06-460048-3

Manufactured in the United States of America

78 79 80   12 11 10 9 8

PREFACE

This Outline has been prepared with three fundamental objectives in mind: 1st, to furnish enough of the standard tools of the Calculus to enable the reader to make computations in the main branches of the subject met with in a first study; 2nd, to present some of the simpler proofs and derivations so as to encourage the serious student in his efforts toward obtaining at least a partial understanding of the basic principles involved; and 3rd, to make the presentation in a self-explanatory outline form designed for self-instruction.

The Calculus is, in essence, a study of infinitesimals and of limiting processes — entirely new ideas to the person who has had only limited training in high school mathematics. It would require many books the size of this to make a full and detailed analysis of these operations.

Even the mathematically inclined will have difficulty in his study of the Calculus unless he has a fair understanding of the usual subject matter found in a freshman college course in Algebra, Trigonometry, and Analytic Geometry. For a quick review of this material and as a convenient source of information, Chapter I is devoted wholly to Reference Formulae and Graphs pertaining to these fields.

Throughout we have made an attempt not only to illuminate the discussions in the main body of the Outline but also to support the worked-out Illustrations by means of clearly and accurately drawn figures and to present typical and standard problems in the Exercises for which answers are supplied. These problems cover a wide range of applications in both pure and applied mathematics and they, along with the examination questions in Appendix A, should furnish the student with adequate review material for quizzes and final tests. Appendix B contains a short table of the most useful elementary integrals.

GREEK ALPHABET

Letters		Names	Letters		Names	Letters		Names
A	α	Alpha	I	ι	Iota	P	ρ	Rho
B	β	Beta	K	κ	Kappa	Σ	σ	Sigma
Γ	γ	Gamma	Λ	λ	Lambda	T	τ	Tau
Δ	δ	Delta	M	μ	Mu	Υ	υ	Upsilon
E	ε	Epsilon	N	ν	Nu	Φ	φ	Phi
Z	ζ	Zeta	Ξ	ξ	Xi	X	χ	Chi
H	η	Eta	O	o	Omicron	Ψ	ψ	Psi
Θ	θ	Theta	Π	π	Pi	Ω	ω	Omega

TABLE OF CONTENTS

THE CALCULUS

CHAPTER I

REFERENCE FORMULAE AND GRAPHS

1. Basic Formulae. In a study of the calculus, the student will find constant need of a list of formulae of reference. For this reason we begin this Outline with a selection of the more important formulae taken from the fields of algebra, geometry, trigonometry, and analytic geometry of two and three dimensions. We also list the equations and graphs of many of the standard curves, a knowledge of which will be of great aid to the student.

2. Algebra.

(1) *Quadratic equation.* The roots (solutions) of the quadratic equation $ax^2 + bx + c = 0$ are

$$x = \frac{-b \pm \sqrt{b^2 - 4\,ac}}{2\,a}.$$

The expression $\Delta = b^2 - 4\,ac$ is called the discriminant.
(a) If $\Delta > 0$, the roots are real and distinct;
(b) If $\Delta = 0$, the roots are real and equal;
(c) If $\Delta < 0$, the roots are complex.

(2) *Factorial notation.* The symbol $n!$, called "n factorial," stands for the product of the first n (positive) integers.

(a) $n! = 1 \cdot 2 \cdot 3 \cdots n$;   (b) $0! = 1$, by definition.

(3) *Binomial theorem.* The expansion of $(a + b)^n$, where n is a positive integer, is

(a) $(a + b)^n = a^n + na^{n-1}b + \dfrac{n(n-1)}{2!}\,a^{n-2}b^2$

$$+ \frac{n(n-1)(n-2)}{3!}\,a^{n-3}b^3 + \cdots$$

$$+ \frac{n(n-1)(n-2) \cdots (n-r+2)}{(r-1)!}\,a^{n-r+1}b^{r-1}$$

$$+ \cdots + b^n;$$

(b) The rth term in this expansion is

$$\frac{n(n-1)(n-2)\cdots(n-r+2)}{(r-1)!}\,a^{n-r+1}b^{r-1}.$$

(4) *Logarithms.*

(a) If $a^b = x$, then, by definition of logarithm, $\log_a x = b$,

(b) $\log_b a = \dfrac{1}{\log_a b}$,

To any base:

(c) $\log MN = \log M + \log N$,

(d) $\log M^A = A \log M$,

(e) $\log \dfrac{M}{N} = \log MN^{-1} = \log M - \log N$,

(f) $\log \sqrt[n]{M} = \log M^{\frac{1}{n}} = \dfrac{1}{n} \log M$.

3. Geometry.

(1) *Relation between degree measure and radian measure:*

$$360° = 2\pi \text{ radians} = 1 \text{ revolution.}$$

(2) *Mensuration formulae.* Let r denote radius; θ, central angle in radians; S, arc; h, altitude; b, length of base; s, slant height; A, area of base.

	CIRCUMFERENCE	AREA	VOLUME
(a) Circle	$2\pi r$	πr^2	
(b) Circular sector		$\frac{1}{2} r^2\theta$	
(c) Triangle		$\frac{1}{2} bh$	
(d) Trapezoid		$\frac{1}{2}(b_1 + b_2)h$	
(e) Prism			Ah
(f) Right circular cylinder (limiting case of a prism)	$2\pi rh$		$Ah = \pi r^2 h$
(g) Pyramid			$\frac{1}{3} Ah$
(h) Right circular cone (limiting case of a pyramid)		$\pi rs = \pi r\sqrt{r^2 + h^2}$	$\frac{1}{3}\pi r^2 h$
(i) Sphere		$4\pi r^2$	$\frac{4}{3}\pi r^3$

4. Trigonometry.

(1) *Fundamental identities.*

(a) $\sin^2 x + \cos^2 x = 1$, (b) $1 + \tan^2 x = \sec^2 x$,
  (c) $1 + \cot^2 x = \csc^2 x$.

(2) *Reduction formulae rule:*

1st. Any trigonometric function of the angle $\left(k\dfrac{\pi}{2} \pm \alpha\right)$ is equal to $(\pm)$ the same function of α, if k is even, and is equal to $(\pm)$ the cofunction of α if k is odd.

2nd. The " $+$ " sign is used if the original function of the original angle $\left(k\dfrac{\pi}{2} \pm \alpha\right)$ is positive; the " $-$ " sign is used if the original function is negative. The sign of the original function of $\left(k\dfrac{\pi}{2} \pm \alpha\right)$ is determined by the usual quadrantal conventions. To summarize

$$\text{Any function of } \left(k\frac{\pi}{2} \pm \alpha\right) = \pm \begin{cases} \text{Same function of } \alpha, \text{ if } k \text{ is even; co-} \\ \text{function of } \alpha, \text{ if } k \text{ is odd. Use sign} \\ \text{of original function of } \left(k\frac{\pi}{2} \pm \alpha\right). \end{cases}$$

(3) *Functions of the sum and difference of two angles.*

(a) $\sin (x \pm y) = \sin x \cos y \pm \cos x \sin y$,

(b) $\cos (x \pm y) = \cos x \cos y \mp \sin x \sin y$,

(c) $\tan (x \pm y) = \dfrac{\tan x \pm \tan y}{1 \mp \tan x \tan y}$.

(4) *Multiple angle formulae.*

(a) $\sin 2x = 2 \sin x \cos x$,

(b) $\cos 2x = \cos^2 x - \sin^2 x = 2 \cos^2 x - 1 = 1 - 2 \sin^2 x$,

(c) $\tan 2x = \dfrac{2 \tan x}{1 - \tan^2 x}$,

(d) $\sin \dfrac{x}{2} = \sqrt{\dfrac{1 - \cos x}{2}}$,

(e) $\cos \dfrac{x}{2} = \sqrt{\dfrac{1 + \cos x}{2}}$,

(f) $\tan \dfrac{x}{2} = \sqrt{\dfrac{1 - \cos x}{1 + \cos x}} = \dfrac{1 - \cos x}{\sin x} = \dfrac{\sin x}{1 + \cos x}$.

(5) *Sum and product formulae.*

(a) $\sin x + \sin y = 2 \sin \frac{1}{2}(x + y) \cos \frac{1}{2}(x - y)$,

(b) $\sin x - \sin y = 2 \cos \frac{1}{2}(x + y) \sin \frac{1}{2}(x - y)$,

(c) $\cos x + \cos y = 2 \cos \frac{1}{2}(x + y) \cos \frac{1}{2}(x - y)$,

(d) $\cos x - \cos y = -2 \sin \frac{1}{2}(x + y) \sin \frac{1}{2}(x - y)$,

(e) $\sin x \sin y = \frac{1}{2} \cos (x - y) - \frac{1}{2} \cos (x + y)$,

(f) $\sin x \cos y = \frac{1}{2} \sin (x - y) + \frac{1}{2} \sin (x + y)$,

(g) $\cos x \cos y = \frac{1}{2} \cos (x - y) + \frac{1}{2} \cos (x + y)$.

(6) *Formulae for plane triangles.* Let a, b, c be sides; A, B, C opposite angles; $s = \dfrac{a + b + c}{2}$, semi-perimeter; $r = \sqrt{\dfrac{(s - a)(s - b)(s - c)}{s}}$, radius of the inscribed circle; R, radius of the circumscribed circle; K, area.

(a) Law of sines: $\dfrac{a}{\sin A} = \dfrac{b}{\sin B} = \dfrac{c}{\sin C} = 2R$,

(b) Law of cosines: $a^2 = b^2 + c^2 - 2bc \cos A$,

(c) Law of tangents: $\dfrac{a + b}{a - b} = \dfrac{\tan \frac{1}{2}(A + B)}{\tan \frac{1}{2}(A - B)}$,

(d) Tangent of half angle: $\tan \frac{1}{2} A = \dfrac{r}{s - a}$,

(e) Area: $K = \frac{1}{2} ab \sin C = \sqrt{s(s - a)(s - b)(s - c)} = rs = \dfrac{abc}{4R}$.

5. Plane Analytic Geometry.

(1) *Distance between two points:* $d = \sqrt{(x_2 - x_1)^2 + (y_2 - y_1)^2}$.

(2) *Slope of line through two points:* $m = \dfrac{y_2 - y_1}{x_2 - x_1}$.

(3) *Angle between two lines:*

(a) $\tan \theta_{12} = \dfrac{m_2 - m_1}{1 + m_1 m_2}$, where θ_{12} designates the angle from line 1 to line 2 (counterclockwise);

(b) $\cos \theta = \lambda_1 \lambda_2 + \mu_1 \mu_2$, where λ_1 is the cosine of the angle between the first line and the X-axis and μ_1 is the cosine of the angle between the first line and the Y-axis, and similarly for λ_2 and μ_2.

(4) *Two lines are parallel if* $m_1 = m_2$ (slopes) or if $\lambda_1 \lambda_2 + \mu_1 \mu_2 = 1$ (direction cosines).

(5) *Two lines are perpendicular* if $m_1 = -\dfrac{1}{m_2}$ (slopes) **or if**
$\lambda_1\lambda_2 + \mu_1\mu_2 = 0$ (direction cosines).

(6) *Forms of the equation of a straight line and their graphs.*

(a) General: $ax + by + c = 0$,

(b) Two-point: $\dfrac{y - y_1}{x - x_1} = \dfrac{y_2 - y_1}{x_2 - x_1}$,

(c) Point-slope: $y - y_1 = m(x - x_1)$,

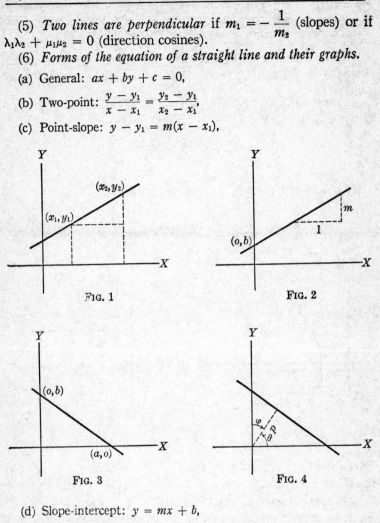

FIG. 1   FIG. 2

FIG. 3   FIG. 4

(d) Slope-intercept: $y = mx + b$,

(e) Intercept: $\dfrac{x}{a} + \dfrac{y}{b} = 1$,

(f) Parallel to Y-axis: $x = k$,

(g) Parallel to X-axis: $y = k$,

(h) Normal form: $x \cos \theta + y \sin \theta - p = 0$.

Note that (h) could also be written $x \cos \theta + y \cos \varphi - p = 0$,
where φ is the angle between the normal and the Y-axis. Or, writing

$\lambda = \cos\theta$, $\mu = \cos\varphi$, we have $\lambda x + \mu y - p = 0$, λ and μ being direction cosines of the normal to the line. Note that $\lambda^2 + \mu^2 = 1$.

(7) *To reduce the general equation $ax + by + c = 0$ to normal form* divide through by $\pm\sqrt{a^2 + b^2}$ and choose sign opposite to that of c.

(8) *The distance from a line $ax + by + c = 0$ to a point $P(x_1, y_1)$ is given by*

$$d = \frac{ax_1 + by_1 + c}{\pm\sqrt{a^2 + b^2}}.$$

(9) *Standard forms of the conic sections.*

(a) PARABOLA

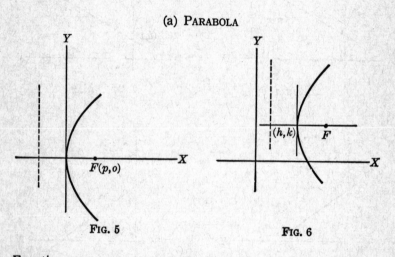

FIG. 5   FIG. 6

Equation:	$y^2 = 4px$	$(y - k)^2 = 4p(x - h)$
Coordinates of vertex:	$V(0, 0)$	$V(h, k)$
Coordinates of focus:	$F(p, 0)$	$F(h + p, k)$
Equation of directrix:	$x = -p$	$x = h - p$
Length of latus rectum:	$LL' = 4p$	$LL' = 4p$

(b) CIRCLE

Equation:	$x^2 + y^2 = r^2$	$(x - h)^2 + (y - k)^2 = r^2$
Coordinates of center:	$C(0, 0)$	$C(h, k)$
Radius:	r	r

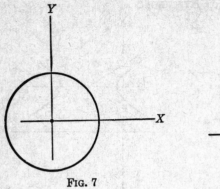

FIG. 7

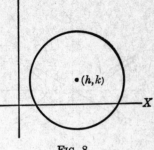

FIG. 8

(c) ELLIPSE

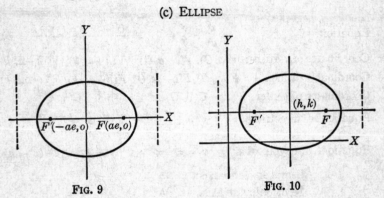

FIG. 9

FIG. 10

Equation:	$\dfrac{x^2}{a^2} + \dfrac{y^2}{b^2} = 1$	$\dfrac{(x-h)^2}{a^2} + \dfrac{(y-k)^2}{b^2} = 1$
Coordinates of vertices:	$V(a, O), V'(-a, O)$	$V(h+a, k), V'(h-a, k)$
Coordinates of foci:	$F(ae, O), F'(-ae, O)$	$F(h+ae, k), F'(h-ae, k)$
Coordinates of center:	$C(O, O)$	$C(h, k)$
Equations of directrices:	$x = \pm \dfrac{a}{e}$	$x = h \pm \dfrac{a}{e}$
Semimajor axis:	a	
Semiminor axis:	b	
Eccentricity:	$e = \dfrac{\sqrt{a^2 - b^2}}{a} < 1$	
Length of latus rectum:	$LL' = \dfrac{2\,b^2}{a}$	

(d) HYPERBOLA

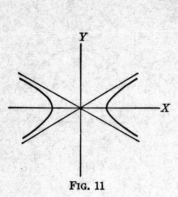

FIG. 11

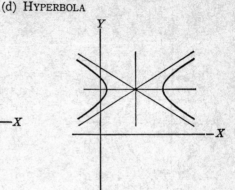

FIG. 12

Equation: $\dfrac{x^2}{a^2} - \dfrac{y^2}{b^2} = 1$ $\dfrac{(x-h)^2}{a^2} - \dfrac{(y-k)^2}{b^2} = 1$

Coordinates of vertices: $V(a, O), V'(-a, O)$ $V(h+a, k), V'(h-a, k)$

Coordinates of foci: $F(ae, O), F'(-ae, O)$ $F(h+ae, k), F'(h-ae, k)$

Coordinates of center: $C(O, O)$ $C(h, k)$

Equations of directrices: $x = \pm \dfrac{a}{e}$ $x = h \pm \dfrac{a}{e}$

Equations of asymptotes: $y = \pm \dfrac{b}{a} x$ $y - k = \pm \dfrac{b}{a}(x - h)$

Semitransverse axis: a

Semiconjugate axis: b

Eccentricity: $e = \dfrac{\sqrt{a^2 + b^2}}{a} > 1$

Length of latus rectum: $LL' = \dfrac{2 b^2}{a}$

(e) Polar equation of a conic with focus at the pole and directrix perpendicular to the polar axis.

$$\rho = \frac{\pm\, ep}{1 \mp e \cos \theta}.$$

6. Solid Analytic Geometry.

(1) *Distance between two points:*

$$d = \sqrt{(x_2 - x_1)^2 + (y_2 - y_1)^2 + (z_2 - z_1)^2}.$$

(2) *Direction cosines of a line:* λ, μ, ν.

$$\lambda = \cos \alpha, \; \mu = \cos \beta, \; \nu = \cos \gamma,$$

α, β, γ being the angles made by the line and the positive directions of the coordinate axes X, Y, Z, respectively; and $\lambda^2 + \mu^2 + \nu^2 = 1$.

(3) *Direction numbers a, b, c* are proportional to the direction cosines when $a = k\lambda$, $b = k\mu$, $c = k\nu$.

(4) *Equation of a plane.*

(a) General: $ax + by + cz + d = 0$,

a, b, c are direction numbers of a line perpendicular to the plane;

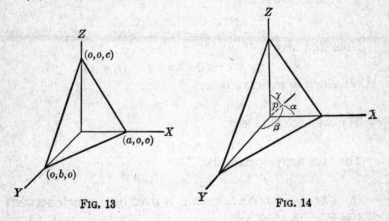

FIG. 13   FIG. 14

(b) Intercept: $\dfrac{x}{a} + \dfrac{y}{b} + \dfrac{z}{c} = 1$;

(c) Normal form: $\lambda x + \mu y + \nu z - p = 0$.

To reduce the general equation $ax + by + cz + d = 0$ to normal form divide through by $\pm \sqrt{a^2 + b^2 + c^2}$ and choose sign opposite to that of d:

$$\frac{ax + by + cz + d}{\pm \sqrt{a^2 + b^2 + c^2}} = 0.$$

(5) *The distance from a plane* $ax + by + cz + d = 0$ *to a point* $P(x_1, y_1, z_1)$ is given by

$$D = \frac{ax_1 + by_1 + cz_1 + d}{\pm \sqrt{a^2 + b^2 + c^2}}.$$

(6) *Equations of a line.*

(a) Intersection of two planes:

$$\begin{cases} a_1x + b_1y + c_1z + d_1 = 0, \\ a_2x + b_2y + c_2z + d_2 = 0. \end{cases}$$

For this line

$$\lambda : \mu : \nu = \begin{vmatrix} b_1 & c_1 \\ b_2 & c_2 \end{vmatrix} : - \begin{vmatrix} a_1 & c_1 \\ a_2 & c_2 \end{vmatrix} : \begin{vmatrix} a_1 & b_1 \\ a_2 & b_2 \end{vmatrix}.$$

(b) Through (x_1, y_1, z_1) with direction numbers a, b, c:

$$\frac{x - x_1}{a} = \frac{y - y_1}{b} = \frac{z - z_1}{c}.$$

This is sometimes called the symmetric form.

(c) Through two points:

$$\frac{x - x_1}{x_2 - x_1} = \frac{y - y_1}{y_2 - y_1} = \frac{z - z_1}{z_2 - z_1}.$$

Note that here

$$\lambda : \mu : \nu = (x_2 - x_1) : (y_2 - y_1) : (z_2 - z_1).$$

(7) *Angle between two lines.*

$$\cos \theta = \lambda_1\lambda_2 + \mu_1\mu_2 + \nu_1\nu_2.$$

The lines are parallel if

$$\lambda_1\lambda_2 + \mu_1\mu_2 + \nu_1\nu_2 = 1.$$

The lines are perpendicular if

$$\lambda_1\lambda_2 + \mu_1\mu_2 + \nu_1\nu_2 = 0.$$

(8) *The angle between two planes* is given by the angle between normals to the planes.

(9) *Standard forms of the quadric surfaces.*

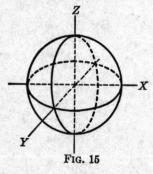

FIG. 15

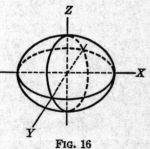

FIG. 16

(a) SPHERE: $x^2 + y^2 + z^2 = r^2$ **(b)** ELLIPSOID: $\dfrac{x^2}{a^2} + \dfrac{y^2}{b^2} + \dfrac{z^2}{c^2} = 1$

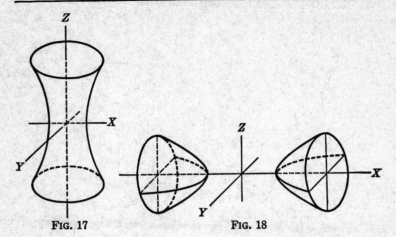

FIG. 17

FIG. 18

(c) HYPERBOLOID OF ONE SHEET:

$$\frac{x^2}{a^2} + \frac{y^2}{b^2} - \frac{z^2}{c^2} = 1$$

(d) HYPERBOLOID OF TWO SHEETS:

$$\frac{x^2}{a^2} - \frac{y^2}{b^2} - \frac{z^2}{c^2} = 1$$

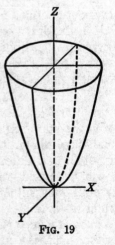

FIG. 19

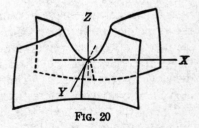

FIG. 20

(e) ELLIPTIC PARABOLOID:

$$\frac{x^2}{a^2} + \frac{y^2}{b^2} = cz$$

(f) HYPERBOLIC PARABOLOID:

$$\frac{x^2}{a^2} - \frac{y^2}{b^2} = cz$$

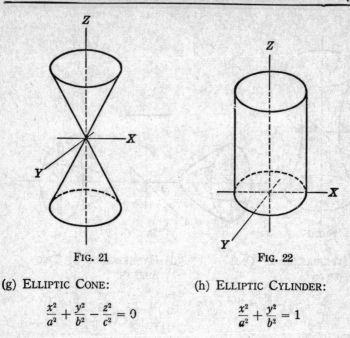

FIG. 21   FIG. 22

(g) ELLIPTIC CONE: (h) ELLIPTIC CYLINDER:

$$\frac{x^2}{a^2} + \frac{y^2}{b^2} - \frac{z^2}{c^2} = 0$$ $$\frac{x^2}{a^2} + \frac{y^2}{b^2} = 1$$

Note that the equation of the elliptic cylinder contains only two variables and that the cylinder extends in the direction of the axis of the missing variable. This is typical: the equation of any cylindrical surface whose elements are parallel to one of the coordinate axes will not contain the variable of that axis.

7. Principles of Graphing. Since it is essential that the student of the calculus have a sound basic working knowledge of the principles of graphing both in two and three dimensions, we now give a quick review and summary of them. Later to these algebraic and geometric methods will be added those developed in the calculus. The combined set of tools will make curve tracing a more interesting and a lighter task.

To plot the function $y = f(x)$, X- and Y-axes are taken at right angles (rectangular coordinates). The horizontal axis is usually designated X. A point A (see Fig. 23) is placed in the plane above a point x_1 on the X-axis at a height which corresponds to the value y_1 of the function. The coordinates of A are x_1 and

y_1, written $A(x_1, y_1)$ or simply (x_1, y_1). The graph of $y = f(x)$ is the curve obtained by joining consecutive points A, B, etc.

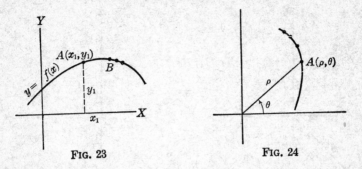

FIG. 23   FIG. 24

To plot the function $\rho = f(\theta)$ polar coordinates are indicated (see Fig. 24). For a given angle θ (radians) ρ is determined as a distance from the pole (origin) along the radius vector. The point A has coordinates (ρ, θ); A also has coordinates $(-\rho, \theta + \pi)$. The graph is the locus of points which satisfy the relation $\rho = f(\theta)$.

In either rectangular or polar coordinates parametric equations might be used: $x = f(t)$, $y = g(t)$; or $\rho = f(t)$, $\theta = g(t)$. In either case corresponding values of x and y, ρ and θ, are determined by assigning arbitrary values to the parameter t; these number pairs (x, y), (ρ, θ) are then plotted as before.

The main items of consideration in the tracing of a curve are:

(1) *Intercepts.* Plot the points where the curve crosses the axes.

(2) *Symmetry.*

(a) The curve is symmetric with respect to the X-axis if the equation remains unchanged when $-y$ is substituted for $+y$.

(b) The curve is symmetric with respect to the Y-axis if the equation remains unchanged when $-x$ is substituted for $+x$.

(c) The curve is symmetric with respect to the origin if the equation remains unchanged when $-x$ and $-y$ are substituted for $+x$ and $+y$ respectively.

(3) *Extent.*

(a) Determine whether the graph lies wholly in a finite portion of space.

(b) Indicate the points of discontinuity.

(c) Determine and sketch the asymptotes.

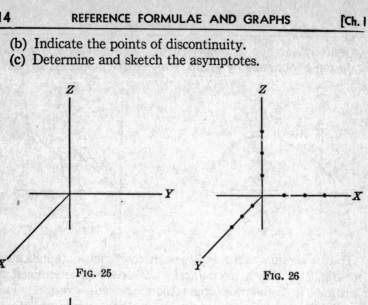

FIG. 25

FIG. 26

FIG. 27

FIG. 28

To plot the surface represented by the function $z = f(x, y)$ we may take (rectangular coordinates) a right-handed system of axes as in Fig. 25 or a left-handed system as in Fig. 26. Or cylindrical coordinates may be indicated (Fig. 27) where the given function is of the form $z = f(\rho, \theta)$. Again a spherical system of coordinates is used (Fig. 28) where the function is of the form $r = f(\theta, \varphi)$. No matter what system is used care must be exercised in the choice of units. For example note that in Fig. 26 the x and the z units are geometrically equal in length since these axes lie in the plane of the paper; but the y unit is indicated by a smaller segment since there is foreshortening in the y direction. *It is worth mentioning that the surfaces drawn will not be in true perspective but nevertheless will look something like perspective figures.*

The main items of consideration in the sketching of surfaces are:

(4) *Intercepts.*

(a) Plot the points where the surface crosses the axes.

(b) Plot the traces in the coordinate planes.

(c) Determine the character of the traces in planes parallel to the coordinate planes even though these curves may not be included in the graph.

(5) *Symmetry.*

The surface is symmetric with respect to the XY-plane if the equation remains unchanged when $-z$ is substituted for $+z$. Similarly for the other coordinate planes.

(6) *Extent.*

8. Graphs for Reference. We have already drawn the graphs of certain standard equations studied in analytic geometry. The student should be familiar with them and with the graphs of the trigonometric functions (Figs. 29–40). He should also develop at least a passing acquaintance with certain other equations and their graphs as he proceeds in his study of the calculus. We reproduce these in Figs. 41–66.

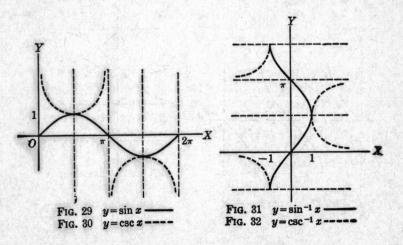

FIG. 29 $y = \sin x$ ———
FIG. 30 $y = \csc x$ - - - -

FIG. 31 $y = \sin^{-1} x$ ———
FIG. 32 $y = \csc^{-1} x$ - - - - -

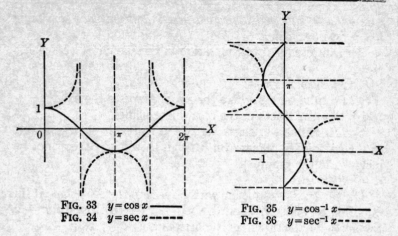

FIG. 33 $y = \cos x$ ——
FIG. 34 $y = \sec x$ - - - -

FIG. 35 $y = \cos^{-1} x$ ——
FIG. 36 $y = \sec^{-1} x$ - - - -

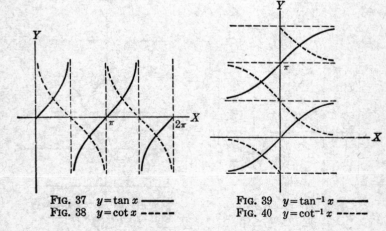

FIG. 37 $y = \tan x$ ——
FIG. 38 $y = \cot x$ - - - -

FIG. 39 $y = \tan^{-1} x$ ——
FIG. 40 $y = \cot^{-1} x$ - - - -

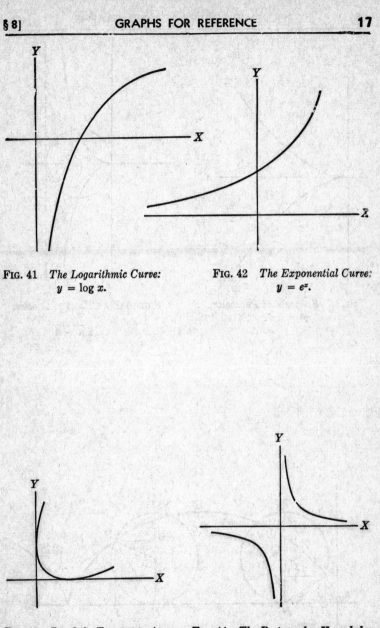

FIG. 41   *The Logarithmic Curve:*
$y = \log x$.

FIG. 42   *The Exponential Curve:*
$y = e^x$.

FIG. 43   *Parabola Tangent to Axes:*
$x^{\frac{1}{2}} + y^{\frac{1}{2}} = a^{\frac{1}{2}}$.

FIG. 44   *The Rectangular Hyperbola:*
$y = \dfrac{1}{x}$.

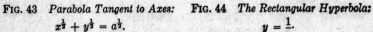

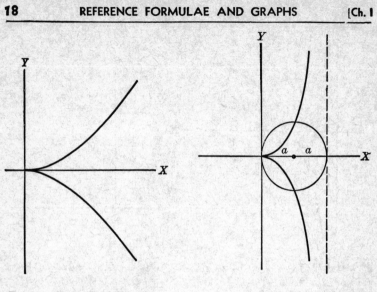

FIG. 45   *Semicubical Parabola:*
$$y^2 = ax^3.$$

FIG. 46 *The Cissoid of Diocles:*
$$y^2 = \frac{x^3}{2\,a - x}.$$

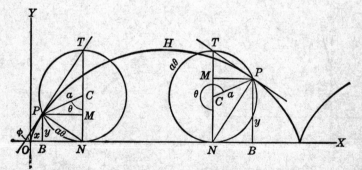

FIG. 47   *The Cycloid:*
$$x = a(\theta - \sin \theta), \quad y = a(1 - \cos \theta).$$

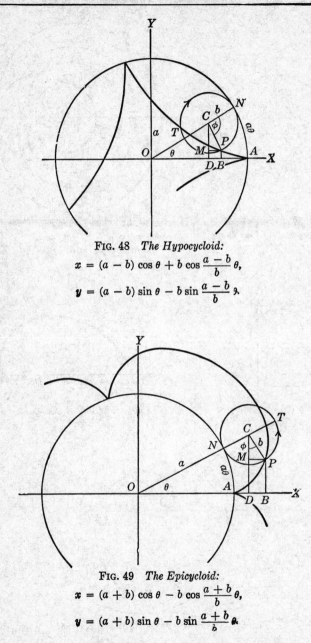

FIG. 48   *The Hypocycloid:*

$$x = (a - b) \cos \theta + b \cos \frac{a - b}{b} \theta,$$

$$y = (a - b) \sin \theta - b \sin \frac{a - b}{b} \theta.$$

FIG. 49   *The Epicycloid:*

$$x = (a + b) \cos \theta - b \cos \frac{a + b}{b} \theta,$$

$$y = (a + b) \sin \theta - b \sin \frac{a + b}{b} \theta.$$

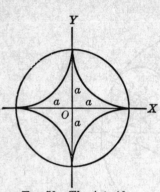

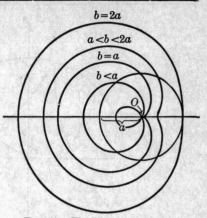

FIG. 50 *The Astroid:*
(Hypocycloid of four cusps)
$$x^{\frac{2}{3}} + y^{\frac{2}{3}} = a^{\frac{2}{3}}.$$

FIG. 51 *The Limaçon of Pascal:*
$$\rho = b - a \cos \theta.$$
(Cardioid if $b = a$. See FIG. 52.)

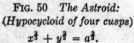

FIG. 52 *The Cardioid:*
$$\rho = a(1 - \cos \theta).$$

FIG. 53 *The Logarithmic or Equiangular Spiral:*
$$\rho = a e^{b\theta}.$$

The figure is drawn for $b = \frac{1}{2}$

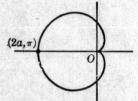

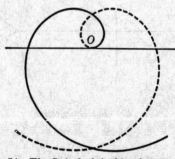

FIG. 54 *The Spiral of Archimedes:* $\rho = a\theta.$

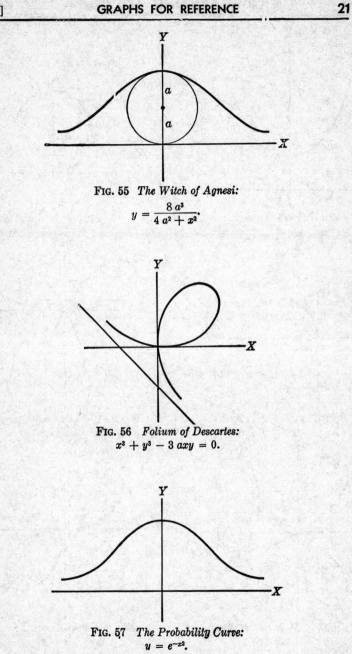

FIG. 55   *The Witch of Agnesi:*
$$y = \frac{8\,a^3}{4\,a^2 + x^2}.$$

FIG. 56   *Folium of Descartes:*
$$x^3 + y^3 - 3\,axy = 0.$$

FIG. 57   *The Probability Curve:*
$$u = e^{-x^2}.$$

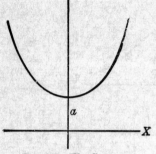

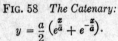

Fig. 58   *The Catenary:*
$$y = \frac{a}{2}\left(e^{\frac{x}{a}} + e^{-\frac{x}{a}}\right).$$

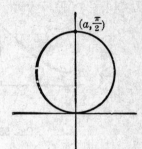

Fig. 59 $\rho = a \sin \theta.$

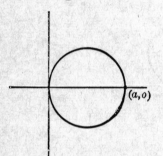

Fig. 60 $\rho = a \cos \theta.$

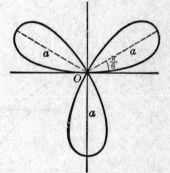

Fig. 61   *Three-Leaved Rose:*
$$\rho = a \sin 3\theta.$$

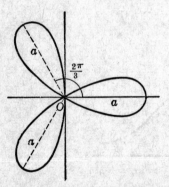

Fig. 62   *Three-Leaved Rose:*
$$\rho = a \cos 3\theta.$$

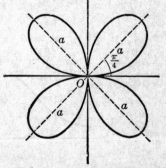

Fig. 63   *Four-Leaved Rose:*
$$\rho = a \sin 2\theta.$$

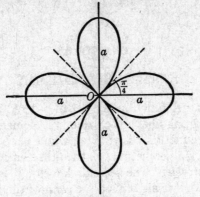

FIG. 64 *Four-Leaved Rose:*
$\rho = a \cos 2\theta.$

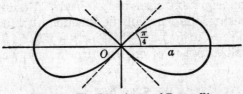

FIG. 65 *The Lemniscate of Bernoulli:*
$$\rho^2 = a^2 \cos 2\theta;$$
$$x = a \cos \theta \sqrt{\cos 2\theta}, \quad y = a \sin \theta \sqrt{\cos 2\theta}.$$

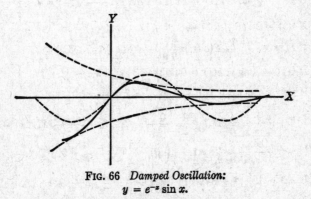

FIG. 66 *Damped Oscillation:*
$y = e^{-x} \sin x.$

CHAPTER II

FUNCTIONS AND LIMITS

9. Functions. A function is a set of ordered pairs such that no two ordered pairs have the same first element. A common notation for a function f is $f: (x,y)$, where each ordered pair is of the form (x,y). Sometimes x, the first element, is called the *independent variable*. The second element, y, is called the *dependent variable*; it is also called the *value* of the function. The set X of admissible values of x is called the *domain* of the function, and the set Y of corresponding values of y is called the *range* of the function. A function is established when a rule exists which determines y for each x. Often the rule is given by an equation such as $y = f(x)$. Although $f(x)$ is, strictly speaking, the value of the function at x, it is not uncommon to refer to $f(x)$ as "the function $f(x)$." These notations generalize to sets of ordered triplets, and we write $z = f(x,y)$, etc.

EXERCISES

1. If $f(x) = x^2$, $f(1) = 1$, $f(3) = 9$, $f(-2) = 4$.

2. If $f(t) = -\dfrac{1}{t^2}$, $f(1) = -\dfrac{1}{1}$, $f(2) = -\dfrac{1}{4}$, $f(-3) = -\dfrac{1}{9}$.

3. If $g(x) = 7 \sin x$, $g(1) = 7 \sin 1^{(r)} = 7 \sin \dfrac{180°}{\pi}$, $g\left(\dfrac{\pi}{2}\right) = 7$.

4. If $\theta(x) = 2^x$, $\theta(3) = 2^3 = 8$, $\theta(-1) = ?$, $\theta(\sqrt{7}) = ?$

5. If $F(x) = \dfrac{x+1}{x^2+1}$, $F(3\,t) = \dfrac{3\,t+1}{9\,t^2+1}$, $F(2\,z) = ?$, $F(x^2) = ?$

6. If $h(y) = 3 \log y$, $h(1) = 0$, $h(2) = 3 \log 2$, $h(1-x) = ?$

7. If $f(\theta) = \theta + \tan \theta$, $f(0) = 0$, $f\left(\dfrac{\pi}{2}\right) = ?$, $f(1) = ?$

8. If $Z = \dfrac{x+y}{x-y}$, $Z(2, 0) = \dfrac{2+0}{2-0} = 1$, $Z(a, 3) = \dfrac{a+3}{a-3}$, $Z(y, x) = ?$

9. If $y = \dfrac{x_1 + x_2 + x_3}{2 - x_1^2 + x_3}$, $y(1, -1, 0) = \dfrac{1-1+0}{2-1+0} = 0$, $y(2, 3, -5) = ?$

10. If $\varphi(t) = 1 - t^2 + 3\,t^4$, $\varphi\left(\dfrac{1}{t}\right) = 1 - \dfrac{1}{t^2} + \dfrac{3}{t^4}$, $\varphi[\varphi(t)] = ?$

10. Limits. A function $f(x)$ is said to approach b as a limit, when x approaches a, if the value of $|f(x) - b|$ becomes and remains less than any preassigned quantity. This is sometimes written $|f(x) - b| < \epsilon$ when $|x - a| < \delta$. Again the notation $f(x) \rightarrow b$, when $x \rightarrow a$ is used; this is read "$f(x)$ approaches b when x approaches a." The notation most widely adopted in books on the calculus is, however,

$$\lim_{x \to a} f(x) = b;$$

this is read "the limiting value of $f(x)$, as x approaches a, equals b."

The following theorems on limits are important.

If $\lim_{x \to a} f(x) = b$ and $\lim_{x \to a} g(x) = c$, then

(1) $\lim_{x \to a} [f(x) \pm g(x)] = b \pm c$,   [The limit of a (finite) sum equals the sum of the limits.]

(2) $\lim_{x \to a} f(x) \cdot g(x) = b \cdot c$,   [The limit of a product equals the product of the limits.]

(3) $\lim_{x \to a} \dfrac{f(x)}{g(x)} = \dfrac{b}{c}$, if $c \neq 0$.   [The limit of a quotient is the quotient of the limits provided the limit of the denominator is not zero.]

DEFINITION. A function $f(x)$ is said to be *continuous at the point a* if $\lim_{x \to a} f(x) = f(a)$, that is to say if the limiting value of the function, as x approaches a, actually equals the value of the function at the point a. (For example the function $f(x) = x^2$, $x \leq 0$, $f(x) = 0$, $x > 0$, is a continuous function at the point $x = 0$ since $\lim_{x \to 0} x^2 = 0 = f(0)$.) If $\lim_{x \to a} f(x) \neq f(a)$ the function is said to be *discontinuous at the point a*. (For example $f(x) = x^2$, $x \neq 0$, $f(0) = 1$, is discontinuous at the point $x = 0$ since $\lim_{x \to 0} (x^2) = 0$, but $f(0) = 1$.)

A function is *continuous in an interval* $x_0 \leq x \leq x_1$ if it is continuous at every point in the interval.

If $f(x)$ and $g(x)$ are two continuous functions, then $g[f(x)]$ is continuous and we write

(4) $\lim_{x \to a} g[f(x)] = g[\lim_{x \to a} f(x)] = g[f(a)]$.

These facts are used in the evaluation of limits. (See l'Hospital's Rule, Chap. VIII, § 33 for further information regarding limits and indeterminate forms.)

The student should become quite clear in his own mind as to the use and meaning of the three expressions $\frac{0}{a}, \frac{a}{0}, \frac{0}{0}$. First, zero divided by a number $a(\neq 0)$ is zero. Next consider $\frac{a}{0}$; this we should write $\lim_{x \to 0} \frac{a}{x} = \infty$ (no limit, infinite limit). The last, $\frac{0}{0}$, is meaningless in that form; that is to say it is indeterminate. For a quick arithmetic check of these facts consider writing these ratios $\left(\text{each of the form } \frac{A}{B} = C\right)$ in the form $A = BC$. Then we have

(5) $\frac{0}{a} = C$,   or $0 = a \cdot C$, $\therefore C = 0$, i.e., $\frac{0}{a} = 0$.

(6) $\frac{a}{0} = C$,   or $a = 0 \cdot C$, $\therefore C = \infty$ (C can be equal to no finite number; C is infinitely large), i.e., $\frac{a}{0} = \infty$.

(7) $\frac{0}{0} = C$,   or $0 = 0 \cdot C$, $\therefore C$ could be any number, i.e., $\frac{0}{0} = $ indeterminate.

There are three especially important limits that we should consider before turning to the subject of differentiation where these limits are used. They are

(8) $\lim_{x \to 0} \dfrac{\sin x}{x} = 1$, ($x$ measured in radians);

(9) $\lim_{x \to 0} \dfrac{1 - \cos x}{x} = 0$, ($x$ measured in radians);

(10) $\lim_{x \to 0} (1 + x)^{\frac{1}{x}} = e = 2.71828 \cdots$.

Now $\lim_{x \to 0} \sin x = 0$ and $\lim_{x \to 0} x = 0$. Hence theorem (3) cannot be applied to (8); if it were applied we would merely have (7) above $\left(\frac{0}{0}\right)$ which would tell us nothing. That $\lim_{x \to 0} \dfrac{\sin x}{x} = 1$,

can readily be proved as follows.   From Fig. 67 it is evident
that

area $OAD >$ area $OAC >$ area OBC,
area $OAD = \frac{1}{2} OA \cdot DA = \frac{1}{2} \tan x$,
area $OAC = \frac{1}{2} rx = \frac{1}{2} x$, ($x$ measured in radians, $r = 1$).
area $OBC = \frac{1}{2} OB \cdot BC = \frac{1}{2} \cos x \sin x$.

Hence $\tan x > x > \cos x \sin x$,

or $\dfrac{1}{\cos x} > \dfrac{x}{\sin x} > \cos x$,

or again $\cos x < \dfrac{\sin x}{x} < \dfrac{1}{\cos x}$.

Since $\dfrac{\sin x}{x}$ always lies between $\cos x$ and $\dfrac{1}{\cos x}$, each of which

approaches unity as x approaches zero, therefore $\lim\limits_{x \to 0} \dfrac{\sin x}{x} = 1$
and the proposition is proved.

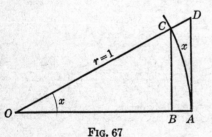

FIG. 67

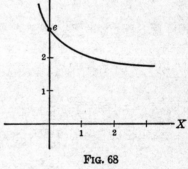

FIG. 68

For (9) write

$$1 - \cos x = \frac{1 - \cos^2 x}{1 + \cos x} = \frac{\sin^2 x}{1 + \cos x} < \sin^2 x,$$

therefore $\dfrac{1 - \cos x}{x} < \dfrac{\sin^2 x}{x}$, x positive.

Hence $\lim\limits_{x \to 0} \dfrac{1 - \cos x}{x} \leq \lim\limits_{x \to 0} \dfrac{\sin x}{x} \sin x = 1 \cdot 0 = 0.$

A rigorous proof of (10) is complicated and is usually found
only in advanced mathematical treatises.   However, if a table
of values of the function $(1 + x)^x$ is prepared for values of x

near zero, it will seem plausible that this limit does exist and is in the neighborhood of 2.7. The student should check, by logarithms, the entries in the following table.

x	2	1	.1	.01	.001	.0001	−.01	−.001
$y = (1 + x)^{\frac{1}{x}}$	1.732	2.000	2.594	2.705	2.717	?	2.732	?

From this information we sketch a portion of the graph of this function (Fig. 68). Later, in Chapter XVII on expansions of functions in infinite series, more information about the number e will be gained; but the earnest student will find profit now in expanding $(1 + x)^{\frac{1}{x}}$ by the binomial theorem, thinking of $\frac{1}{x}$ as an integer. Let x approach zero by taking on the successive values $\frac{1}{2}, \frac{1}{3}, \frac{1}{4}, \cdots$ and consider what happens in the limit.

EXERCISES

1. $\lim_{x \to 1} (x^2 - 1) = 0; \; \lim_{x \to 0} (x^2 - 1) = -1.$

2. $\lim_{x \to \infty} \frac{1}{x} = 0; \; \lim_{x \to 0} \frac{1}{x} = \infty$ (infinite limit).

3. $\lim_{t \to 0} \frac{3t - 5}{t + 2} = -\frac{5}{2}; \; \lim_{t \to \infty} \frac{3t^2 - 5t + 4}{t^2 + 2} = \lim_{t \to \infty} \frac{3 - \frac{5}{t} + \frac{4}{t^2}}{1 + \frac{2}{t^2}} = 3.$

4. $\lim_{x \to 0} \frac{ax^n + bx^{n-1} + \cdots + c}{Ax^n + Bx^{n-1} + \cdots + C} = \frac{c}{C}; \; \lim_{x \to \infty} \frac{ax^n + bx^{n-1} + \cdots + c}{Ax^n + Bx^{n-1} + \cdots + C} = \frac{a}{A}.$

5. $\lim_{x \to \frac{\pi}{2}} \tan x = \lim_{x \to \frac{\pi}{2}} \frac{\sin x}{\cos x} = \frac{1}{0} = \infty$ (infinite limit).

6. $\lim_{x \to \infty} \sin x = $ no limit; $\lim_{x \to 0} \sin \frac{1}{x} = $ no limit; $\lim_{x \to 0} x \sin \frac{1}{x} = 0.$

7. $\lim_{h \to 0} a^{x+h} = a^x; \; \lim_{x \to 2} x^{-4} = \frac{1}{16}; \; \lim_{x \to -2} x^4 = 16.$

8. $\lim_{x \to -\infty} 2^x = \lim_{x \to \infty} 2^{-x} = 0; \; \lim_{h \to 0} 2^{-h} = 1.$

9. $\lim_{t \to \infty} e^{-t} = ? \; \lim_{t \to 0} \frac{e^t + e^{-t}}{2} = ?$

10. $\lim_{x \to 0} \frac{x - y}{x + y} = -\frac{y}{y} = ? \; \lim_{y \to 0} \frac{x - y}{x + y} = ?$

CHAPTER III

THE DERIVATIVE

11. Definition of Derivative. The essence of the differential calculus is contained in the notion of the derivative of a function, the fundamental ideas and the definition being as follows.

Consider a function $y = f(x)$. The value of this function, at $x = x_0$, is $y_0 = f(x_0)$, and at $x = x_1$ is $y_1 = f(x_1)$. (See Fig. 69.)

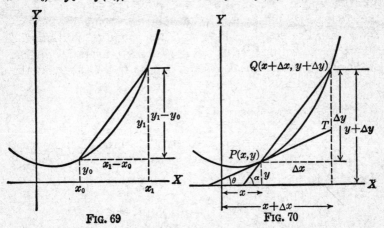

FIG. 69   FIG. 70

Let us suppose x_0 a fixed point but consider x_1 as a variable point and let x_1 approach x_0. *The derivative of $f(x)$ with respect to x at the point x_0 is defined as*

$$\lim_{x_1 \to x_0} \frac{f(x_1) - f(x_0)}{x_1 - x_0}.$$

Since x_0 is any point, we might drop the subscript and talk about the derivative of $f(x)$ with respect to x (at any point x) as being

$$\lim_{x_1 \to x} \frac{f(x_1) - f(x)}{x_1 - x}.$$

More frequently the following notations are used. Let $x_1 - x = \Delta x$, $f(x_1) - f(x) = \Delta y$; Δx and Δy are called incre-

29

independent and dependent variables respectively.
~~rivative~~ of y with respect to x is written

$$\lim_{\Delta x \to 0} \frac{\Delta y}{\Delta x} = \lim_{\Delta x \to 0} \frac{f(x + \Delta x) - f(x)}{\Delta x}.$$

Various symbols are in constant use for this limit:

$$\frac{dy}{dx} = \frac{df}{dx} = y' = f' = D_x y = \lim_{\Delta x \to 0} \frac{\Delta y}{\Delta x}.$$

Examine Fig. 70 very carefully. Note that, geometrically, $\frac{\Delta y}{\Delta x} = \tan \alpha$, where α is the angle made by the secant line PQ and the X-axis. As $\Delta x \to 0$, $Q \to P$ along the curve and hence the secant PQ approaches the tangent, the point of tangency being P. Therefore we have the important result that the derivative of a function represents the trigonometric tangent of the angle between the geometric tangent to the curve and the X-axis. That is

$$\frac{dy}{dx} = \tan \theta = \text{slope of the tangent line } PT.$$

Or again we could interpret the derivative in the following way. As x changes by an amount Δx, y changes by an amount Δy. Hence $\frac{\Delta y}{\Delta x}$ is the average amount by which y changes.

$$\frac{\Delta y}{\Delta x} = \frac{\text{average rate of change in } y \text{ per unit}}{\text{change in } x, \text{ in interval } \Delta x.}$$

From this it follows that

$$\frac{dy}{dx} = \lim_{\Delta x \to 0} \frac{\Delta y}{\Delta x} = \frac{\text{instantaneous rate of change in } y}{\text{per unit change in } x, \text{ at point } x.}$$

The principal steps in the differentiation process — the so called Δ-process of differentiation — are:

(1) Consider $\qquad\qquad y = f(x).$

(2) Give increments to x and y and write $\quad y + \Delta y = f(x + \Delta x).$

(3) Subtract (1) from (2) $\quad \Delta y = f(x + \Delta x) - f(x).$

(4) Divide by Δx $\qquad \dfrac{\Delta y}{\Delta x} = \dfrac{f(x + \Delta x) - f(x)}{\Delta x}.$

(5)   Take limit
$$\frac{dy}{dx} = \lim_{\Delta x \to 0} \frac{\Delta y}{\Delta x} = \lim_{\Delta x \to 0} \frac{f(x + \Delta x) - f(x)}{\Delta x}.$$

Note that since $\Delta y \to 0$, as $\Delta x \to 0$, $\lim\limits_{\Delta x \to 0} \frac{\Delta y}{\Delta x}$ is of the form $\frac{0}{0}$. The difficulties of Δ-process differentiation occur in steps (not indicated) between (2) and (5) since it is essential that (5) be in a form which actually yields something, not just $\frac{0}{0}$, when limits are taken.   These intermediate steps usually involve algebraic and trigonometric operations which do transform (4) into a form amenable to limits.   Many of these special devices are explained in the next chapter where certain rules of differentiation are developed by the fundamental Δ-process.

Several things should be pointed out at this time.

1st.   The increment Δx can be positive or negative and $\lim\limits_{\Delta x \to 0} \frac{\Delta y}{\Delta x}$ must be independent of the way in which Δx approaches zero.

2nd.   A given function $f(x)$ will have a derivative when and only when the operations in steps (1) to (5) can be carried through.   That is to say

3rd.   A necessary and sufficient condition for differentiability is that (a) $\lim\limits_{\Delta x \to 0} \frac{\Delta y}{\Delta x}$ exist.   This is more stringent than the corresponding necessary and sufficient condition for continuity, (b) $\lim\limits_{\Delta x \to 0} f(x + \Delta x) = f(x)$, since conceivably (b) might hold and yet (a) fail.   This is the case: not all continuous functions have derivatives.

4th.   For the most part the material in this outline deals only with functions that are continuous and differentiable (except perhaps for functions that have isolated points of discontinuity).

5th.   The student should be wary of functions that behave in an unorthodox fashion; functions that jump about a lot and whose actions are quite disconnected, functions that have an infinite number of kinks and quirks may be, like people with similar symptoms, pathological.

CHAPTER IV

RULES OF DIFFERENTIATION

12. Derivation of Rules of Differentiation. To establish rules by which functions can be differentiated at sight, the defining Δ-process is employed. This process, as it is applied again and again in the following cases, should be thoroughly mastered and the results should be memorized. The differentiation is with respect to x unless otherwise noted.

I.

$$1. \qquad y = c$$
$$2. \quad y + \Delta y = c$$
$$3. \qquad \Delta y = 0$$
$$4. \qquad \frac{\Delta y}{\Delta x} = 0$$
$$5. \qquad \frac{dy}{dx} = \lim_{\Delta x \to 0} \frac{\Delta y}{\Delta x} = 0$$

The derivative of a constant is zero.

II.

$$1. \qquad y = x$$
$$2. \quad y + \Delta y = x + \Delta x$$
$$3. \qquad \Delta y = (x + \Delta x) - x = \Delta x$$
$$4. \qquad \frac{\Delta y}{\Delta x} = 1$$
$$5. \qquad \frac{dy}{dx} = \lim_{\Delta x \to 0} \frac{\Delta y}{\Delta x} = 1$$

The derivative of the independent variable with respect to itself is unity; or $\frac{dx}{dx} = 1$.

III.

$$1. \qquad y = ax$$
$$2. \quad y + \Delta y = a(x + \Delta x)$$
$$3. \qquad \Delta y = ax + a\,\Delta x - ax = a\,\Delta x$$

4. $\quad \dfrac{\Delta y}{\Delta x} = a$

5. $\quad \dfrac{dy}{dx} = \lim\limits_{\Delta x \to 0} \dfrac{\Delta y}{\Delta x} = a$

IV.

1. $\quad y = x^n$

2. $y + \Delta y = (x + \Delta x)^n$

$$= x^n + nx^{n-1}\,\Delta x + \frac{n(n-1)}{2!}\,x^{n-2}\,\overline{\Delta x}^2 + \cdots + \overline{\Delta x}^n$$

(See Binomial Theorem, Chap. I, § 2, (3).)

3. $\quad \Delta y = nx^{n-1}\,\Delta x + \dfrac{n(n-1)}{2!}\,x^{n-2}\,\overline{\Delta x}^2 + \cdots + \overline{\Delta x}^n$

4. $\quad \dfrac{\Delta y}{\Delta x} = nx^{n-1} + \dfrac{n(n-1)}{2!}\,x^{n-2}\,\Delta x + \cdots + \overline{\Delta x}^{n-1}$

5. $\quad \dfrac{dy}{dx} = \lim\limits_{\Delta x \to 0} \dfrac{\Delta y}{\Delta x} = nx^{n-1}$

Even though this rule has been developed by the binomial theorem for a positive whole number n, the result itself holds for any whatsoever constant value of n as can be shown by other methods. The student should apply the rule for any n.

V. Let u and v be functions of x and consider

1. $\quad y = u + v$

2. $y + \Delta y = u + \Delta u + v + \Delta v$

3. $\quad \Delta y = \Delta u + \Delta v$

4. $\quad \dfrac{\Delta y}{\Delta x} = \dfrac{\Delta u}{\Delta x} + \dfrac{\Delta v}{\Delta x}$

5. $\quad \dfrac{dy}{dx} = \lim\limits_{\Delta x \to 0} \dfrac{\Delta y}{\Delta x} = \lim\limits_{\Delta x \to 0} \left(\dfrac{\Delta u}{\Delta x} + \dfrac{\Delta v}{\Delta x} \right) = \dfrac{du}{dx} + \dfrac{dv}{dx}$

The derivative of a (finite) sum is the sum of the derivatives.

VI.

1. $\quad y = u \cdot v$

2. $y + \Delta y = (u + \Delta u)(v + \Delta v) = u \cdot v + u\,\Delta v + v\,\Delta u + \Delta u\,\Delta v$

3. $\quad \Delta y = u\,\Delta v + v\,\Delta u + \Delta u\,\Delta v$

4. $\quad \dfrac{\Delta y}{\Delta x} = u\dfrac{\Delta v}{\Delta x} + v\dfrac{\Delta u}{\Delta x} + \dfrac{\Delta u\,\Delta v}{\Delta x}$

5. $\quad \dfrac{dy}{dx} = \lim\limits_{\Delta x \to 0} \dfrac{\Delta y}{\Delta x} = u\dfrac{dv}{dx} + v\dfrac{du}{dx}$

Since this rule involves the derivatives of u and v separately, it cannot be applied in the event u and/or v does not have a derivative.

VII.

$$1. \qquad y = \frac{u}{v}$$

$$2. \quad y + \Delta y = \frac{u + \Delta u}{v + \Delta v}$$

$$3. \qquad \Delta y = \frac{u + \Delta u}{v + \Delta v} - \frac{u}{v} = \frac{v\,\Delta u - u\,\Delta v}{v(v + \Delta v)}$$

$$4. \qquad \frac{\Delta y}{\Delta x} = \frac{v\dfrac{\Delta u}{\Delta x} - u\dfrac{\Delta v}{\Delta x}}{v(v + \Delta v)}$$

$$5. \qquad \frac{dy}{dx} = \lim_{\Delta x \to 0} \frac{\Delta y}{\Delta x} = \frac{v\dfrac{du}{dx} - u\dfrac{dv}{dx}}{v^2}$$

VIII. Since

$$1. \quad \frac{\Delta y}{\Delta x} = \frac{1}{\dfrac{\Delta x}{\Delta y}}$$

therefore

$$2. \quad \frac{dy}{dx} = \frac{1}{\dfrac{dx}{dy}}$$

IX. Suppose $y = f(u)$, where $u = g(x)$. Now

$$1. \quad \frac{\Delta y}{\Delta x} = \frac{\Delta y}{\Delta u} \cdot \frac{\Delta u}{\Delta x}$$

Therefore, taking limits, we have the very important relation

$$2. \quad \frac{dy}{dx} = \frac{dy}{du} \cdot \frac{du}{dx}$$

X. Using rule IX, we effect the differentiation of parametric equations. For if

$$1. \quad x = f(t), \; y = g(t)$$

then $\dfrac{dx}{dt}$ and $\dfrac{dy}{dt}$ can be determined and

$$2. \quad \frac{dy}{dx} = \frac{dy}{dt} \cdot \frac{dt}{dx} = \frac{\dfrac{dy}{dt}}{\dfrac{dx}{dt}}$$

XI. Using rules IV and IX, we get the derivative of the nth power of a function of x.

$$1. \quad y = u^n$$

$$2. \quad \frac{dy}{dx} = nu^{n-1}\frac{du}{dx}$$

XII.

$$1. \qquad y = \log_a u$$

$$2. \quad y + \Delta y = \log_a (u + \Delta u)$$

$$3. \qquad \Delta y = \log_a (u + \Delta u) - \log_a u = \log_a \left(\frac{u + \Delta u}{u}\right)$$

$$= \log_a \left(1 + \frac{\Delta u}{u}\right)$$

$$4. \qquad \frac{\Delta y}{\Delta u} = \frac{1}{\Delta u} \log_a \left(1 + \frac{\Delta u}{u}\right) = \frac{1}{u} \log_a \left(1 + \frac{\Delta u}{u}\right)^{\frac{u}{\Delta u}}$$

Now the $\lim\limits_{k \to 0} (1 + k)^{\frac{1}{k}} = e \sim 2.718.$ (The mathematical symbol $\sim$ stands for "is approximately equal to." See Chap. II, § 10.) Hence

$$5. \qquad \frac{dy}{du} = \frac{1}{u} \lim_{\Delta u \to 0} \log_a \left(1 + \frac{\Delta u}{u}\right)^{\frac{u}{\Delta u}}$$

$$= \frac{1}{u} \log_a e$$

$$6. \qquad \frac{dy}{dx} = \frac{1}{u} \log_a e \frac{du}{dx}$$

If base e logarithms are used, $\log_e e = 1$, and this reduces to

$$7. \quad \frac{d \log_e u}{dx} = \frac{1}{u}\frac{du}{dx}$$

This is one reason for base e ("natural") logarithms — their use simplifies the differentiation of the logarithmic function. In the future where no base is mentioned, base e will always be understood.

XIII.

$$1. \qquad y = a^u$$

$$2. \quad \log y = u \log a$$

$$3. \quad \frac{1}{v}\frac{dy}{dx} = \log a \frac{du}{dx},$$

by differentiating both sides of 2.

$$4. \quad \frac{dy}{dx} = a^u \log a \frac{du}{dx}$$

If $a = e$, we have, as a very important special case,

$$5. \quad \frac{de^u}{dx} = e^u \frac{du}{dx}$$

XIV.

1. $y = u^v$

2. $\log y = v \log u$

3. $\dfrac{1}{y}\dfrac{dy}{dx} = v \cdot \dfrac{1}{u}\dfrac{du}{dx} + \log u \dfrac{dv}{dx}$

4. $\dfrac{dy}{dx} = vu^{v-1}\dfrac{du}{dx} + u^v \log u \dfrac{dv}{dx}$

It is worth noting that the two parts of this formula are the expressions for the derivative of u^v, v being thought of as a constant, and for the derivative of u^v, u being thought of as a constant respectively. (See XI and XIII above.)

XV.

1. $y = \sin u$

2. $y + \Delta y = \sin (u + \Delta u) = \sin u \cos \Delta u + \cos u \sin \Delta u$

3. $\Delta y = \sin u (\cos \Delta u - 1) + \cos u \sin \Delta u$

4. $\dfrac{\Delta y}{\Delta u} = \sin u \left(\dfrac{\cos \Delta u - 1}{\Delta u}\right) + \cos u \dfrac{\sin \Delta u}{\Delta u}$

Now $\lim\limits_{\Delta u \to 0} \dfrac{\cos \Delta u - 1}{\Delta u} = 0$, and $\lim\limits_{\Delta u \to 0} \dfrac{\sin \Delta u}{\Delta u} = 1$, provided radian measure is used. (See Chap. II, § 10.) Hence

$$5. \quad \frac{dy}{du} = \cos u$$

$$6. \quad \frac{dy}{dx} = \cos u \frac{du}{dx}$$

This is one reason why radian measure is used: it simplifies the differentiation of the trigonometric functions. Where trigonometric functions are involved, radian measure will be used unless otherwise noted.

XVI. To differentiate cosine we note that

    1. $y = \cos u = \sin\left(\dfrac{\pi}{2} - u\right)$

Hence, by XV,

    2. $\dfrac{dy}{dx} = \cos\left(\dfrac{\pi}{2} - u\right)\dfrac{d}{dx}\left(\dfrac{\pi}{2} - u\right) = -\cos\left(\dfrac{\pi}{2} - u\right)\dfrac{du}{dx}$

        $= -\sin u\,\dfrac{du}{dx}$

XVII.

    1. $y = \tan u = \dfrac{\sin u}{\cos u}$

    2. $\dfrac{dy}{du} = \dfrac{\cos^2 u + \sin^2 u}{\cos^2 u} = \sec^2 u$

    3. $\dfrac{dy}{dx} = \sec^2 u\,\dfrac{du}{dx}$

XVIII.

    1. $y = \cot u = \dfrac{1}{\tan u}$

Differentiating this as a quotient, we get

    2. $\dfrac{dy}{du} = \dfrac{0 - \sec^2 u}{\tan^2 u} = -\csc^2 u$

    3. $\dfrac{dy}{dx} = -\csc^2 u\,\dfrac{du}{dx}$

XIX.

    1. $y = \sec u = \dfrac{1}{\cos u}$

    2. $\dfrac{dy}{du} = \dfrac{0 + \sin u}{\cos^2 u}$

        $= \sec u \tan u$

    3. $\dfrac{dy}{dx} = \sec u \tan u\,\dfrac{du}{dx}$

XX.

    1. $y = \csc u = \dfrac{1}{\sin u}$

    2. $\dfrac{dy}{du} = -\dfrac{\cos u}{\sin^2 u}$

        $= -\csc u \cot u$

    3. $\dfrac{dy}{dx} = -\csc u \cot u\,\dfrac{du}{dx}$

XXI.

    1. $y = \sin^{-1} u$

    2. $u = \sin y$

    3. $\dfrac{du}{dy} = \cos y$

Now cos y will be positive if y is a first or fourth quadrantal angle and will be negative if the terminal side of the angle y lies in the second or third quadrant.   Hence

    4. $\dfrac{dy}{du} = \dfrac{1}{\cos y} = \pm \dfrac{1}{\sqrt{1 - u^2}}$

    5. $\dfrac{dy}{dx} = \pm \dfrac{1}{\sqrt{1 - u^2}} \dfrac{du}{dx}$

    6. $\dfrac{dy}{dx} = \dfrac{1}{\sqrt{1 - u^2}} \dfrac{du}{dx}, \quad -\dfrac{\pi}{2} \le \operatorname{Sin}^{-1} u \le \dfrac{\pi}{2}$

The notation $\operatorname{Sin}^{-1} u$ is used to indicate the principal values of $\sin^{-1} u$; those authors who use arc sin u as the notation for the inverse sin u generally adopt Arc sin u to indicate principal values.

XXII.

    1. $y = \cos^{-1} u$

    2. $u = \cos y$

    3. $\dfrac{du}{dy} = -\sin y$

          $= \mp \sqrt{1 - u^2},$

where the minus sign is to be chosen if y is in the first or second quadrant, and the positive sign chosen if y is in the third or fourth quadrant.

    4. $\dfrac{dy}{du} = \dfrac{\mp 1}{\sqrt{1 - u^2}}$

    5. $\dfrac{dy}{dx} = \dfrac{\mp 1}{\sqrt{1 - u^2}} \dfrac{du}{dx}$

    6. $\dfrac{dy}{dx} = \dfrac{-1}{\sqrt{1 - u^2}} \dfrac{du}{dx}, \quad 0 \le \operatorname{Cos}^{-1} u \le \pi$

XXIII.

1. $y = \tan^{-1} u$

2. $u = \tan y$

3. $\dfrac{du}{dy} = \sec^2 y = 1 + u^2$

4. $\dfrac{dy}{du} = \dfrac{1}{1 + u^2}$

5. $\dfrac{dy}{dx} = \dfrac{1}{1 + u^2} \dfrac{du}{dx}$

XXIV.

1. $y = \cot^{-1} u$

2. $u = \cot y$

3. $\dfrac{du}{dy} = - \csc^2 y = - (1 + u^2)$

4. $\dfrac{dy}{du} = \dfrac{-1}{1 + u^2}$

5. $\dfrac{dy}{dx} = \dfrac{-1}{1 + u^2} \dfrac{du}{dx}$

XXV.

1. $y = \sec^{-1} u$

2. $u = \sec y$

3. $\dfrac{du}{dy} = \sec y \tan y = \pm\, u \sqrt{u^2 - 1}$

4. $\dfrac{dy}{du} = \dfrac{\pm 1}{u \sqrt{u^2 - 1}}$

5. $\dfrac{dy}{dx} = \dfrac{\pm 1}{u \sqrt{u^2 - 1}} \dfrac{du}{dx}$

Here the plus sign is to be used if the angle y is in the first or third quadrant, and the minus sign used if the angle is in the second or fourth quadrant.

6. $\dfrac{dy}{dx} = \dfrac{1}{u \sqrt{u^2 - 1}} \dfrac{du}{dx}, \quad -\pi \le \operatorname{Sec}^{-1} u \le -\dfrac{\pi}{2},\ 0 \le \operatorname{Sec}^{-1} u \le \dfrac{\pi}{2}$

VI.

1. $y = \csc^{-1} u$

2. $u = \csc y$

3. $\dfrac{du}{dy} = -\csc y \cot y = \mp\, u\sqrt{u^2 - 1}$

4. $\dfrac{dy}{du} = \dfrac{\mp 1}{u\sqrt{u^2 - 1}}$

5. $\dfrac{dy}{dx} = \dfrac{\mp 1}{u\sqrt{u^2 - 1}}\dfrac{du}{dx}$

Here the minus sign holds when y is in the first or third quadrant and the plus sign when y is in the second or fourth quadrant.

6. $\dfrac{dy}{dx} = \dfrac{-1}{u\sqrt{u^2 - 1}}\dfrac{du}{dx}$, $\quad -\pi \le \mathrm{Csc}^{-1}\, u \le -\dfrac{\pi}{2},\ 0 \le \mathrm{Csc}^{-1}\, u \le \dfrac{\pi}{2}$

This completes the list of the fundamental elementary functions; their derivatives should be memorized. The rules and the results will be needed for further work in differentiation.

13. Tabular Form of Rules of Differentiation. We summarize the rules of differentiation in the following condensed table of derivatives.

	THE FUNCTION	THE DERIVATIVE
1.	$y = x^n$	$\dfrac{dy}{dx} = nx^{n-1}$
2.	$y = u + v$	$\dfrac{dy}{dx} = \dfrac{du}{dx} + \dfrac{dv}{dx}$
3.	$y = u \cdot v$	$\dfrac{dy}{dx} = u\dfrac{dv}{dx} + v\dfrac{du}{dx}$
4.	$y = \dfrac{u}{v}$	$\dfrac{dy}{dx} = \dfrac{v\dfrac{du}{dx} - u\dfrac{dv}{dx}}{v^2}$
5.	$y = f(u),\ u = g(x)$	$\dfrac{dy}{dx} = \dfrac{dy}{du}\cdot\dfrac{du}{dx}$
6.	$y = u^n$	$\dfrac{dy}{dx} = nu^{n-1}\dfrac{du}{dx}$

	THE FUNCTION	THE DERIVATIVE
7.	$y = \log u$	$\dfrac{dy}{dx} = \dfrac{1}{u}\dfrac{du}{dx}$
8.	$y = a^u$	$\dfrac{dy}{dx} = a^u \log a \dfrac{du}{dx}$
9.	$y = e^u$	$\dfrac{dy}{dx} = e^u \dfrac{du}{dx}$
10.	$y = u^v$	$\dfrac{dy}{dx} = vu^{v-1}\dfrac{du}{dx} + u^v \log u \dfrac{dv}{dx}$
11.	$y = \sin u$	$\dfrac{dy}{dx} = \cos u \dfrac{du}{dx}$
12.	$y = \cos u$	$\dfrac{dy}{dx} = -\sin u \dfrac{du}{dx}$
13.	$y = \tan u$	$\dfrac{dy}{dx} = \sec^2 u \dfrac{du}{dx}$
14.	$y = \cot u$	$\dfrac{dy}{dx} = -\csc^2 u \dfrac{du}{dx}$
15.	$y = \sec u$	$\dfrac{dy}{dx} = \sec u \tan u \dfrac{du}{dx}$
16.	$y = \csc u$	$\dfrac{dy}{dx} = -\csc u \cot u \dfrac{du}{dx}$
17.	$y = \operatorname{Sin}^{-1} u$	$\dfrac{dy}{dx} = \dfrac{1}{\sqrt{1 - u^2}}\dfrac{du}{dx}$
18.	$y = \operatorname{Cos}^{-1} u$	$\dfrac{dy}{dx} = \dfrac{-1}{\sqrt{1 - u^2}}\dfrac{du}{dx}$
19.	$y = \operatorname{Tan}^{-1} u$	$\dfrac{dy}{dx} = \dfrac{1}{1 + u^2}\dfrac{du}{dx}$
20.	$y = \operatorname{Cot}^{-1} u$	$\dfrac{dy}{dx} = \dfrac{-1}{1 + u^2}\dfrac{du}{dx}$
21.	$y = \operatorname{Sec}^{-1} u$	$\dfrac{dy}{dx} = \dfrac{1}{u\sqrt{u^2 - 1}}\dfrac{du}{dx}$
22.	$y = \operatorname{Csc}^{-1} u$	$\dfrac{dy}{dx} = \dfrac{-1}{u\sqrt{u^2 - 1}}\dfrac{du}{dx}$

14. Implicit Differentiation. Where y is given explicitly as a function of x there is no difficulty in obtaining $\dfrac{dy}{dx}$ since if

$y = f(x)$, $\frac{dy}{dx} = f'(x)$. But in the event y is given implicitly as a function of x, i.e., $F(x, y) = 0$, then, instead of first trying to solve for y, it is generally preferable to differentiate immediately as the equation stands and then later to solve for $\frac{dy}{dx}$ (in terms of x and y). Such differentiation is termed implicit differentiation.

Illustration 1. Given $x^5 + x^2y^3 - y^6 + 7 = 0$, find $\frac{dy}{dx}$.

Solution. Differentiating implicitly, we get

$$5\,x^4 + 2\,xy^3 + 3\,x^2y^2\frac{dy}{dx} - 6\,y^5\frac{dy}{dx} = 0.$$

Solving this for $\frac{dy}{dx}$ gives the answer

$$\frac{dy}{dx} = \frac{5\,x^4 + 2\,xy^3}{6\,y^5 - 3\,x^2y^2}.$$

Illustration 2. Given $y = e^{xy} + \sin x$, find y'.

Solution. Implicit differentiation yields

$$y' = ye^{xy} + xy'e^{xy} + \cos x.$$

Hence
$$y' = \frac{ye^{xy} + \cos x}{1 - xe^{xy}}.$$

15. Derivatives of Higher Order. Since the derivative $\frac{dy}{dx}$ of a function y is itself a function, its derivative can be found in turn. We write

$$\frac{d}{dx}\left(\frac{dy}{dx}\right) = \frac{d^2y}{dx^2} = y'' = f'' = D_x^2y.$$

This is called the second derivative of the original function. Similarly the third derivative is indicated by $y''' = \frac{d^3y}{dx^3}$; and the nth derivative by $y^{[n]} = \frac{d^ny}{dx^n}$.

Illustration.

$$y = x^7 + 3\,e^{x^2} - \sin 2\,x,$$
$$y' = 7\,x^6 + 6\,xe^{x^2} - 2\cos 2\,x,$$
$$y'' = 42\,x^5 + 6\,e^{x^2} + 12\,x^2e^{x^2} + 4\sin 2\,x.$$

EXERCISES

FUNCTION	DERIVATIVE

1. $y = 7 + \sqrt{2} - 3x^0 + 5c$ $\quad \dfrac{dy}{dx} = 0$

2. $y = 6x - 4a$ $\quad y' = 6$

3. $y = \sqrt{5}\,x^{\frac{3}{2}} + x^{\frac{1}{2}} - kx^{-2}$ $\quad D_x y = \dfrac{3\sqrt{5}}{2}\,x^{\frac{1}{2}} + \dfrac{1}{2\sqrt{x}} + 2kx^{-3}$

4. $s = \sqrt{3}\,t + \dfrac{9}{t^3}$ $\quad \dfrac{ds}{dt} = \dfrac{\sqrt{3}}{2\sqrt{t}} - \dfrac{27}{t^4}$

5. $r = 1 + \dfrac{1}{\theta} + \dfrac{1}{\theta^2}$ $\quad \dfrac{dr}{d\theta} = -\dfrac{1}{\theta^2} - \dfrac{2}{\theta^3}$

6. $w = (4z + 3)(z^2 - 7)$ $\quad \dfrac{dw}{dz} = (4z + 3)(2z) + 4(z^2 - 7)$

7. $y = (1-x)(1+x^2)(2-x^3)$ $\quad y' = (1-x)(1+x^2)(-3x^2)$
$$+ (1-x)(2-x^3)(2x) - (1+x^2)(2-x^3)$$

8. $y = \dfrac{4x-1}{x^2 - x^5}$ $\quad y' = \dfrac{(x^2 - x^5)4 - (4x-1)(2x - 5x^4)}{(x^2 - x^5)^2}$

9. $y = (5 - 3x^2)^9$ $\quad y' = 9(5 - 3x^2)^8(-6x)$

10. $y = (1 - 2x)(x^2 - 2)^3$ $\quad y' = (1 - 2x)6x(x^2 - 2)^2 - 2(x^2 - 2)^3$

11. $y = 2^{(x+1)}$ $\quad y' = 2^{(x+1)}\log 2$

12. $y = e^{2-x} - \log \sin x$ $\quad y' = -e^{2-x} - \dfrac{\cos x}{\sin x}$

13. $y = \tan \dfrac{x^2}{2} - \sec^2\left(\dfrac{\pi}{3} - x\right)$ $\quad y' = x\sec^2\dfrac{x^2}{2} + 2\sec^2\left(\dfrac{\pi}{3} - x\right)\tan\left(\dfrac{\pi}{3} - x\right)$

14. $y = 3\cos^{-1}2x$ $\quad y' = \dfrac{-6}{\sqrt{1 - 4x^2}}$

15. $y = \tan^{-1}\dfrac{x}{a}$ $\quad y' = \dfrac{a}{a^2 + x^2}$

16. $y = x^3 - \cos 3x - \log x^5$ $\quad y' = ?,\ y'' = ?$

17. $y = \dfrac{e^x + e^{-x}}{e^x - e^{-x}}$ $\quad y' = ?,\ y'' = ?$

18. $y = \dfrac{x}{2}\sqrt{1 - x^2} + \tfrac{1}{2}\sin^{-1}x$ $\quad y' = ?,\ y'' = ?$

19. $y = \log \tan\left(\dfrac{\pi}{4} + \dfrac{x}{2}\right)$ $\quad y' = ?,\ y'' = ?$

20. $y = \log \dfrac{x - a}{x + a}$ $\quad y' = ?,\ y'' = ?$

CHAPTER V

APPLICATIONS OF DIFFERENTIATION

16. Slopes. As we have already seen in Chap. III, § 11, $y' = \dfrac{dy}{dx} = m = \tan \theta =$ slope of the tangent to the curve $y = f(x)$. This we define to be the slope of the curve itself.

Illustration 1. Find the slope of the curve $y = 4x^3 - 3x + 1$ at the point for which $x = -1$.

Solution.
$$y' = 12x^2 - 3$$
$$y'(-1) = 9$$

Illustration 2. Find the point(s) at which the tangent to the curve $x^2 + 3y^2 = 1$ makes 60° with the X-axis.

Solution.
$$2x + 6yy' = 0$$
$$y' = -\frac{x}{3y} = \pm\frac{x}{\sqrt{3}\sqrt{1-x^2}}$$

Setting this equal to $\tan 60° = \sqrt{3}$, we have

$$\pm\frac{x}{\sqrt{3}\sqrt{1-x^2}} = \sqrt{3}$$
$$\pm x = 3\sqrt{1-x^2}$$
$$x^2 = 9(1-x^2)$$
$$x = \pm\tfrac{3}{10}\sqrt{10}$$
$$y = \pm\frac{\sqrt{30}}{30}$$

Upon proper pairing of signs we find the points to be

$$\left(\tfrac{3}{10}\sqrt{10}, -\frac{\sqrt{30}}{30}\right) \text{ and } \left(-\tfrac{3}{10}\sqrt{10}, \frac{\sqrt{30}}{30}\right).$$

17. Tangents and Normals. To find the equation of the tangent to a curve we use the point-slope form of the equation of the straight line, namely

(1) $\qquad y - y_1 = m(x - x_1), \; \textit{Equation of Tangent,}$

where $m = y'$ evaluated at the point (x_1, y_1). Since a line perpendicular to this would have the slope $-\dfrac{1}{m}$, the equation of the normal becomes

(2) $y - y_1 = -\dfrac{1}{m}(x - x_1)$, *Equation of Normal.*

Illustration 1. Find (a) the equation of the tangent and (b) the equation of the normal to the curve $y^2 = 5x - 1$ at the point $(1, -2)$.

Solution. (a) The equation of the tangent will be of the form $y + 2 = m(x - 1)$ where $m = y'$ evaluated at $(1, -2)$. Now $2yy' = 5$, or $y' = \dfrac{5}{2y}$. Hence our equation becomes

$$y + 2 = -\tfrac{5}{4}(x - 1).$$

(b) The equation of the normal will be

$$y + 2 = \tfrac{4}{5}(x - 1).$$

Refer to Fig. 71 for the following definitions

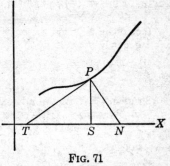

Length of subtangent $= ST$,
Length of subnormal $= SN$,
Length of tangent $\quad = PT$,
Length of normal $\quad = PN$.

FIG. 71

If in the equation of the tangent (1) we set $y = 0$ and solve for x, we get the coordinates of T, $T(x_1 - \dfrac{y_1}{m}, 0)$; similarly for $N(x_1 + my_1, 0)$. With this information the lengths ST, etc., can be readily determined. They are

$$\text{Length of subtangent} = \left| x_1 - \left(x_1 - \frac{y_1}{m}\right) \right| = \left| \frac{y_1}{m} \right|$$

$$\text{Length of subnormal} = |(x_1 + my_1) - x_1| = |my_1|$$

$$\text{Length of tangent} \quad = \left| \frac{y_1\sqrt{1 + m^2}}{m} \right|$$

$$\text{Length of normal} \quad = |y_1\sqrt{1 + m^2}|$$

Illustration 2. Find the lengths of the tangent and subnormal to the curve $y = x^5 - 2x + 3$ at $(1, 2)$.

Solution.
$$y' = 5x^4 - 2,$$
$$y'(1) = 3.$$

Hence

$$\text{Length of tangent} = \frac{2\sqrt{1+9}}{3} = \tfrac{2}{3}\sqrt{10}$$

$$\text{Length of subnormal} = 3 \cdot 2 = 6.$$

18. Angle between Two Curves. The angle between two curves will be the angle between the tangents. This angle is best given by formula (3) (a), § 5, Chap. I:

$$\tan \theta_{12} = \frac{m_2 - m_1}{1 + m_1 m_2},$$

where θ_{12} is the angle measured counterclockwise *from* the tangent to curve (1) *to* the tangent to curve (2).

Illustration 1. Find the angle at which the curves intersect in the first quadrant.

(1) $$x^2 + y^2 = 9,$$
(2) $$y^2 = 8x.$$

Solution. The point of intersection is gotten by solving the two equations simultaneously. This yields $x^2 + 8x = 9$, or $x = 1, -9$. The point of intersection in the first quadrant, therefore, has coordinates $(1, 2\sqrt{2})$. For (1), $y' = -\frac{x}{y}$; for (2), $y' = \frac{4}{y}$. Hence at $(1, 2\sqrt{2})$, $m_1 = -\tfrac{1}{4}\sqrt{2}$ and $m_2 = \sqrt{2}$. Therefore

$$\tan \theta_{12} = \frac{\sqrt{2} + \tfrac{1}{4}\sqrt{2}}{1 - \tfrac{1}{2}} = \tfrac{5}{2}\sqrt{2},$$

and the angle of intersection is given by

$$\theta_{12} = \tan^{-1} \tfrac{5}{2}\sqrt{2}.$$

Illustration 2. Show that (1) $x^2 - xy + y^2 - 3 = 0$, and (2) $x + y = 0$ intersect at right angles.

Solution. The points of intersection are readily found to be $(1, -1)$ and $(-1, 1)$. For (1), $y' = \frac{2x - y}{x - 2y}$ and at either point $m_1 = 1$. For (2), $y' = -1$ and $m_2 = -1$. Hence

$$\tan \theta_{12} = \frac{-1 - 1}{1 - 1} = \frac{-2}{0}.$$

Therefore the angle of intersection is 90°. Or again, since $m_1 = -\frac{1}{m_2}$, the lines are perpendicular.

19. Maxima and Minima.   We first define a critical point on the curve $y = f(x)$ to be a point where $y' = 0$, i.e., where the tangent to the curve is horizontal.   Or we say that a critical value of x is a value such that $f'(x) = 0$.   All roots of $f'(x) = 0$ are critical values of x.   The corresponding values of y are called the critical values of the function.

Next we say that the function has a maximum value y_1 at the point $x = x_1$ if $f(x) < y_1$ for all values of x near x_1.   Similarly for a minimum y_2 at $x = x_2$ we have $f(x) > y_2$ for all values of

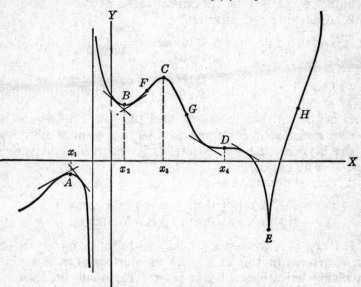

FIG. 72

x near x_2.   In Fig. 72 A, B, C, D are critical points; x_1, x_2, x_3, x_4 are critical values of x; y' is zero at each point A, B, C, D; A and C are maximum points, B is a minimum, D is neither since for some values of x in the neighborhood of x_4 $f(x) < y_4$ and for others $f(x) > y_4$.

Further we note that the slope y' is positive immediately before (to the left of) a maximum point and negative immediately after (to the right of); that for a minimum, the slope y' is negative before and positive after.   In special instances a maximum or a minimum may occur when $y' \neq 0$, as at E where $y' = \infty$.

The points D, F, G, H are called points of inflection which are, by definition, points where the slope is a maximum or minimum. The values of x for points of inflection satisfy $f''(x) = 0$ but not all roots of this equation lead to points of inflection.

And finally we point out that if $y'' \neq 0$ at a critical point, then y'' is negative at a maximum point and is positive at a minimum. We summarize:

To determine the relative extreme values of $y = f(x)$.

1. Solve $f'(x) = 0$ for the critical values of x.
2. Apply first derivative test:

$$\text{(a) If } f'(x) \begin{Bmatrix} > 0 \text{ before} \\ < 0 \text{ after} \end{Bmatrix} \quad \text{Maximum,}$$

$$\text{(b) If } f'(x) \begin{Bmatrix} < 0 \text{ before} \\ > 0 \text{ after} \end{Bmatrix} \quad \text{Minimum.}$$

If neither (a) nor (b) holds, then the point in question is neither a maximum nor a minimum but is a point of inflection with a horizontal tangent. Instead of using the first derivative test we may use the

3. Second derivative test:

$$\text{If } f''(x_1) < 0, \text{ then } f(x_1) \text{ is a Maximum,}$$
$$\text{If } f''(x_1) > 0, \text{ then } f(x_1) \text{ is a Minimum.}$$

If $f''(x_1) = 0$, the test fails and $f(x_1)$ might or might not be an extreme. In this case there are further tests available involving derivatives of higher order. The results are these:

4. Let $\quad f'(x_1) = f''(x_1) = f'''(x_1) = \cdots = f^{[n-1]}(x_1) = 0,$
$f^{[n]}(x_1) \neq 0.$

Then,

$$\text{(a) } n, \text{ even} \begin{cases} \text{If } f^{[n]}(x_1) < 0, f(x_1) \text{ is a Maximum,} \\ \text{If } f^{[n]}(x_1) > 0, f(x_1) \text{ is a Minimum;} \end{cases}$$

(b) n, odd $f(x_1)$ will be neither a maximum nor a minimum.

Illustration 1. Examine $y = 2x^3 + 3x^2 - 12x - 15$ for extreme values. (Fig. 73.)

Solution. $\quad y' = 6x^2 + 6x - 12$
$\qquad\qquad = 6(x + 2)(x - 1) = 0$
$\qquad\qquad x = -2, 1, \text{ critical values}$

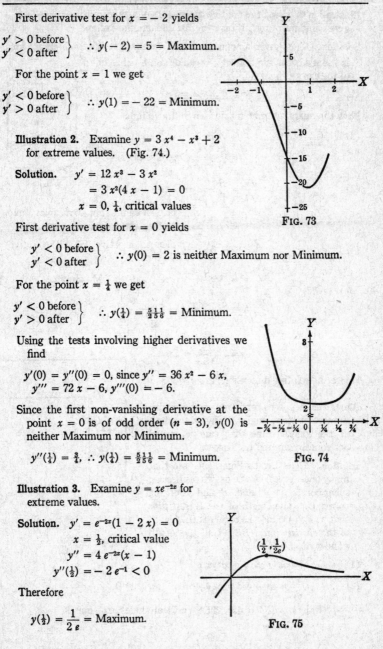

First derivative test for $x = -2$ yields

$\left.\begin{array}{l} y' > 0 \text{ before} \\ y' < 0 \text{ after} \end{array}\right\} \quad \therefore y(-2) = 5 = \text{Maximum.}$

For the point $x = 1$ we get

$\left.\begin{array}{l} y' < 0 \text{ before} \\ y' > 0 \text{ after} \end{array}\right\} \quad \therefore y(1) = -22 = \text{Minimum.}$

Illustration 2. Examine $y = 3x^4 - x^3 + 2$ for extreme values. (Fig. 74.)

Solution. $\quad y' = 12x^3 - 3x^2$
$$= 3x^2(4x - 1) = 0$$
$$x = 0, \tfrac{1}{4}, \text{ critical values}$$

Fig. 73

First derivative test for $x = 0$ yields

$\left.\begin{array}{l} y' < 0 \text{ before} \\ y' < 0 \text{ after} \end{array}\right\} \quad \therefore y(0) = 2 \text{ is neither Maximum nor Minimum.}$

For the point $x = \tfrac{1}{4}$ we get

$\left.\begin{array}{l} y' < 0 \text{ before} \\ y' > 0 \text{ after} \end{array}\right\} \quad \therefore y(\tfrac{1}{4}) = \tfrac{511}{256} = \text{Minimum.}$

Using the tests involving higher derivatives we find

$y'(0) = y''(0) = 0$, since $y'' = 36x^2 - 6x$,
$y''' = 72x - 6$, $y'''(0) = -6$.

Since the first non-vanishing derivative at the point $x = 0$ is of odd order ($n = 3$), $y(0)$ is neither Maximum nor Minimum.

$y''(\tfrac{1}{4}) = \tfrac{3}{4}, \therefore y(\tfrac{1}{4}) = \tfrac{511}{256} = \text{Minimum.}$

Fig. 74

Illustration 3. Examine $y = xe^{-2x}$ for extreme values.

Solution. $y' = e^{-2x}(1 - 2x) = 0$
$$x = \tfrac{1}{2}, \text{ critical value}$$
$$y'' = 4e^{-2x}(x - 1)$$
$$y''(\tfrac{1}{2}) = -2e^{-1} < 0$$

Therefore

$$y(\tfrac{1}{2}) = \frac{1}{2e} = \text{Maximum.}$$

Fig. 75

Illustration 4.   Find the relative dimensions of a tin can, to be made from a given amount of metal, that will have maximum volume.

Solution.   The "given amount of metal" means that the total surface area is specified; call it S and let r = radius and h = height of the can.   Then

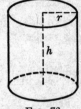

(1) $$S = 2\pi rh + 2\pi r^2$$

Now the quantity to be maximized is the volume

(2) $$V = \pi r^2 h$$
$$= \frac{Sr}{2} - \pi r^3 \text{ because of (1)}$$

(3) $$\frac{dV}{dr} = \frac{S}{2} - 3\pi r^2 = 0$$

FIG. 76

$$r = \pm \sqrt{\frac{S}{6\pi}}, \quad \text{critical values; but no meaning, here, to the minus sign.}$$

(4) $$\frac{d^2V}{dr^2} = -6\pi r, \quad \text{which is negative for all (positive) values of } r.$$

$$\therefore r = \sqrt{\frac{S}{6\pi}} \quad \text{corresponds to a Maximum.}$$

$$h = \frac{S - 2\pi r^2}{2\pi r} = S \frac{\frac{2}{3}}{2\pi \sqrt{\frac{S}{6\pi}}}$$

$$= 2\sqrt{\frac{S}{6\pi}} = 2r$$

Hence the relative dimensions are $h = 2r$.

Illustration 5.   Two corridors, each of width a, meet at right angles.   Find the length of the longest pipe that can be passed horizontally around the corner.

Solution.   Referring to Fig. 77 we see that many lines (pipes) can be drawn connecting such points as A and B and touching corner C.   The length of the *longest pipe* that will go around the corner is the length of the *shortest line ABC*.   Call the length l and write $l = l_1 + l_2$.

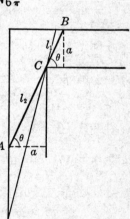

FIG. 77

(1) $$l = a \csc \theta + a \sec \theta$$

(2) $$l' = \frac{dl}{d\theta} = a(-\csc \theta \cot \theta + \sec \theta \tan \theta) = 0$$

$$\tan^3 \theta = 1, \; \theta = 45°, \; 225°, \quad \text{critical values; the one of interest is } \theta = 45°$$

Testing at, say, 30° (before) and 60° (after), we get

$$l'(30°) = a(-2\sqrt{3} + \tfrac{2}{3}) < 0,$$
$$l'(60°) = a(2\sqrt{3} - \tfrac{2}{3}) > 0.$$

Hence

$$l(45°) = 2\,a\sqrt{2}, \quad \textit{Minimum length of line} \text{ and a } \textit{Maximum length of pipe} \text{ that will go around the corner.}$$

Illustration 6. Find the point where the slope of the curve whose parametric equations are $x = 2\,t^2 - 1$, $y = 3\,t^3 + t$ is a minimum.

Solution. The slope m will be given by $\dfrac{dy}{dx} = y'$.

(1) $$\frac{dx}{dt} = 4\,t$$

(2) $$\frac{dy}{dt} = 9\,t^2 + 1$$

(3) $$m = \frac{dy}{dx} = \frac{\dfrac{dy}{dt}}{\dfrac{dx}{dt}} = \frac{9\,t^2 + 1}{4\,t} = \frac{9}{4}t + \frac{1}{4\,t}$$

It is the slope that is to be minimized; therefore we must find $\dfrac{dy'}{dx} = y''$

and set this equal to zero in order to obtain the critical points for slope.

(4) $$y'' = \frac{d^2y}{dx^2} = \frac{d}{dx}\left(\frac{dy}{dx}\right) = \frac{d}{dt}\left(\frac{dy}{dx}\right) \cdot \frac{dt}{dx}$$

$$= \left(\frac{9}{4} - \frac{1}{4\,t^2}\right) \cdot \frac{1}{4\,t} = \frac{1}{16\,t^3}\,(9\,t^2 - 1) = 0$$

$$\therefore t = \pm\,\tfrac{1}{3}$$

There are two critical points, namely for $t = \tfrac{1}{3}$, P $(-\tfrac{7}{9}, \tfrac{4}{9})$ and, for $t = -\tfrac{1}{3}$, Q $(-\tfrac{7}{9}, -\tfrac{4}{9})$. In testing we vary x slightly and keep in mind that "before" and "after" refer to values of x, not t.

Testing at P, $y'' < 0$ before ⎫
$\qquad\qquad y'' > 0$ after ⎬ $\quad\therefore$ Slope is Minimum.

Testing at Q, $y'' > 0$ before ⎫
$\qquad\qquad y'' < 0$ after ⎬ $\quad\therefore$ Slope is Maximum.

The test used, though involving y'', is the *first derivative test; y''* is the *first derivative of y'*, whose extreme values are being investigated.

EXERCISES

1. Given $y = x^3 + 6\,x^2 - 2\,x + 8$. Find the coordinates of the point of inflection and the value of the slope there.   *Ans.* $(-2, 28)$; $m = -14$.

2. Find the angle of intersection of the two curves $y = x^2$ and $y^2 = x$.
     Ans. $\theta = \tan^{-1}\tfrac{3}{4}$, at $(1, 1)$; $\theta = 90°$ at $(0, 0)$.

3. Find the equation of the tangent T to the curve $y^2 = x$ at any point $P(x_1, y_1)$ on the curve.

$$Ans. \ y - y_1 = \frac{1}{2 \, y_1} (x - x_1).$$

Show that the line passing through P and the focus F and the line through P parallel to the X-axis make equal angles with the tangent T.

4. Find the length of the subnormal to $y = xe^{-x}$ at the point of inflection.

Ans. $2 \, e^{-4}$.

5. Find the maximum value of $y = \sin x + \cos x$. *Ans.* $\sqrt{2}$.

6. An open cylindrical cup with a given volume is to be made out of the least possible amount of tin. Find the relative dimensions.

Ans. Radius r = height h.

7. A picture 8′ high hangs on a wall with the bottom of the picture 7′ from the floor. How far back from the wall should a person stand whose eyes are 5′ from the floor so as to make the picture subtend the largest visual angle?

Ans. $2\sqrt{5}$ ft.

8. A messenger in a boat directly off shore 1 mile wishes to reach a point farther on down the shore in the least possible time. On water he can travel 30 mi./hr. while on land he can travel 50 mi./hr. Consider the shore straight and find where he should land.

Ans. ¾ of a mile on down the shore toward his objective if his objective is greater than ¾ of a mile down the shore. If his objective is ¾ of a mile or less down the shore he should travel entirely by water for minimum time.

9. What is the volume of the right circular cylinder of greatest volume that can be inscribed in a right circular cone of radius r and height h? *Ans.* $\frac{4}{27} \pi r^2 h$.

10. In strip mining the cost increases directly as the depth. Suppose that the value of the product increases as the square root of the depth and that at a depth of 25 feet the cost of mining is \$1.25/cu. unit and the value \$5.00/cu. unit. At what depth will the greatest profit be made and what is that profit?

Ans. Depth 100 ft.; profit \$5.00/cu. unit.

20. Straight-Line Motion. Various problems in kinematics can be solved by the use of the derivative. If a particle moves along a straight line so that its distance s from some fixed point is a function of time, then $s = f(t)$, the velocity $v = \dfrac{ds}{dt}$, and the acceleration $a = \dfrac{dv}{dt} = \dfrac{d^2s}{dt^2}$.

Illustration 1. The height s feet after t seconds of a certain body thrown vertically upward is given by $s = 96 \, t - 16 \, t^2$. Find (a) the velocity and acceleration at any time t; (b) the initial velocity; (c) the maximum height reached by the body; (d) the velocity at the end of 1 sec.; (e) the time when it returned to the ground and its velocity then.

Solution. (a) $v = 96 - 32\,t$ ft./sec.

$a = -32$ ft./sec^2.

(b)   At $t = 0$, $v = 96$ ft./sec.

(c) Maximum height is attained when $\dfrac{ds}{dt} = v = 0$

$96 - 32\,t = 0$, $t = 3$ sec.

Maximum $s = 96 \cdot 3 - 16 \cdot 9 = 144$ ft.

(d) $v(1) = 64$ ft./sec.

(e) $s = 0 = 96\,t - 16\,t^2$, $t = 0$ (body started up),

$t = 6$ (body returned to the ground).

$v(6) = -96$ ft./sec.

Illustration 2. A particle moves in a straight line so that $s = A \cos (kt + \theta)$. Find the velocity at any time t and show that the acceleration is proportional to s.

Solution. $v = \dfrac{ds}{dt} = -kA \sin (kt + \theta)$

$$a = \dfrac{dv}{dt} = -k^2 A \cos (kt + \theta) = -k^2 s.$$

Such a motion, with the acceleration proportional to displacement, is termed *simple harmonic motion*. The amplitude of the motion is A; the period $= \dfrac{1}{\text{frequency}} = \dfrac{2\pi}{k}$; the phase constant is θ.

21. Curvilinear Motion. When a particle moves along a curve, the expressions for velocity and acceleration are a little more complicated. Let the equation of the curve be given in

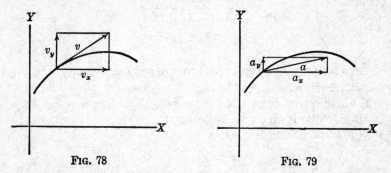

Fig. 78   Fig. 79

parametric form $x = f(t)$, $y = g(t)$ where the parameter t represents time. The velocity v is a vector quantity and has components $v_x = \dfrac{dx}{dt}$, and $v_y = \dfrac{dy}{dt}$.

The magnitude of v (speed) is

$$|v| = \sqrt{v_x^2 + v_y^2},$$

The direction of v is given by

$$\tan \theta = \frac{v_y}{v_x} = \frac{dy}{dx}.$$

The velocity vector is tangent to the curve of motion.

Similarly for the x- and y-components of acceleration we have

$$a_x = \frac{dv_x}{dt} = \frac{d^2x}{dt^2}, \quad a_y = \frac{dv_y}{dt} = \frac{d^2y}{dt^2}.$$

The magnitude of a is

$$|a| = \sqrt{a_x^2 + a_y^2},$$

The direction of a is given by

$$\tan \varphi = \frac{a_y}{a_x}.$$

The acceleration vector is not, in general, tangent to the curve of motion.

Sometimes it is important to resolve the acceleration vector into components tangent and normal respectively to the curve. The tangential component a_T, and the normal component a_N are given by

$$a_T = \frac{v_x a_x + v_y a_y}{|v|},$$

$$a_N = \frac{v_x a_y - v_y a_x}{|v|}.$$

Another important concept is that of angular velocity. When a particle moves along the circumference of a circle the central angle θ, measured from some fixed direction, is a function of time t. We define angular velocity ω as the rate of change of θ with respect to time t and write

$$\omega = \frac{d\theta}{dt}.$$

Likewise angular acceleration α is denoted by

$$\alpha = \frac{d\omega}{dt} = \frac{d^2\theta}{dt^2}.$$

Or again we speak of the angular velocity and angular acceleration of a vector OP drawn from the origin O to a point P as P
moves along a curve.

Illustration 1. A particle moves along the parabola $y = x^2$ with a constant
speed of 10 ft./sec. Find v_y when v_x is 2 ft./sec. Also find the corresponding point on the curve and the x- and y-components of acceleration
there.

Solution.   (1) $v^2 = v_x{}^2 + v_y{}^2$
$$100 = 4 + v_y{}^2, \qquad v_y = \pm\, 4\sqrt{6} \text{ ft./sec.}$$

Differentiating the equation of the curve of motion with respect to time t
we get

$$\frac{dy}{dt} = 2\,x\,\frac{dx}{dt}, \qquad (2)\ v_y = 2\,xv_x$$

$$\pm\, 4\sqrt{6} = 4\,x, \qquad\qquad x = \pm\sqrt{6},\ y = 6.$$

Differentiating (1) and (2) with respect to t we arrive at two equations in
the unknowns a_x and a_y, namely

$$0 = v_x a_x + v_y a_y, \quad a_y = 2\,x a_x + 2\,v_x{}^2.$$

Solving these simultaneously we get

$$a_x = \mp\, \tfrac{16}{25}\sqrt{6} \text{ ft./sec}^2., \quad a_y = \tfrac{8}{25} \text{ ft./sec}^2.$$

Illustration 2. A particle moves so that its x- and y-coordinates are given
by $x = a \cos 2\,t$, $y = b \sin 2\,t$. Find (a) its velocity and acceleration
x- and y-components, and (b) the magnitude and direction of the velocity
and acceleration vectors. Show (c) that the path is an ellipse. Find
(d) when a_y is a maximum. (Let t be both time in seconds and radian
measure; x and y are to be measured in feet.)

Solution.   (a) $v_x = -\,2\,a \sin 2\,t \text{ ft./sec.}$
$$v_y = 2\,b \cos 2\,t \text{ ft./sec.}$$
$$a_x = -\,4\,a \cos 2\,t \text{ ft./sec}^2.$$
$$a_y = -\,4\,b \sin 2\,t \text{ ft./sec}^2.$$

(b) $|v| = \sqrt{v_x{}^2 + v_y{}^2} = 2\sqrt{a^2 \sin^2 2\,t + b^2 \cos^2 2\,t}$
$$|a| = \sqrt{a_x{}^2 + a_y{}^2} = 4\sqrt{a^2 \cos^2 2\,t + b^2 \sin^2 2\,t}$$

$$\tan \theta = \frac{v_y}{v_x} = -\,\frac{b}{a} \cot 2\,t$$

$$\tan \varphi = \frac{a_y}{a_x} = \frac{b}{a} \tan 2\,t$$

(c) $\dfrac{x}{a} = \cos 2\,t, \quad \dfrac{y}{b} = \sin 2\,t$

Hence $\dfrac{x^2}{a^2} + \dfrac{y^2}{b^2} = 1$, the equation of an ellipse.

(d) $\dfrac{da_y}{dt} = -\,8\,b \cos 2\,t = 0, \quad t = \dfrac{\pi}{4},\ \dfrac{3\,\pi}{4}$

Using the second derivative test we have

$$\frac{d^2 a_y}{dt^2} = 16\, b \sin 2\, t$$

At $t = \frac{\pi}{4}$, this is plus, therefore a_y is a Minimum;

At $t = \frac{3\pi}{4}$, this is minus, therefore a_y is a Maximum.

The particle is moving around the curve counterclockwise and has maximum a_y at the lower end of the minor axis. Note that here $a_x = 0$.

Illustration 3. A particle P moves around the circumference of a circle with constant angular velocity. Find $v_x, v_y, a_x, a_y, a_T, a_N$.

Solution. Let the equation of the circle be given in parametric form

$$x = r \cos \theta, \qquad y = r \sin \theta$$

Then $v_x = -r \sin \theta \dfrac{d\theta}{dt}, \quad v_y = r \cos \theta \dfrac{d\theta}{dt}$

$$= -r\omega \sin \theta, \qquad = r\omega \cos \theta$$

$$a_x = -r\omega^2 \cos \theta, \quad a_y = -r\omega^2 \sin \theta$$

$$a_T = \frac{v_x a_x + v_y a_y}{|v|}$$

$$= \frac{(-r\omega \sin \theta)(-r\omega^2 \cos \theta) + (r\omega \cos \theta)(-r\omega^2 \sin \theta)}{|v|} = 0$$

$$a_N = \frac{v_x a_y - v_y a_x}{|v|}$$

$$= \frac{(-r\omega \sin \theta)(-r\omega^2 \sin \theta) - (r\omega \cos \theta)(-r\omega^2 \cos \theta)}{\sqrt{r^2\omega^2 \sin^2 \theta + r^2\omega^2 \cos^2 \theta}}$$

$$= r\omega^2$$

Thus all of the acceleration is directed toward the center. The projection of P upon a diameter executes simple harmonic motion since $a_x = -\omega^2 x$; that is, the acceleration in the x direction is proportional to the displacement in that direction. (See Illustration 2, § 20.)

Illustration 4. (a) Find the angular velocity and angular acceleration of a particle which moves along the curve $y^2 = x^3$ in such a way that v_x is constant and equal to 2 ft./sec.
(b) Find ω and α at the point (1, 1).

Solution. (a) Now $\theta = \tan^{-1}\dfrac{y}{x} = \tan^{-1} x^{\frac{1}{2}}$

$$\omega = \frac{d\theta}{dt} = \frac{1}{1 + x}\left(\tfrac{1}{2} x^{-\frac{1}{2}} \frac{dx}{dt}\right)$$

$$= \frac{1}{\sqrt{x}(1 + x)}$$

$$\alpha = \frac{d^2\theta}{dt^2} = \frac{-\left(\frac{1}{2}x^{-\frac{1}{2}} + \frac{3}{2}x^{\frac{1}{2}}\right)}{x(1+x)^2}\frac{dx}{dt}$$

$$= -\frac{1+3x}{x^{\frac{3}{2}}(1+x)^2}$$

(b)
$$\omega \mid_{(1,1)} = \tfrac{1}{2}\text{ rad./sec.}$$
$$\alpha \mid_{(1,1)} = -1\text{ rad./sec}^2.$$

22. Related Rates.

Suppose that a relation exists between two variables u and v each of which depends upon time t. Then $\frac{du}{dt}$ and $\frac{dv}{dt}$ represent respectively the rates of change of u and v with respect to time. Since u and v are related so will $\frac{du}{dt}$ and $\frac{dv}{dt}$ be related and these relations may be used to solve a variety of problems.

Illustration 1. A boat is being hauled toward a pier which is 20 ft. above the water. The rope is pulled in at the rate of 6 ft./sec. How fast is the boat approaching the base of the pier when 25 ft. of rope remain to be pulled in?

Solution. At any time t we have

$$20^2 + x^2 = z^2$$

Hence

$$x\frac{dx}{dt} = z\frac{dz}{dt}$$

FIG. 80

When $z = 25$, $x = 15$; therefore

$$15\frac{dx}{dt} = 25(-6)$$

$$\frac{dx}{dt} = -10\text{ ft./sec.}$$

(The boat approaches base at 10 ft./sec.)

Illustration 2. A conical filter is 3″ in radius and 4″ deep. Liquid escapes through the filter at the rate of 2 cc/sec. How fast is the level of the liquid falling when the depth of the liquid is 3″?

Solution. Let h be the depth of the liquid at any time t and let r be the corresponding radius. Then, at any time t,

$$\frac{r}{h} = \frac{3}{4}, \quad r = \frac{3}{4}h$$

Since we seek $\dfrac{dh}{dt}$, it is best to express V as a function of h.

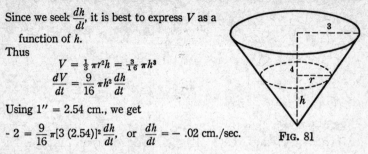

Thus

$$V = \tfrac{1}{3}\pi r^2 h = \tfrac{3}{16}\pi h^3$$
$$\frac{dV}{dt} = \frac{9}{16}\pi h^2 \frac{dh}{dt}$$

Using $1'' = 2.54$ cm., we get

$$-2 = \frac{9}{16}\pi[3\,(2.54)]^2 \frac{dh}{dt}, \quad \text{or} \quad \frac{dh}{dt} = -\,.02 \text{ cm./sec.}$$

Fig. 81

The liquid level falls at the rate of .02 cm./sec.

Illustration 3. A man 6 ft. tall walks at 4 mi./hr. directly away from a light that hangs 18 ft. above the ground. (a) How fast does his shadow lengthen? (b) At what rate is the head of the shadow moving away from the base of the light?

Solution. (a) $\dfrac{x+y}{18} = \dfrac{y}{6}$

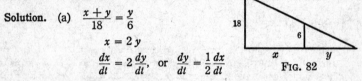

$$x = 2y$$
$$\frac{dx}{dt} = 2\frac{dy}{dt}, \quad \text{or} \quad \frac{dy}{dt} = \frac{1}{2}\frac{dx}{dt}$$

Fig. 82

This says that the shadow lengthens at a rate equal to one-half that of the walker and is independent of position. Therefore, at any time

$$\frac{dy}{dt} = 2 \text{ mi./hr.}$$

(b) Now the head of the shadow moves at a rate equal to the sum of the rates of the walker and of the lengthening of the shadow. Call $L = x + y$. Then

$$\frac{dL}{dt} = \frac{dx}{dt} + \frac{dy}{dt}$$
$$= 6 \text{ mi./hr.}$$

This also is independent of position.

Illustration 4. A dive bomber loses altitude at the rate of 400 mi./hr. How fast is the visible surface of the earth decreasing when the bomber is one mile high?

Solution. First call the radius of the earth r and call the height of the bomber x; let z be, as in Fig. 83, the distance from the center to the base of the visible spherical cap. We have

$$\frac{r}{r+x} = \frac{z}{r}, \text{ since each equals } \cos\alpha.$$

Whence

$$z = \frac{r^2}{r + x}$$

Now the area of the spherical cap cut off by a plane
z units from the center is

$$A = 2 \pi r (r - z)$$

$$= 2 \pi r^2 - \frac{2 \pi r^3}{r + x}$$

$$\frac{dA}{dt} = \frac{2 \pi r^3}{(r + x)^2} \frac{dx}{dt}$$

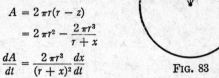

FIG. 83

Putting $r = 4{,}000$, $x = 1$, $\frac{dx}{dt} = -400$, we can evaluate $\frac{dA}{dt}$ exactly. However, since $r + x$ is approximately equal to r, we can get an approximation
for $\frac{dA}{dt}$ with little work.

$$\frac{dA}{dt} \sim 2 \pi r \frac{dx}{dt} = 2 \pi\, 4{,}000(-400)$$

$$\sim -32 \pi\, 10^5 \text{ sq. mi./hr.}$$

$$\sim -\frac{32 \cdot 22 \cdot 10^5}{7 \cdot 60 \cdot 60} \text{ sq. mi./sec.}$$

$$\sim -2{,}800 \text{ sq. mi./sec.}$$

The visible area decreases at the rate of approximately 2,800 sq. mi./sec.

EXERCISES

1. A body moves in a straight line in such a way that $s = t^2 - 5 t + 6$.
(a) Where is the body at $t = \frac{5}{2}$? (b) What is its velocity then? (c) When
will its velocity be positive?	*Ans.* (a) $s = -\frac{1}{4}$; (b) $v = 0$; (c) $t > \frac{5}{2}$.

2. A body moves in a straight line so that $s = t^3 - 3 t^2 - 9 t + 5$. Find
when both the velocity and acceleration are positive.	*Ans.* $t > 3$.

3. A particle moves around the ellipse $x^2 + 2 y^2 = 1$. Where will the two
components of velocity be equal?

Ans. $v_x = v_y$ at $\left(\frac{\sqrt{6}}{3}, -\frac{\sqrt{6}}{6}\right)$ and at $\left(-\frac{\sqrt{6}}{3}, \frac{\sqrt{6}}{6}\right)$.

4. A projectile, when acted on only by the force of gravity, has the following
path: $x = v_0 t \cos \alpha$, $y = v_0 t \sin \alpha - \frac{1}{2} g t^2$, where $v_x = v_0 \cos \alpha$, $v_y = v_0 \sin \alpha - gt$,
and α is the angle the direction of fire makes with the horizontal. How far
will the projectile travel in a horizontal direction?

Ans. Horizontal range $= \frac{v_0^2}{g} \sin 2 \alpha$.

Show that this range is a maximum for $\alpha = 45°$.

5. If a particle moves along a curve with constant speed, show that the
tangential component of acceleration $a_T = 0$.

6. Show that for motion along the cycloid $x = b(t - \sin t)$, $y = b(1 - \cos t)$,
the magnitude of the acceleration $|a|$ is constant.

7. Gas is let into a balloon at the constant rate of 3 cu. in./sec. How fast is the surface area changing when the radius is 10 in.?   *Ans.* $\frac{3}{5}$ sq. in./sec.

8. An airplane, flying due north at an elevation of 1 mile and with a speed of 300 mi./hr., passes directly over a ship traveling due west at 30 mi./hr. How fast are they separating 2 minutes later?   *Ans.* $\dfrac{3{,}030}{\sqrt{102}}$ mi./hr.

23. Polar Coordinates.   Whereas in rectangular coordinates $\dfrac{dy}{dx}$ represents the slope of the curve $y = f(x)$, in polar coordinates $\dfrac{d\rho}{d\theta}$ does not represent the slope of the curve $\rho = f(\theta)$.   It merely represents the rate of change of the radius vector ρ with respect to the angle θ.   In order to determine slope in polar coordinates we make use of the relations between rectangular coordinates (x, y) and polar coordinates (ρ, θ).   These are

$$x = \rho \cos \theta, \quad y = \rho \sin \theta.$$

Hence

$$\frac{dx}{d\theta} = \frac{d\rho}{d\theta} \cos \theta - \rho \sin \theta$$

$$\frac{dy}{d\theta} = \frac{d\rho}{d\theta} \sin \theta + \rho \cos \theta$$

$$\text{Slope} = \frac{dy}{dx} = \frac{\dfrac{d\rho}{d\theta} \sin \theta + \rho \cos \theta}{\dfrac{d\rho}{d\theta} \cos \theta - \rho \sin \theta}$$

This reduces, when numerator and denominator are both divided by $\dfrac{d\rho}{d\theta} \cos \theta$, to

$$(1) \qquad \text{Slope} = \frac{\tan \theta + \dfrac{\rho}{\rho'}}{1 - \tan \theta \cdot \dfrac{\rho}{\rho'}}, \quad \text{where } \rho' = \frac{d\rho}{d\theta}$$

With this formula we can readily find the slope of a curve whose equation is given in polar coordinates.

An important angle is the angle, ψ, between the radius vector and the tangent measured counterclockwise from the radius vector to the tangent.   (Fig. 84.)   Now

Slope $= \tan \tau$

$= \tan (\theta + \psi)$

(2) $\qquad = \dfrac{\tan \theta + \tan \psi}{1 - \tan \theta \tan \psi}$

Comparing (1) and (2) we find

(3) $\qquad \tan \psi = \dfrac{\rho}{\rho'}.$

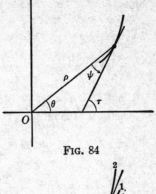

The angle between two curves would then be given by (Fig. 85)

$$\theta_{12} = \psi_2 - \psi_1$$

where θ_{12} is the angle measured counterclockwise from curve 1 to curve 2. Hence

$$\tan \theta_{12} = \tan (\psi_2 - \psi_1)$$

(4) $\qquad = \dfrac{\tan \psi_2 - \tan \psi_1}{1 + \tan \psi_1 \tan \psi_2}$

Formula (3) is used to evaluate $\tan \psi_1$ and $\tan \psi_2$.

Fig. 84

Fig. 85

Illustration 1. Find the slope of the curve $\rho = 2 - \cos \theta$, (a) at any point, (b) at $\theta = \dfrac{\pi}{4}$.

Solution. (a) $\qquad$ Slope $= \dfrac{\tan \theta + \dfrac{\rho}{\rho'}}{1 - \tan \theta \dfrac{\rho}{\rho'}}$

$= \dfrac{\tan \theta + \dfrac{2 - \cos \theta}{\sin \theta}}{1 - \tan \theta \dfrac{2 - \cos \theta}{\sin \theta}}$

$= \dfrac{\sin \theta \tan \theta + 2 - \cos \theta}{2(\sin \theta - \tan \theta)}.$

(b) $\qquad$ Slope $= \dfrac{\dfrac{\sqrt{2}}{2} + 2 - \dfrac{\sqrt{2}}{2}}{\sqrt{2} - 2}$

$= \dfrac{2}{\sqrt{2} - 2},$ at $\theta = \dfrac{\pi}{4}.$

Illustration 2. Find the angle of intersection of the curves (1) $\rho = \sin \theta$, and (2) $\rho = 1 + \cos \theta$.

Solution. For (1) we have $\tan \psi_1 = \dfrac{\rho}{\rho'} = \dfrac{\sin \theta}{\cos \theta} = \tan \theta$

For (2) we have $\tan \psi_2 = \dfrac{\rho}{\rho'} = \dfrac{1 + \cos \theta}{-\sin \theta}$

Curve (1) is a circle; curve (2) is a cardioid. They intersect in the two points $\left(1, \dfrac{\pi}{2}\right)$ and $(0, \pi)$. For any common point we have

$$\tan \theta_{12} = \frac{\tan \psi_2 - \tan \psi_1}{1 + \tan \psi_1 \tan \psi_2}$$

$$= \frac{\dfrac{1 + \cos \theta}{-\sin \theta} - \tan \theta}{1 + \left(\dfrac{1 + \cos \theta}{-\sin \theta}\right) \tan \theta}$$

$$= \frac{1 + \cos \theta}{\sin \theta}.$$

At the first point of intersection this reduces to

$$\tan \theta_{12} = \frac{1 + \cos \dfrac{\pi}{2}}{\sin \dfrac{\pi}{2}} = 1,$$

therefore $\theta_{12} = \dfrac{\pi}{4}$

At the second point

$$\tan \theta_{12} = \frac{1 + \cos \pi}{\sin \pi} = \frac{0}{0}, \text{ an indeterminate form.}$$

But $\dfrac{1 + \cos \theta}{\sin \theta} = \cot \dfrac{\theta}{2}$, and $\cot \dfrac{\pi}{2} = 0$.

Hence $\theta_{12} = 0$ and the curves are tangent.

EXERCISES

1. Find the slope of the curve $\rho = a \sin 2\theta$ at the point $\left(a, \dfrac{\pi}{4}\right)$. (Fig. 63.)

Ans. -1.

2. Find the angle between the radius vector and the tangent to the curve $\rho = a\theta$ at the point $\left(\dfrac{a\pi}{2}, \dfrac{\pi}{2}\right)$.

Ans. $\tan^{-1} \dfrac{\pi}{2}$

3. Find the angle of intersection of the curves $\rho = a(1 - \sin \theta)$, $\rho = a(1 + \sin \theta)$, at the point (a, π).

Ans. $\dfrac{\pi}{2}$

CHAPTER VI

THE DIFFERENTIAL

24. Differentials. Up to this point we have considered $\dfrac{dy}{dx}$ as a single symbol and not as a fraction. But it is clear, however, that since $\dfrac{dy}{dx}$ is the tangent of a certain angle it could be represented as a fraction if we so desired. Further we could choose arbitrarily any value for the denominator, say, of this fraction; then, of course, the numerator would be fixed so that the ratio would be equal to $\dfrac{dy}{dx}$. The symbol itself suggests that we define quantities dy and dx and then take the ratio of these for the derivative of y with respect to x. Let us recall that

$$\frac{dy}{dx} = \lim_{\Delta x \to 0} \frac{\Delta y}{\Delta x} = f'(x).$$

Now

$$\frac{\Delta y}{\Delta x} = \tan \alpha,$$

Δy and Δx being increments of the dependent and independent variables respectively. Hence

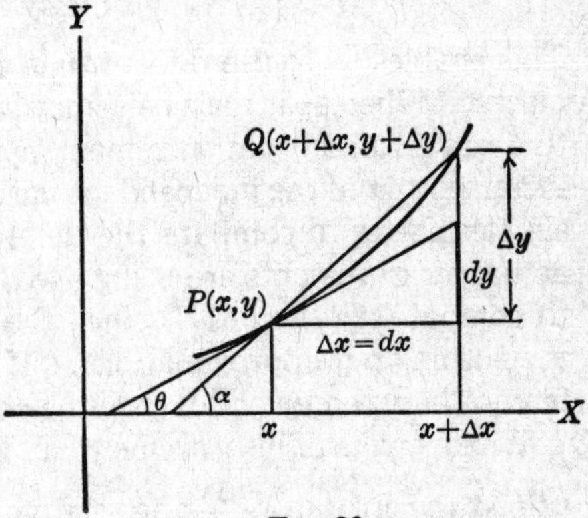

Fig. 86

$\dfrac{\Delta y}{\Delta x}$ is the ratio of two increments. But $\dfrac{dy}{dx} = \tan \theta$, in like manner could be called a ratio. If we set $\Delta x = dx$ and call this the differential of the independent variable x, then $\dfrac{dy}{dx} = f'(x)$ or $dy = f'(x)\, dx = \dfrac{dy}{dx}\, dx$. We define dy as the differential of the function. *The differential of a function*, therefore, *equals the derivative of the function multiplied by the differential of the independent variable.*

EXERCISES

FUNCTION	DIFFERENTIAL
1. $y = x^3 + 7$	$dy = 3 x^2 dx$
2. $y = 4 \sin 3 x$	$dy = 12 \cos 3 x \, dx$
3. $y = e^{x^2} - \log x$	$dy = \left(2 x e^{x^2} - \dfrac{1}{x}\right) dx$
4. $y = x e^x$	$dy = e^x(1 + x) \, dx$
5. $y + \log y + \tan 2 x = 5$	$dy + \dfrac{1}{y} dy + 2 \sec^2 2 x \, dx = 0$

25. Approximations by Means of Differentials. Since the limit of $\dfrac{\Delta y}{\Delta x}$, as $\Delta x \to 0$, is equal to $\dfrac{dy}{dx}$, then by the very notion of a limit it follows that for sufficiently small values of Δx we have, approximately (the symbol $\sim$ stands for "approximately equal to")

$$dy \sim \Delta y.$$

This enables us to use differentials as approximations to increments. Whereas it may be somewhat troublesome to compute the exact value of an increment Δy of a function for a given increment Δx of the independent variable, it may be a relatively simple matter to compute the differential dy. Further, where actual measurements are being used, it would usually be foolish to compute Δy "exactly" since the measurements themselves are nothing but approximations. If Δx is small enough the difference between dy and Δy will be small.

Where errors of measurement are involved, it is customary to call Δy the error in y, $\dfrac{\Delta y}{y}$ the relative error, and $100 \dfrac{\Delta y}{y}$ the percentage error. Approximations to these are

$$dy \sim \text{the error in } y,$$

$$\frac{dy}{y} \sim \text{the relative error,}$$

$$100 \frac{dy}{y} \sim \text{the percentage error.}$$

Note that if $\log y$ is first computed then the relative error is automatically introduced upon taking differentials since the differential of $\log y$ is $\dfrac{1}{y} dy$.

Illustration 1. A spherical ball bearing when new measures 3.00 inches in radius. What is the approximate volume of metal lost after it wears down to $r = 2.98$ inches?

Solution.
$$V = \tfrac{4}{3} \pi r^3$$
$$dV = 4 \pi r^2 \, dr$$
$$= 4 \pi (3^2)(.02) = .72 \pi$$
$$= 2.26 \text{ cu. in.}$$

If we assume that the figures $r = 3.00''$ and $r = 2.98''$ are exact, then the exact answer would be

$$\Delta V = \tfrac{4}{3} \pi [3^3 - (2.98)^3]$$
$$= (.71521066 \cdots)\pi$$
$$= 2.26 \text{ cu. in. to two decimal places.}$$

Illustration 2. Find (a) the error, and (b) the percentage error made in computing the volume of a cube if a 1% error is made in computing the length of an edge.

Solution. $V = x^3$
$$dV = 3 x^2 \, dx$$

Now we are given $100 \dfrac{dx}{x} = 1$, i.e. $\dfrac{dx}{x} = .01$. Therefore we must modify dV to read

$$dV = 3 x^3 \frac{dx}{x} \quad \text{by multiplying and dividing by } x.$$

(a) $dV = 3 x^3(.01)$
$$= .03 x^3 \quad \text{which depends, necessarily, upon } x.$$

(b) $\dfrac{dV}{V} = \dfrac{3 x^2}{x^3} dx$

$$= 3 \frac{dx}{x}$$

$$= .03$$

Hence a 3% error in the calculation of the volume will be made if a 1% error is made in the measurement of an edge.

Illustration 3. Kinetic energy is given by $E = \tfrac{1}{2} mv^2$. If E is known only to within 2% for a given mass m, find (a) the relative error and (b) the percentage error made in estimating the velocity v from this equation.

Solution.

$$E = \tfrac{1}{2} mv^2$$

$$\log E = \log \tfrac{1}{2} m + 2 \log v$$

$$\frac{dE}{E} = 2 \frac{dv}{v}$$

$$.02 = 2 \frac{dv}{v}$$

(a)
$$\frac{dv}{v} = .01$$

(b)
$$100 \frac{dv}{v} = 1\%.$$

EXERCISES

1. Approximately what would be the area of a circular ring of radius r and width dr?   *Ans.* $dA = 2 \pi r \, dr$.

2. Find, by using differentials, an approximate value for $\sqrt[3]{509}$. (*Hint:* Let $y = \sqrt[3]{x}$ and find dy.)   *Ans.* 7.984 correct to 3 decimals.

3. Approximately what is the allowable percentage error in the measurement of the diameter of a sphere if the volume is not to be in error by more than 3%?   *Ans.* 1%.

4. A painter, in making up his bid for painting an observatory's hemispherical dome, estimates the radius of the dome to be 28′ when it is actually 29′. If the cost of painting is 2¢/sq. ft., approximately how much extra will it cost him to give the dome 2 coats?   *Ans.* $14.08.

5. The period t (time, in seconds, for one complete oscillation) of a pendulum is $t = 2\pi\sqrt{\dfrac{l}{g}}$, $g = 32.2$ ft./sec²., $l = $ length of the pendulum in feet.

(a) If a pendulum takes 4 sec. for a complete oscillation (two sec. for "tick," two sec. for "tock"), find its length. (b) If, because of extremely cold weather, the pendulum of such a great-grandfather clock should shrink to 13′, how much time would it gain or lose in a day?

Ans. (a) 13.05 ft.; (b) Gain about 2.7 min./day.

CHAPTER VII

CURVATURE

26. Differentiation of Arc Length. We seek the instantaneous rate of change of arc length per unit change in x. This will evidently be given by

$$\frac{ds}{dx} = \lim_{\Delta x \to 0} \frac{\Delta s}{\Delta x},$$

where s represents the length of arc measured from some fixed point P on the curve. (See Fig. 87.) In order to determine $\frac{ds}{dx}$ we note that

$$z^2 = \overline{\Delta x}^2 + \overline{\Delta y}^2.$$

We have

$$\frac{\Delta s}{\Delta x} = \frac{\Delta s}{z} \cdot \frac{z}{\Delta x},$$

$$= \frac{\Delta s}{z} \frac{\sqrt{\overline{\Delta x}^2 + \overline{\Delta y}^2}}{\Delta x},$$

$$= \frac{\Delta s}{z} \sqrt{1 + \left(\frac{\Delta y}{\Delta x}\right)^2}.$$

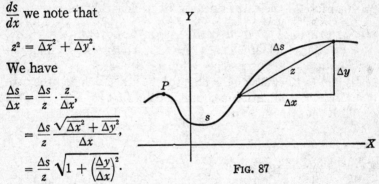

FIG. 87

Although we shall not prove it here it is true that $\lim\limits_{\Delta x \to 0} \dfrac{\Delta s}{z} = \lim\limits_{\text{arc} \to 0} \dfrac{\text{arc}}{\text{chord}} = 1$. Hence

$$\lim_{\Delta x \to 0} \frac{\Delta s}{\Delta x} = \lim_{\Delta x \to 0} \sqrt{1 + \left(\frac{\Delta y}{\Delta x}\right)^2},$$

(1) $$\frac{ds}{dx} = \sqrt{1 + \left(\frac{dy}{dx}\right)^2}.$$

This could be written, in terms of differentials,

(2) $$ds = \sqrt{1 + y'^2}\, dx$$

or again

(3) $$ds^2 = dx^2 + dy^2.$$

67

These are important forms and the student should realize that essentially they say that ds, dx, and dy play the role of the sides of a right triangle. Intuitively this seems very reasonable since arc approaches chord as arc tends to zero. A little reflection will make it clear why the situation is quite different in polar coordinates where the expression corresponding to (3) is

$$(4) \qquad\qquad ds^2 = d\rho^2 + \rho^2 \, d\theta^2.$$

This follows from (3) immediately upon transforming from rectangular to polar coordinates by means of the relations $x = \rho \cos \theta$, $y = \rho \sin \theta$. The student should become thoroughly familiar with these formulae since considerable use will be made of them later.

27. Curvature. In the preceding article we developed the formula for $\dfrac{ds}{dx}$, the rate of change of arc length with respect to unit change in x. A more useful notion, however, is that of the rate of change of arc length per unit change in inclination. (Inclination $= \theta$, where slope $= \tan \theta$; see Fig. 88.) We should really prefer to consider the reciprocal of this, namely, the rate of change of inclination per unit change in arc length. This would be in symbol

$$K = \frac{d\theta}{ds} = \lim_{\Delta s \to 0} \frac{\Delta \theta}{\Delta s}$$

and is defined as *curvature* (at a point P).

We shall now derive a formula for K in terms of the more familiar quantities y' and y''. To do this we write

$$\theta = \tan^{-1} y'$$

and differentiate this with respect to x getting

$$\frac{d\theta}{dx} = \frac{1}{1 + y'^2} y''$$

Then

$$\frac{d\theta}{ds} = \frac{d\theta}{dx} \cdot \frac{dx}{ds},$$

$$= \frac{y''}{1 + y'^2} \left(\frac{1}{1 + y'^2} \right)^{\frac{1}{2}}.$$

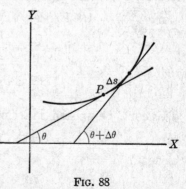

FIG. 88

by (1) § 26.   Finally curvature

(1) $$K = \frac{y''}{(1 + y'^2)^{\frac{3}{2}}}.$$

In general the sign of K is chosen as that of y'' although many authors treat K as always being positive.

Curvature measures the rate at which the tangent line turns per unit distance moved along the curve. Or, simply, it measures the rate of change of direction of the curve.

Illustration 1.   Find the curvature of a circle of radius r.

First Solution.   Let the equation of the circle be

$$x^2 + y^2 = r^2$$

Then $2x + 2yy' = 0$

$$y' = -\frac{x}{y}$$

$$y'' = -\frac{y - xy'}{y^2} = -\frac{y - x\left(-\dfrac{x}{y}\right)}{y^2}$$

$$= -\frac{r^2}{y^3}$$

$$K = \frac{-\dfrac{r^2}{y^3}}{\left(1 + \dfrac{x^2}{y^2}\right)^{\frac{3}{2}}}$$

$$= -\frac{1}{r} \text{ where } y'' < 0, \text{ i.e. for } y > 0,$$

$$= \frac{1}{r} \text{ where } y'' > 0, \text{ i.e. for } y < 0.$$

Normally, however, curvature of a circle is considered positive everywhere since this is the result we should obtain if we were to compute curvature directly from the fundamental definition. We do this in the

FIG. 89

Second Solution.

$$K = \lim_{\Delta s \to 0} \frac{\Delta \theta}{\Delta s}$$

Recalling that $s = r\theta$ for a circle we have

$$K = \lim_{\Delta s \to 0} \frac{\frac{\Delta s}{r}}{\Delta s}$$

$$= \frac{1}{r}$$

Thus curvature is a constant for a circle and is equal to the reciprocal of the radius.

By making use of (4) § 26 we arrive at the following formula for curvature in polar coordinates

(2) $$K = \frac{\rho^2 + 2\rho'^2 - \rho\rho''}{(\rho^2 + \rho'^2)^{\frac{3}{2}}} .$$

Illustration 2. Find the curvature of the spiral $\rho = a\theta$.

Solution.
$$\rho = a\theta$$
$$\rho' = a$$
$$\rho'' = 0$$
$$K = \frac{a^2\theta^2 + 2a^2}{(a^2\theta^2 + a^2)^{\frac{3}{2}}}$$
$$= \frac{1}{a}\frac{\theta^2 + 2}{(\theta^2 + 1)^{\frac{3}{2}}}.$$

Illustration 3. Find the curvature of the cardioid $\rho = a(1 - \cos\theta)$ at the point $\left(a, \frac{\pi}{2}\right)$.

Solution. $\rho = a(1 - \cos\theta)$
$$\rho' = a\sin\theta$$
$$\rho'' = a\cos\theta$$
$$K = \frac{a^2(1 - \cos\theta)^2 + 2a^2\sin^2\theta - a(1 - \cos\theta)(a\cos\theta)}{[a^2(1 - \cos\theta)^2 + a^2\sin^2\theta]^{\frac{3}{2}}}$$
$$= \frac{3 - 3\cos\theta}{2\sqrt{2}\,a(1 - \cos\theta)^{\frac{3}{2}}} = \frac{3}{2\sqrt{2}\,a\rho}.$$
$$K = \frac{3\sqrt{2}}{4a} \quad \text{at the point } \left(a, \frac{\pi}{2}\right).$$

28. Circle of Curvature. In Illustration 1 we found that curvature of a circle is the reciprocal of the radius of the circle. Similarly, for any curve, we define *the radius of curvature as the absolute value of the reciprocal of curvature.* That is, for any point on the curve.

(1) $$R = \frac{1}{|K|}$$

(2) $$R = \frac{(1 + y'^2)^{\frac{3}{2}}}{y''}, \text{ rectangular coordinates,}$$

(3) $$R = \frac{(\rho^2 + \rho'^2)^{\frac{3}{2}}}{\rho^2 + 2\rho'^2 - \rho\rho''}, \text{ polar coordinates.}$$

The student should memorize the definition (1) but should **not** try to remember (2) and (3); if the formulae for curvature are known, it is a simple matter to compute the radius of curvature from $R = \dfrac{1}{|K|}$.

A circle drawn with this radius R and with center on the normal to the curve on the concave side will have the same curvature as the curve itself. This circle is called the circle of curvature; it is an aid to the understanding of the geometric significance of curvature.

29. Center of Curvature. In order to find the coordinates of the center of the circle of curvature, referred to briefly as center of curvature, we proceed as follows. Let the equation of the circle be

(1) $$(x - \alpha)^2 + (y - \beta)^2 = R^2,$$

where $R^2 = \dfrac{1}{K^2}$. Upon differentiating (1) two times we get upon simplifying

(2) $$y' = -\frac{x - \alpha}{y - \beta},$$

(3) $$y'' = -\frac{R^2}{(y - \beta)^3}.$$

Solving (2) and (3) simultaneously for α and β, making use of the value of R, we get

(4) $$\alpha = x - \frac{y'(1 + y'^2)}{y''},$$

(5) $$\beta = y + \frac{1 + y'^2}{y''}.$$

Thus the coordinates of the circle of curvature are given in terms of x, y, y', and y''.

Illustration. Find the coordinates of the center of curvature of the cubical parabola $y = x^3$ at the point $(1, 1)$.

Solution.
$$y = x^3$$
$$y' = 3x^2$$
$$y'' = 6x$$
$$\alpha = x - \frac{3x^2(1 + 9x^4)}{6x}$$
$$\beta = y + \frac{1 + 9x^4}{6x}$$
$$\alpha = 1 - \frac{3(1 + 9)}{6} = -4$$
$$\beta = 1 + \frac{10}{6} = \frac{8}{3}.$$

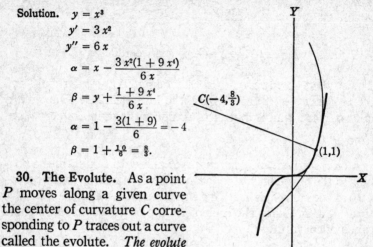

FIG. 90

30. The Evolute. As a point P moves along a given curve the center of curvature C corresponding to P traces out a curve called the evolute. *The evolute is* therefore *the locus of centers of curvature* and we might consider equations (4) and (5) § 29 as the parametric equations of the evolute, the variables being α and β, the parameter being x (y, y', and y'' are all functions of x). The regular Cartesian equation of the evolute would result from the elimination, if possible, of x from the parametric equations.

Illustration 1. Find the evolute of the parabola $y = x^2$.

Solution.
$$y = x^2$$
$$y' = 2x$$
$$y'' = 2$$
$$\alpha = x - \frac{2x(1 + 4x^2)}{2}$$
$$\beta = x^2 + \frac{1 + 4x^2}{2}$$
$$\left. \begin{array}{l} \alpha = -4x^3 \\ \beta = \frac{1}{2} + 3x^2 \end{array} \right\} \text{ parametric equations of the evolute.}$$

The rectangular equation of the evolute would be gotten by eliminating x from these equations. This yields $\beta = \frac{1}{2} + 3\left(-\frac{\alpha}{4}\right)^{\frac{2}{3}}$.

Illustration 2. Find the parametric equations of the evolute of the curve $x = 3t, y = t^2 - 2$.

Solution.

$$dx = 3\,dt, \quad dy = 2t\,dt$$

$$y' = \frac{dy}{dx} = \frac{2}{3}t$$

$$y'' = \frac{d^2y}{dx^2} = \frac{dy'}{dt} \cdot \frac{dt}{dx} = \frac{2}{3} \cdot \frac{1}{3}$$

$$= \tfrac{2}{9}$$

$$\alpha = 3t - \frac{\frac{2}{3}t(1 + \frac{4}{9}t^2)}{\frac{2}{9}}$$

$$\beta = t^2 - 2 + \frac{1 + \frac{4}{9}t^2}{\frac{2}{9}}$$

$$\alpha = -\tfrac{4}{3}t^3$$
$$\beta = 3t^2 + \tfrac{5}{2}.$$

We list in the following exercises some of the standard curves along with the radius of curvature R, the coordinates α and β of the center of curvature, and the Cartesian equation of the evolute E where simple or where interesting. We should always interpret α and β as the parametric equations of the evolute. Note that in some cases α and β involve only the parameter x but that in other cases y is also present. Allowing y to be present rather than eliminating it does no harm since y is a function of x and hence is determined for each value of x; it merely simplifies matters to retain y in some instances.

EXERCISES

Find R, α, β, and E for the following. (In E write x, y instead of α, β.)

1. Parabola
$y^2 = 4px$
(FIG. 5)

$$R = \frac{2(p + x)^{\frac{3}{2}}}{\sqrt{p}}$$

$$\alpha = 3x + 2p, \ \beta = -\frac{y^3}{4p^2}$$

$$E : 27py^2 = 4(x - 2p)^3$$

2. Semicubical parabola
$y^2 = x^3$
(FIG. 45)

$$R = \frac{\sqrt{x}}{6}(4 + 9x)^{\frac{3}{2}}$$

$$\alpha = -\frac{x}{2}(9x + 2), \ \beta = \tfrac{4}{3}\sqrt{x}(3x + 1)$$

3. Catenary
$y = \frac{a}{2}\left(e^{\frac{x}{a}} + e^{-\frac{x}{a}}\right)$
(FIG. 58)

$$R = \frac{y^2}{a}$$

$$\alpha = x - \frac{y}{a}\sqrt{y^2 - a^2}, \ \beta = 2y$$

4. Exponential
$y = e^x$
(FIG. 42)

$$R = \frac{(1 + e^{2x})^{\frac{3}{2}}}{e^x}$$

$\alpha = x - 1 - e^{2x}, \; \beta = 2 e^x + e^{-x}$

5. Ellipse
$b^2x^2 + a^2y^2 = a^2b^2$
(FIG. 9)

$$R = \frac{(a^2 - e^2x^2)^{\frac{3}{2}}}{ab}, \; (e = \text{eccentricity})$$

$\alpha = \dfrac{a^2 - b^2}{a^4} x^3, \; \beta = -\dfrac{a^2 - b^2}{b^4} y^3$

$E : (ax)^{\frac{2}{3}} + (by)^{\frac{2}{3}} = (a^2 - b^2)^{\frac{2}{3}}$

6. Hyperbola
$b^2x^2 - a^2y^2 = a^2b^2$
(FIG. 11)

$$R = \frac{(e^2x^2 - a^2)^{\frac{3}{2}}}{ab}, \; (e = \text{eccentricity})$$

$\alpha = \dfrac{a^2 + b^2}{a^4} x^3, \; \beta = -\dfrac{a^2 + b^2}{b^4} y^3$

$E : (ax)^{\frac{2}{3}} - (by)^{\frac{2}{3}} = (a^2 + b^2)^{\frac{2}{3}}$

7. Four cusped hypocycloid
$x^{\frac{2}{3}} + y^{\frac{2}{3}} = a^{\frac{2}{3}}$
(FIG. 50)

$R = 3(axy)^{\frac{1}{3}}$

$\alpha = x + 3 x^{\frac{1}{3}}y^{\frac{2}{3}}, \; \beta = y + 3 x^{\frac{2}{3}}y^{\frac{1}{3}}$

$E : (x + y)^{\frac{2}{3}} + (x - y)^{\frac{2}{3}} = 2 a^{\frac{2}{3}}$

8. Lemniscate
$x = a \cos \theta \sqrt{\cos 2\theta}$
$y = a \sin \theta \sqrt{\cos 2\theta}$
(FIG. 65)

$$R = \frac{a}{3\sqrt{\cos 2\theta}}$$

$\alpha = \dfrac{2 a \cos^3 \theta}{3\sqrt{\cos 2\theta}}, \; \beta = -\dfrac{2 a \sin^3 \theta}{3\sqrt{\cos 2\theta}}$

9. Cycloid
$x = a(\theta - \sin \theta)$
$y = a(1 - \cos \theta)$
(FIG. 47)

$R = 2\sqrt{2 ay} = 4 a \sin \dfrac{\theta}{2}$

$\alpha = a(\theta + \sin \theta), \; \beta = - a(1 - \cos \theta)$

10. Logarithmic curve
$y = \log x$
(FIG. 41)

$R = ?$
$\alpha = ?, \beta = ?$

CHAPTER VIII

INDETERMINATE FORMS

31. The Law of the Mean. Let $y = f(x)$ be a curve with a unique tangent at every point in the interval (a, b), $a \leq x \leq b$ (Fig. 91). Let P have coordinates $[a, f(a)]$ and Q have coordinates $[b, f(b)]$. It seems geometrically evident then that at

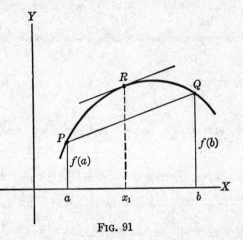

FIG. 91

some point $R[x_1, f(x_1)]$, interior to (a, b), the tangent to the curve will be parallel to the chord PQ. This fact, known as the mean value theorem or the law of the mean, can be stated and proved analytically.

THE LAW OF THE MEAN. *Let $f(x)$ have a unique derivative at every point in the interval (a, b). There exists an interior point x_1 such that*

$$\frac{f(b) - f(a)}{b - a} = f'(x_1), \quad a < x_1 < b.$$

In particular if $f(a) = 0 = f(b)$ we have $f'(x_1) = 0$ which states that if a function vanishes at the endpoints a and b, then there is an interior point at which the derivative is zero. Or again, geometrically this would say that if a curve crosses the X-axis at $x = a$ and at $x = b$, then at some point between a and b the tangent to the curve is horizontal (parallel to the X-axis). This special case is known as Rolle's Theorem.

32. Extended Law of the Mean. The Law of the Mean can be extended so as to include two functions $f(x)$ and $g(x)$. Analytically the statement of the extended law is as follows.

THE EXTENDED LAW OF THE MEAN. *Let $f(x)$ and $g(x)$ each have a unique derivative at every point in the interval (a, b) and let $g(x) \neq 0$ at every interior point. Then there exists an interior point x_1 such that*

$$(1) \qquad \frac{f(b) - f(a)}{g(b) - g(a)} = \frac{f'(x_1)}{g'(x_1)}, \quad a < x_1 < b.$$

This theorem is of value in the evaluation of indeterminate forms.

33. Indeterminate Forms. We have already met (Chap. II) an indeterminate form of the type $\frac{0}{0}$. [See (8) and (9), p. 26.] There, by special methods, we proved that $\lim\limits_{x \to 0} \frac{\sin x}{x} = 1$ and $\lim\limits_{x \to 0} \frac{1 - \cos x}{x} = 0$. We shall now develop a general method whereby indeterminate forms of this type $\left(\frac{0}{0}\right)$ can be evaluated.

To do this we make use of the Extended Law of the Mean and suppose that $f(a) = 0 = g(a)$ and write x for b. Then (1) § 32 becomes

$$(1) \qquad \frac{f(x)}{g(x)} = \frac{f'(x_1)}{g'(x_1)}$$

where $a < x_1 < x$. Now $\lim\limits_{x \to a} \frac{f(x)}{g(x)} = \frac{0}{0}$ in form since $f(a) = 0 = g(a)$. But, clearly, $x_1 \to a$ as $x \to a$. Therefore, taking limits of both sides of (1) we get

$$(2) \qquad \lim_{x \to a} \frac{f(x)}{g(x)} = \lim_{x \to a} \frac{f'(x)}{g'(x)}$$

provided this last limit exists. This relation (2) is known as *l'Hospital's Rule* and holds whether a is finite or infinite. It should be emphasized that here, in order to determine $\lim\limits_{x \to a} \dfrac{f(x)}{g(x)}$ we actually take the derivative of the numerator and the derivative of the denominator separately and then evaluate the quotient of the derivatives, i.e., compute $\lim\limits_{x \to a} \dfrac{f'(x)}{g'(x)}$ provided this is not again indeterminate. The student should be warned not to confuse this operation with that of differentiating a quotient.

If $\lim\limits_{x \to a} \dfrac{f'(x)}{g'(x)}$ is itself an indeterminate form, then we may start over again and apply l'Hospital's Rule to this getting $\lim\limits_{x \to a} \dfrac{f'(x)}{g'(x)} = \lim\limits_{x \to a} \dfrac{f''(x)}{g''(x)}$, etc. Most of the problems that the student will ordinarily meet will yield to a finite number of repeated applications of this rule.

L'Hospital's Rule also applies to indeterminate forms of the type $\dfrac{\infty}{\infty}$, i.e., to the case where $\lim\limits_{x \to a} \dfrac{f(x)}{g(x)} = \dfrac{\infty}{\infty}$. In either type, $\dfrac{0}{0}$ or $\dfrac{\infty}{\infty}$, the point a may be finite or infinite.

But there are indeterminate forms of other types, namely, $\infty \cdot 0$, 1^{∞}, 0^{0}, ∞^{0}, and $\infty - \infty$. It is evident that if $\lim\limits_{x \to a} f(x)g(x) = \infty \cdot 0$, where $\lim\limits_{x \to a} f(x) = \infty$, $\lim\limits_{x \to a} g(x) = 0$, then $\lim\limits_{x \to a} \dfrac{f(x)}{\dfrac{1}{g(x)}}$ is of type $\dfrac{\infty}{\infty}$ and we resort to l'Hospital's Rule. Next consider $\lim\limits_{x \to a} f(x)^{g(x)} = 1^{\infty}$ where $\lim\limits_{x \to a} f(x) = 1$, $\lim\limits_{x \to a} g(x) = \infty$. By taking logarithms of both sides we have (see (4) p. 25) $\log \lim\limits_{x \to a} f(x)^{g(x)} = \lim\limits_{x \to a} \log f(x)^{g(x)} = \lim\limits_{x \to a} g(x) \log f(x) = \infty \cdot 0$. Hence $\lim\limits_{x \to a} \dfrac{\log f(x)}{\dfrac{1}{g(x)}} = \dfrac{0}{0}$ type and we apply l'Hospital's Rule at this point. (Or we write $\lim\limits_{x \to a} \dfrac{g(x)}{\dfrac{1}{\log f(x)}} = \dfrac{\infty}{\infty}$ and apply the rule if this form is easier to handle so far as the differentiation is concerned.) If $\lim\limits_{x \to a} \dfrac{\log f(x)}{\dfrac{1}{g(x)}} = b$, then the answer to the original problem is $\lim\limits_{x \to a} f(x)^{g(x)} = e^b$. In a similar way we treat type

$\lim\limits_{x \to a} f(x)^{g(x)} = 0^0$ since here $\lim\limits_{x \to a} \dfrac{g(x)}{\dfrac{1}{\log f(x)}} = \dfrac{0}{0}$. And again this

method applies to type $\lim\limits_{x \to a} f(x)^{g(x)} = \infty^0$ since $\lim\limits_{x \to a} \dfrac{g(x)}{\dfrac{1}{\log f(x)}} = \dfrac{0}{0}$.

Finally the type $\lim\limits_{x \to a} [f(x) - g(x)] = \infty - \infty$ can be trans-

formed into type $\dfrac{0}{0}$ since we can write $\lim\limits_{x \to a} [f(x) - g(x)] =$

$\lim\limits_{x \to a} \left(\dfrac{1}{\dfrac{1}{f(x)}} - \dfrac{1}{\dfrac{1}{g(x)}} \right) = \lim\limits_{x \to a} \dfrac{\dfrac{1}{g(x)} - \dfrac{1}{f(x)}}{\dfrac{1}{g(x)} \cdot \dfrac{1}{f(x)}} = \dfrac{0}{0}.$

SUMMARY

Type of Indeterminate Form   *Apply l'Hospital's Rule to:*

1. $\lim \dfrac{f}{g} = \dfrac{0}{0}$

2. $\lim \dfrac{f}{g} = \dfrac{\infty}{\infty}$

$\left\{ \begin{array}{l} \lim \dfrac{f}{g} = \lim \dfrac{f'}{g'} = \lim \dfrac{f''}{g''} = \lim \dfrac{f'''}{g'''} = \cdots. \\[6pt] \quad \text{The first one of these which is not} \\ \text{indeterminate will give the answer.} \end{array} \right.$

3. $\lim fg = \infty \cdot 0$

$\left\{ \begin{array}{l} \lim \dfrac{f}{\dfrac{1}{g}} \text{ or to } \lim \dfrac{g}{\dfrac{1}{f}}. \end{array} \right.$

4. $\lim f^g = 1^\infty$

5. $\lim f^g = 0^0$

6. $\lim f^g = \infty^0$

$\left\{ \begin{array}{l} \lim \dfrac{\log f}{\dfrac{1}{g}} \text{ or to } \lim \dfrac{g}{\dfrac{1}{\log f}}. \\[6pt] \quad \text{If l'Hospital's Rule applied to one} \\ \text{of these yields } b \text{ for the limit, then the} \\ \text{answer to the original problem is } e^b. \end{array} \right.$

7. $\lim (f - g) = \infty - \infty$

$\left\{ \begin{array}{l} \lim \dfrac{\dfrac{1}{g} - \dfrac{1}{f}}{\dfrac{1}{g} \cdot \dfrac{1}{f}}. \\[6pt] \quad \text{The answer will be given directly by} \\ \text{l'Hospital's Rule.} \end{array} \right.$

Illustration 1. Find $\lim\limits_{x \to 0} \dfrac{\sin 2x + \tan x}{3x}$.

Solution. This limit is of type $\dfrac{0}{0}$. Applying l'Hospital's Rule we obtain

$$\lim_{x \to 0} \frac{2\cos 2x + \sec^2 x}{3} = 1.$$

Illustration 2. Find $\lim_{x \to 0} \frac{\sin 2x \tan x}{3x}$.

Solution. This limit by l'Hospital's Rule equals

$$\lim_{x \to 0} \frac{\sin 2x \sec^2 x + 2 \cos 2x \tan x}{3} = 0.$$

Illustration 3. Find $\lim_{x \to 0} \frac{\sin 2x + \tan x}{3x^2}$.

Solution. This limit equals $\lim_{x \to 0} \frac{2\cos 2x + \sec^2 x}{6x} = \frac{3}{0} = \infty$.

Illustration 4. Find $\lim_{x \to \infty} \frac{x^n}{e^x}$.

Solution. This is of type $\frac{\infty}{\infty}$. We get

$$\lim_{x \to \infty} \frac{x^n}{e^x} = \lim_{x \to \infty} \frac{nx^{n-1}}{e^x} = \lim_{x \to \infty} \frac{n(n-1)x^{n-2}}{e^x} = \cdots$$

$$= \lim_{x \to \infty} \frac{n!}{e^x} = 0.$$

Illustration 5. Find $\lim_{x \to \infty} (1+x)^{\frac{1}{x}}$.

Solution. This is of type ∞^0. We write

$$\lim_{x \to \infty} \frac{\log(1+x)}{x} = \lim_{x \to \infty} \frac{\frac{1}{1+x}}{1} = 0$$

Therefore $\qquad \lim_{x \to \infty} (1+x)^{\frac{1}{x}} = e^0 = 1.$

Illustration 6. Show that $\lim f^g = 0^\infty$ is not indeterminate but equals 0.

Solution. Write $\qquad A = \lim f^g$

Then $\qquad\qquad \log A = \lim g \log f$

$\qquad\qquad\qquad\quad = \lim (\infty)(-\infty)$

$\qquad\qquad\qquad\quad = -\infty$

Therefore $\qquad\quad A = e^{-\infty} = 0.$

Illustration 7. Evaluate $\lim_{x \to 0} \frac{e^x - e^{-x} - 2x}{x - \sin x}$.

Solution. This equals $\frac{0}{0}$ type.

$$\lim_{x \to 0} \frac{e^x + e^{-x} - 2}{1 - \cos x} = \frac{0}{0} =$$

$$\lim_{x \to 0} \frac{e^x - e^{-x}}{\sin x} = \frac{0}{0} = \lim_{x \to 0} \frac{e^x + e^{-x}}{\cos x} = 2.$$

Illustration 8. Evaluate $\lim\limits_{x \to \frac{\pi}{2}} (\tan x - \sec x)$.

Solution. This is of type $\infty - \infty$. We write

$$\lim_{x \to \frac{\pi}{2}} (\tan x - \sec x)$$

$$= \lim_{x \to \frac{\pi}{2}} \left(\frac{\sin x}{\cos x} - \frac{1}{\cos x} \right)$$

$$= \lim_{x \to \frac{\pi}{2}} \left(\frac{\sin x - 1}{\cos x} \right) = \frac{0}{0}$$

$$= \lim_{x \to \frac{\pi}{2}} \frac{\cos x}{-\sin x} = 0.$$

EXERCISES

Evaluate the following limits.

PROBLEM	ANSWER
1. $\lim\limits_{x \to 1} \dfrac{x^3 - x}{x^4 - 3x^2 + 1}$	0
2. $\lim\limits_{x \to 2} \dfrac{x^3 - 6x + 4}{x^2 + x - 6}$	$\dfrac{6}{5}$
3. $\lim\limits_{\theta \to 0} \dfrac{1 - \cos \theta}{\theta^2}$	$\dfrac{1}{2}$
4. $\lim\limits_{y \to 0} \dfrac{\log \sin y}{\log y}$	1
5. $\lim\limits_{x \to \infty} \dfrac{x^n}{n^x}$	0
6. $\lim\limits_{z \to \infty} z^{\frac{1}{z}}$	1
7. $\lim\limits_{\theta \to 0} \dfrac{\theta}{\sin^{-1} \theta}$	1
8. $\lim\limits_{x \to \infty} \dfrac{a^x}{x^b}$	∞
9. $\lim\limits_{x \to \infty} \dfrac{\log x}{x}$	0
10. $\lim\limits_{x \to \frac{1}{2}} (1 - 2x) \tan \pi x$	

CHAPTER IX

INTEGRATION

34. Indefinite Integrals. In Chapter IV we established rules whereby the derivatives of the standard elementary functions and combinations of them could be obtained. At this time a thorough review of the differentiation formulae on page 41 is desirable. For we are now to study the process inverse to that of differentiation. Suppose, for example, we were given the derivative of some function and were asked to find the function. More specifically let $\frac{dy}{dx} = x^3$. The problem is to find y, some function of x, whose derivative is x^3. Because of our knowledge of the derivatives, we see that y must be something like x^4. But if $y = x^4$ were differentiated, we would have $\frac{dy}{dx} = 4x^3$, which is not what was given. However, $4x^3$ differs from x^3 only in the multiplicative factor 4; hence if we had chosen $y = \frac{1}{4}x^4$, we would then get $\frac{dy}{dx} = x^3$, which is exactly what we were given. There is still another point: if $y = \frac{1}{4}x^4 + c$, where c is any constant, then $\frac{dy}{dx} = x^3$. And $y = \frac{1}{4}x^4 + c$ is the most general function whose derivative is $y' = x^3$. We have thus reversed the process and have found the function y which differentiates into x^3; the function, $y = \frac{1}{4}x^4 + c$, is not unique: c can have any value so long as it is constant. The process of beginning with y' and from it finding y is known as integration and c is called the arbitrary constant of integration. In symbols we write $y = \int x^3\, dx = \frac{1}{4}x^4 + c$. The symbol will be discussed more fully later.

Clearly then we could be given $\frac{dy}{dx} = f(x)$ and be asked to find y. This means that y is some function whose derivative is $f(x)$, a given function. The answer will be given by

$$(1) \qquad\qquad y = \int f(x)\, dx$$

where an arbitrary constant of integration must be added to whatever particular function we find that will differentiate into $f(x)$.

We should like to know the answers (and to memorize them) in the cases of the standard elementary functions with which we normally work. To this end we develop formulae of integration corresponding to the formulae of differentiation derived in Chapter IV.

The symbol (1) for the integral comes about in the following way. When a function, say $f(x)$, is to be differentiated, we must specify the variable with respect to which the differentiation is to take place. The derivative of $f(x)$ with respect to x is $\dfrac{df}{dx}$; the derivative with respect to t is, in symbol, $\dfrac{df}{dt}$ (or this could be written $\dfrac{df}{dx} \cdot \dfrac{dx}{dt}$). So in the reverse process of integration we must integrate with respect to a certain variable. We write

$$(2) \qquad\qquad \frac{dy}{dx} = f(x)$$

$$(3) \qquad\qquad dy = f(x)\, dx$$

Integrating both sides of (3), we get

$$(4) \qquad\qquad y = \int dy = \int f(x)\, dx$$

where differential x, dx, in (4) tells us that the integration of $f(x)$ is to take place with respect to x. This notation will have still more meaning after the material in Chapter X is covered.

The function $f(x)$ in (4) is called the integrand. Note that $\int x^3\, dx = \tfrac{1}{4} x^4 + c$ and that $\int t^3\, dt = \tfrac{1}{4} t^4 + c$ but that $\int x^3\, dt$ cannot be performed until we know what function x is of t. This corresponds directly with the parallel situation in differentiation where $\dfrac{dx^3}{dx} = 3\, x^2$, but $\dfrac{dx^3}{dt} = 3\, x^2 \dfrac{dx}{dt}$ and this cannot be completed until we know the relation between x and t. For example, let $x = e^{2t}$, then $\dfrac{dx^3}{dt} = \dfrac{de^{6t}}{dt} = 6\,e^{6t}$. Similarly $\int x^3\,dt$ would become $\int e^{6t}\,dt = \frac{1}{6}\,e^{6t} + c$ as the student can quickly check by differentiation.

In the development of the formulae for differentiation we generally worked with functions $u(x)$. We shall do likewise in the formulae for integration.

The integrals I–XVII are the direct consequence of our knowledge of the derivatives developed in Chapter IV. They should be memorized.

I. $\int o\,dx = c$

II. $\int k\,dx = k\int dx = kx + c$

III. $\int x^n\,dx = \dfrac{x^{n+1}}{n+1} + c, \quad n \neq -1$

IV. $\int u^n\,du = \dfrac{u^{n+1}}{n+1} + c, \quad n \neq -1$

V. $\int \dfrac{1}{u}\,du = \log u + c$

VI. $\int [u(x) \pm v(x)]\,dx = \int u(x)\,dx \pm \int v(x)\,dx.$

The integral of a (finite) sum is the sum of the integrals.

VII. $\int e^u\,du = e^u + c$

VIII. $\int a^u\,du = \dfrac{a^u}{\log a} + c$

IX. $\int \sin u\,du = -\cos u + c$

X. $\int \cos u\,du = \sin u + c$

XI. $\int \sec^2 u\,du = \tan u + c$

XII. $\int \csc^2 u\,du = -\cot u + c$

XIII. $\int \sec u \tan u\,du = \sec u + c$

XIV. $\int \csc u \cot u \, du = -\csc u + c$

XV. $\int \dfrac{du}{\sqrt{a^2 - u^2}} = \sin^{-1} \dfrac{u}{a} + c$

XVI. $\int \dfrac{du}{a^2 + u^2} = \dfrac{1}{a} \tan^{-1} \dfrac{u}{a} + c$

XVII. $\int \dfrac{du}{u \sqrt{u^2 - a^2}} = \dfrac{1}{a} \sec^{-1} \dfrac{u}{a} + c$

The following integrals are met so frequently that they too should be memorized. It will be noted that they do not come from differentiation formulae that we have considered as the standard elementary ones to be committed to memory. But they are nevertheless very important and a knowledge of them will be of tremendous aid in the integration of more complicated functions.

XVIII. $\int \tan u \, du = \log \sec u + c$

XIX. $\int \cot u \, du = \log \sin u + c$

XX. $\int \sec u \, du = \log (\sec u + \tan u) + c$

XXI. $\int \csc u \, du = \log (\csc u - \cot u) + c$

XXII. $\int \dfrac{du}{u^2 - a^2} = \dfrac{1}{2a} \log \dfrac{u - a}{u + a} + c$

XXIII. $\int \dfrac{du}{a^2 - u^2} = \dfrac{1}{2a} \log \dfrac{a + u}{a - u} + c$

XXIV. $\int \dfrac{du}{\sqrt{u^2 \pm a^2}} = \log (u + \sqrt{u^2 \pm a^2}) + c$

XXV. $\int \sqrt{a^2 - u^2} \, du = \dfrac{u}{2} \sqrt{a^2 - u^2} + \dfrac{a^2}{2} \sin^{-1} \dfrac{u}{a} + c$

XXVI. $\int \sqrt{u^2 \pm a^2} \, du = \dfrac{u}{2} \sqrt{u^2 \pm a^2} \pm \dfrac{a^2}{2} \log (u + \sqrt{u^2 \pm a^2}) + c$

It would be a simple matter to verify these integrals by differentiating the answers, thus obtaining the integrands. But we should derive these answers by way of beginning a discussion of the general methods of integration. To do this we begin with XVIII; offhand we know no function that will differentiate into tan u. But write

(5) $\qquad \int \tan u \, du = \int \dfrac{\sin u}{\cos u} \, du$

and then examine V, which says that the integral of a fraction the numerator of which is the differential (du) of the denominator (u) is log u. The denominator of (5) is cos u, whose differential is $- \sin u \, du$. Hence we could write

(6) $\qquad \int \tan u \, du = -\int \dfrac{- \sin u \, du}{\cos u} = - \log \cos u + c$

Since $- \log \cos u = \log (\cos u)^{-1} = \log \dfrac{1}{\cos u} = \log \sec u$ the form of the answer given in XVIII follows.

Similarly for XIX we have

(7) $\qquad \int \cot u \, du = \int \dfrac{\cos u \, du}{\sin u} = \log \sin u + c$ by V.

To derive XX we write

(8) $\qquad \int \sec u \, du = \int \dfrac{du}{\cos u} = \int \dfrac{\cos u \, du}{\cos^2 u} = \int \dfrac{d(\sin u)}{1 - \sin^2 u}$

which is of the form $\int \dfrac{dv}{1 - v^2}$ (if we set $v = \sin u$) and this in turn is of type XXIII. Therefore

(9) $\qquad \int \sec u \, du = \tfrac{1}{2} \log \dfrac{1 + \sin u}{1 - \sin u} + c$

and this is a perfectly good and standard form for $\int \sec u \, du$. By noting that $\dfrac{1 + \sin u}{1 - \sin u} = (\sec u + \tan u)^2$, a trigonometric identity, the final form XX is obtained.

There is still another useful form for this integral:

$$\int \sec u \, du = \log \tan \left(\dfrac{\pi}{4} + \dfrac{u}{2} \right) + c.$$

This may be derived from (9) by the change in variable $u = v - \dfrac{\pi}{2}$ (in the answer).

The integral in XXI, $\int \csc u \, du$, is derived in a manner exactly analogous to that used for $\int \sec u \, du$ and is left as an exercise for the student.

For formula XXII we make use of partial fractions which might be called a process inverse to that of reducing a fraction to a common denominator. This method is explained in some detail in § 37; at the present it will be sufficient to note that

$$\frac{1}{u^2 - a^2} = \frac{\dfrac{1}{2 a}}{u - a} - \frac{\dfrac{1}{2 a}}{u + a}$$

by reducing the right-hand members to a common denominator, thus obtaining immediately the left-hand member of the equation. Hence

(10) $$\int \frac{du}{u^2 - a^2} = \frac{1}{2 a} \int \frac{du}{u - a} - \frac{1}{2 a} \int \frac{du}{u + a}$$

But each of these last two integrals is of form V. Therefore

(11) $$\int \frac{du}{u^2 - a^2} = \frac{1}{2 a} \log (u - a) - \frac{1}{2 a} \log (u + a) + c$$

$$= \frac{1}{2 a} \log \frac{u - a}{u + a} + c$$

Since XXIII is handled in identically the same way, we leave it to the student as an exercise.

To obtain one of the integrals in XXIV, $\int \dfrac{du}{\sqrt{u^2 + a^2}}$, we make use of the device known as the method of transformations. (See § 36 for a fuller discussion.) Let $u = a \tan v$; then $du = a \sec^2 v \, dv$ and our integral becomes

(12) $$\int \frac{du}{\sqrt{u^2 + a^2}} = \int \frac{a \sec^2 v \, dv}{\sqrt{a^2 \tan^2 v + a^2}}$$

$$= \int \frac{a \sec^2 v \, dv}{a \sec v} = \int \sec v \, dv$$

$$= \log (\sec v + \tan v) + c$$

by XX. But if $u = a \tan v$, $\sec v = \dfrac{\sqrt{u^2 + a^2}}{a}$ and (12) becomes

(13) $$\int \frac{du}{\sqrt{u^2 + a^2}} = \log \left(\frac{u}{a} + \frac{\sqrt{u^2 + a^2}}{a} \right) + c$$

$$= \log \left(\frac{u + \sqrt{u^2 + a^2}}{a} \right) + c$$

$$= \log (u + \sqrt{u^2 + a^2}) - \log a + c$$

But a is a constant and hence we might combine $- \log a + c$, calling it a new constant k. This completes the derivation of the one integral in XXIV and the other, using the minus sign, follows the same pattern.

To perform the integration in XXV we make another transformation, this time setting $u = a \sin v$, $du = a \cos v \, dv$. The integral becomes

(14) $$\int \sqrt{a^2 - u^2} \, du = \int a^2 \cos^2 v \, dv$$

$$= a^2 \int \left(\frac{1 + \cos 2v}{2} \right) dv$$

$$= \frac{a^2}{2} \int (1 + \cos 2v) \, dv$$

$$= \frac{a^2}{2} [v + \tfrac{1}{2} \sin 2v] + c$$

$$= \frac{a^2}{2} [v + \sin v \cos v] + c$$

$$= \frac{a^2}{2} \left[\sin^{-1} \frac{u}{a} + \frac{u}{a} \frac{\sqrt{a^2 - u^2}}{a} \right] + c.$$

This is formula XXV.

Finally the integrals XXVI are best treated by a process called integration by parts which we now explain.

35. Integration by Parts. The method makes use of the simple form of the differential of a product:

(1) $$d(uv) = u \, dv + v \, du$$

or, transposing, we have

(2) $$u \, dv = d(uv) - v \, du$$

Upon integrating (2) we obtain

(3) $$\int u \, dv = uv - \int v \, du.$$

Hence the integral $\int u \, dv$ is made to depend upon the integral $\int v \, du$, which may be more readily handled or may be recognizable as one of the standard forms. We illustrate the method first with a simple example.

Illustration 1. Find $\int xe^x \, dx$.

Solution. This does not immediately come under any of the standard cases. Let us choose $u = x$ and $dv = e^x \, dx$.

Then $du = dx$ and $v = \int e^x \, dx = e^x$. (We shall add our constant of integration later.) Then our integral becomes, integrating by parts

$$\int u \, dv = uv - \int v \, du$$

$$\int xe^x \, dx = xe^x - \int e^x \, dx$$

and this last integral is one of the standard forms. Hence

$$\int xe^x \, dx = xe^x - e^x + c.$$

We shall now derive formula XXVI using the plus sign. First we transform the integral by setting $u = a \tan z$ and du becomes $du = a \sec^2 z \, dz$. The integral therefore becomes

$$(4) \qquad \int \sqrt{u^2 + a^2} \, du = \int a \sec z \; a \sec^2 z \, dz$$

$$(5) \qquad = a^2 \int \sec^3 z \, dz$$

This last integral we integrate by parts, setting $u = \sec z$ and $dv = \sec^2 z \, dz$; hence $du = \sec z \tan z \, dz$ and $v = \int \sec^2 z \, dz = \tan z$. Thus (5) becomes, upon applying the integration by parts formula (3)

$$(6) \quad a^2 \int \sec^3 z \, dz = a^2 \sec z \tan z - a^2 \int \sec z \tan^2 z \, dz$$

$$= a^2 \sec z \tan z - a^2 \int \sec z \, (\sec^2 z - 1) \, dz$$

$$= a^2 \sec z \tan z + a^2 \int \sec z \, dz - a^2 \int \sec^3 z \, dz$$

$$(7) \qquad = a^2 \sec z \tan z + a^2 \log (\sec z + \tan z) - a^2 \int \sec^3 z \, dz$$

upon the use of XX.

But the last member in (7) is the very thing we seek, namely, $\int \sec^3 z \, dz$; but it has the factor $- a^2$. Hence if we bring it over to the left-hand side of the equation we get

(8) $\quad 2 \, a^2 \int \sec^3 z \, dz = a^2 \sec z \tan z + a^2 \log (\sec z + \tan z),$

or, dividing by 2,

(9) $\quad a^2 \int \sec^3 z \, dz = \dfrac{a^2}{2} \sec z \tan z + \dfrac{a^2}{2} \log (\sec z + \tan z).$

Finally transforming this back into the variable u we have XXVI or

$$\int \sqrt{u^2 + a^2} \, du = \frac{u}{2} \sqrt{u^2 + a^2} + \frac{a^2}{2} \log (u + \sqrt{u^2 + a^2}) + c.$$

The student should carry through XXVI when the minus sign is used.

This completes the derivation of the standard formulae of integration I–XXVI and we now further illustrate the principle of integration by parts with

Illustration 2. Find $\int x^2 \sin x \, dx.$

Solution. Set $u = x^2, \, dv = \sin x \, dx$
(The object is so to choose u and dv as *1st* to make *dv* integrable and *2nd* to make $\int v \, du$ simpler than the original $\int u \, dv.$)
Here $du = 2 \, x \, dx$ and $v = - \cos x.$ Then

$$\int x^2 \sin x \, dx = - x^2 \cos x + \int 2 \, x \cos x \, dx.$$

Note that this last integral is of the same type except that we have x instead of x^2 as a multiplier of the trigonometric part. We therefore apply the rule once more (to $\int x \cos x \, dx$) setting $u = x, \, dv = \cos x \, dx$ which gives $du = dx$ and $v = \sin x.$ Our integral becomes

$$\int x^2 \sin x \, dx = - x^2 \cos x + 2[x \sin x - \int \sin x \, dx]$$
$$= - x^2 \cos x + 2 \, x \sin x + 2 \cos x + c.$$

Illustration 3.   Find $\int e^x \sin x \, dx$.

Solution.   Set $u = e^x$, $dv = \sin x \, dx$; then $du = e^x \, dx$, $v = -\cos x$.

$$\int e^x \sin x \, dx = -e^x \cos x + \int e^x \cos x \, dx.$$

For the last integral set $u = e^x$, $dv = \cos x \, dx$; then $du = e^x \, dx$ and $v = \sin x$. Or

$$\int e^x \sin x \, dx = -e^x \cos x + [e^x \sin x - \int e^x \sin x \, dx]$$

Thus, transposing the last integral,

$$2 \int e^x \sin x \, dx = -e^x \cos x + e^x \sin x;$$

or finally

$$\int e^x \sin x \, dx = \frac{e^x}{2} (\sin x - \cos x) + c.$$

Illustration 4.   Find $\int x^3 \sqrt{x^2 - 2} \, dx$.

Solution.   Set $u = x^2$, $dv = x\sqrt{x^2 - 2} \, dx$.

Then $du = 2 x \, dx$ and $v = \frac{1}{3}(x^2 - 2)^{\frac{3}{2}}$ by IV.   Thus

$$\int x^3 \sqrt{x^2 - 2} \, dx = \frac{x^2}{3} (x^2 - 2)^{\frac{3}{2}} - \frac{2}{3} \int x(x^2 - 2)^{\frac{3}{2}} \, dx$$

But this last integral is again one of type IV.   Hence

$$\int x^3 \sqrt{x^2 - 2} \, dx = \frac{x^2}{3} (x^2 - 2)^{\frac{3}{2}} - \frac{2}{15} (x^2 - 2)^{\frac{5}{2}} + c.$$

Only by solving many problems will the student gain proficiency in this method: it is not an easy matter to choose the parts u and dv without wide experience.

It should be said that a particular problem may not yield readily to this method in which case other methods should be tried. Among these is the one of transformations already used in deriving several of the standard formulae.

36. Integration by Transformations. No general rule can be laid down as to what transformation will reduce a given integral to one of recognizable form. But in certain cases particular transformations automatically suggest themselves. Since the Pythagorean Theorem for a right triangle states that the square on the hypotenuse equals the sums of squares of the two sides, an appropriate trigonometric transformation might simplify a given integral involving such quantities as $\sqrt{u^2 - a^2}$, $\sqrt{u^2 + a^2}$, $\sqrt{a^2 - u^2}$. For example:

If $\sqrt{u^2 - a^2}$ is present, try $u = a \csc \theta$.
If $\sqrt{u^2 + a^2}$ is present, try $u = a \tan \theta$.
If $\sqrt{a^2 - u^2}$ is present, try $u = a \sin \theta$.

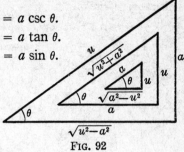

But success is not assured even when such a transformation is used and it may be necessary to apply other methods.

Fig. 92

Illustration 1. Find $\int \dfrac{x^2 \, dx}{\sqrt{4 - x^2}}$.

Solution. Set $x = 2 \sin \theta$, $dx = 2 \cos \theta \, d\theta$.

(The student should draw a figure and note that $\dfrac{x}{\sqrt{4 - x^2}} = \tan \theta$.)

$$\int \frac{x^2 \, dx}{\sqrt{4 - x^2}} = 4 \int \sin \theta \tan \theta \cos \theta \, d\theta$$

$$= 4 \int \sin^2 \theta \, d\theta$$

This last integral is readily handled by writing

$$\sin^2 \theta = \frac{1 - \cos 2\theta}{2}$$

$$\int \frac{x^2 \, dx}{\sqrt{4 - x^2}} = 2 \int (1 - \cos 2\theta) \, d\theta$$

$$= 2\theta - \sin 2\theta + c$$

$$= 2\theta - 2 \sin \theta \cos \theta + c$$

$$= 2 \sin^{-1} \frac{x}{2} - \frac{x}{2} \sqrt{4 - x^2} + c.$$

Illustration 2. Find $\int \dfrac{x \, dx}{(x^2 + 9)^{\frac{5}{2}}}$.

Solution. This requires no transformation since it is already in standard form IV.   Write

$$\int \frac{x \, dx}{(x^2 + 9)^{\frac{5}{2}}} = \frac{1}{2} \int (x^2 + 9)^{-\frac{5}{2}} (2 x \, dx)$$

$$= \frac{1}{2} \frac{(x^2 + 9)^{-\frac{3}{2}}}{-\frac{3}{2}} + c$$

$$= -\frac{1}{3} (x^2 + 9)^{-\frac{3}{2}} + c.$$

Illustration 3. Find $\int \sin^3 x \, dx$.

Solution. Write this as

$$\int (1 - \cos^2 x) \sin x \, dx = \int (\sin x - \cos^2 x \sin x) \, dx$$
$$= - \cos x + \tfrac{1}{3} \cos^3 x + c.$$

Illustration 4. Find $\int \dfrac{dx}{(5 + x^2)^{\frac{3}{2}}}$.

Solution. Set
$$x = \sqrt{5} \tan \theta,$$
$$dx = \sqrt{5} \sec^2 \theta \, d\theta$$

$$\int \frac{dx}{(5 + x^2)^{\frac{3}{2}}} = \int \left(\frac{1}{5^{\frac{3}{2}}} \cos^3 \theta \right) (5^{\frac{1}{2}} \sec^2 \theta \, d\theta)$$

$$= \frac{1}{5} \int \cos \theta \, d\theta$$

$$= \tfrac{1}{5} \sin \theta + c$$

$$= \frac{1}{5} \frac{x}{\sqrt{5 + x^2}} + c.$$

Again some other transformation may be suggested by the particular form of the function to be integrated.

Illustration 5. Find $\int \dfrac{dx}{x + 5 - \sqrt{x + 5}}$.

Solution. Here it seems reasonable to think of $(x + 5)$ as a new variable. Because of the square root term we set $\sqrt{x + 5} = z$; then $x + 5 = z^2$ and $dx = 2 z \, dz$. Our integral becomes

$$\int \frac{dx}{x + 5 - \sqrt{x + 5}} = \int \frac{2 z \, dz}{z^2 - z}$$

$$= 2 \int \frac{dz}{z - 1} = 2 \log (z - 1) + c$$

$$= 2 \log (\sqrt{x + 5} - 1) + c.$$

Illustration 6. Find $\int \dfrac{dx}{\sqrt{x^2 - 3 x + 2}}$.

Solution. If this could be thrown into the form $\int \dfrac{du}{\sqrt{u^2 \pm a^2}}$, this could immediately be integrated by XXIV. That this is possible will be seen after a little reflection upon the process of completing the square. We write

$$\int \frac{dx}{\sqrt{x^2 - 3 x + 2}} = \int \frac{dx}{\sqrt{x^2 - 3 x + \tfrac{9}{4} + 2 - \tfrac{9}{4}}}$$

$$= \int \frac{dx}{\sqrt{(x - \tfrac{3}{2})^2 - \tfrac{1}{4}}}.$$

Now set $x - \frac{3}{2} = z$ and we get

$$= \int \frac{dz}{\sqrt{z^2 - \frac{1}{4}}} = \log (z + \sqrt{z^2 - \frac{1}{4}}) + c$$

$$= \log (x - \frac{3}{2} + \sqrt{x^2 - 3x + 2}) + c.$$

This principle of completing the square should be applied to integrals of the form XV, XVI, XXII–XXVI which contain a linear term cu in addition to the quadratic term u^2 and the constant a^2. We illustrate with another example.

Illustration 7. Find $\int \frac{(3x - 5)\, dx}{x^2 + 2x + 9}$.

Solution. We first write this in the form

(a) $\qquad \frac{3}{2} \int \frac{(2x + 2)\, dx}{x^2 + 2x + 9} - 8 \int \frac{dx}{x^2 + 2x + 9}.$

The factor in the denominators is the same as in the original integral. The numerator of the first integral in (a) is made (chosen) to be the derivative of this denominator. This is done since then that integral is of the standard form V, $\int \frac{du}{u}$. The multiplicative factor $\frac{3}{2}$ will result in giving us the $3x$ term that is needed. Finally $-8 \int \frac{dx}{x^2 + 2x + 9}$ is added so that we get our -5 term in the original integral. A partial answer is, therefore

(b) $\qquad \frac{3}{2} \log (x^2 + 2x + 9) - 8 \int \frac{dx}{x^2 + 2x + 9}.$

We now complete the square in the integral remaining in (b) and this integral becomes

(c) $\qquad \int \frac{dx}{x^2 + 2x + 9} = \int \frac{dx}{(x + 1)^2 + 8}.$

Next let $x + 1 = z, dx = dz$ and (c) becomes

$$\int \frac{dz}{z^2 + 8}$$

which is of form XVI and which equals

$$\frac{1}{2\sqrt{2}} \tan^{-1} \frac{z}{2\sqrt{2}}.$$

The final answer then is

$$\int \frac{3x - 5}{x^2 + 2x + 9} = \frac{3}{2} \log (x^2 + 2x + 9) - 2\sqrt{2} \tan^{-1} \frac{x + 1}{2\sqrt{2}} + c.$$

Illustration 8.   Find $\displaystyle\int \frac{(x+1)\,dx}{2\,x^2 - 4\,x - 5}$.

Solution.   We treat this in the same way we treated the problem in Illustration 7.

$$\int \frac{(x+1)\,dx}{2\,x^2 - 4\,x - 5} = \frac{1}{4}\int \frac{(4\,x-4)\,dx}{2\,x^2 - 4\,x - 5} + 2\int \frac{dx}{2\,x^2 - 4\,x - 5}$$

$$= \frac{1}{4}\log(2\,x^2 - 4\,x - 5) + 2\int \frac{dx}{2(x^2 - 2\,x - \frac{5}{2})}$$

This last integral equals

(a) $$\int \frac{dx}{(x-1)^2 - \frac{7}{2}}.$$

Now set $x - 1 = z$, $dx = dz$, and (a) becomes

$$\int \frac{dz}{z^2 - \frac{7}{2}}$$

which is of type XXII and which equals

$$\frac{1}{2\sqrt{\frac{7}{2}}}\log \frac{z - \sqrt{\frac{7}{2}}}{z + \sqrt{\frac{7}{2}}} = \frac{\sqrt{14}}{14}\log \frac{\sqrt{2}(x-1) - \sqrt{7}}{\sqrt{2}(x-1) + \sqrt{7}}$$

Hence, finally

$$\int \frac{(x+1)\,dx}{2\,x^2 - 4\,x - 5} = \frac{1}{4}\log(2\,x^2 - 4\,x - 5) + \frac{\sqrt{14}}{14}\log \frac{\sqrt{2}(x-1) - \sqrt{7}}{\sqrt{2}(x-1) + \sqrt{7}} + c.$$

Because of the complicated factors involved there seems to be no point in combining these terms.

The important fact to be gained from the last two illustrations is that integrals of the type $\displaystyle\int \frac{(ax+b)\,dx}{px^2 + qx + r}$ always reduce by the methods used in these illustrations to integrals of type V, XVI, and/or XXII (or XXIII) (logarithms and arc tangents).

Illustration 9. $\displaystyle\int x(7 + 3\,x)^{\frac{1}{3}}\,dx.$

Solution.   The substitution $7 + 3\,x = z^3$ seems a reasonable one since this will rationalize the integrand; $dx = z^2\,dz$.

$$\int x(7 + 3\,x)^{\frac{1}{3}}\,dx = \int \frac{z^3 - 7}{3} \cdot z \cdot z^2\,dz$$

$$= \int \left(\frac{z^6}{3} - \frac{7}{3}\,z^3\right)dz$$

$$= \frac{z^7}{21} - \frac{7}{12}\,z^4 + c$$

$$= \frac{(7 + 3\,x)^{\frac{7}{3}}}{21} - \frac{7}{12}\,(7 + 3\,x)^{\frac{4}{3}} + c.$$

Again we repeat that the student will gain knowledge of integration by means of substitutions only after solving many problems and making many false starts; what seems to be the "obvious" substitution to make often proves to be of no aid at all in a particular problem.

There is a third standard method in use in integration beyond the method of integration by parts and the method of transformations.   This we discuss in the next article.

37. Integration by Partial Fractions.   This method is particularly useful in the integration of rational fractions (the quotient of two polynomials) where the denominator has real factors.   Suppose the integrand is of the form $\dfrac{ax+b}{x^2+px+q} \equiv$ $\dfrac{ax+b}{(x-\alpha)(x-\beta)}$, where the factors of x^2+px+q are $(x-\alpha)$, $(x-\beta)$.   We suppose that $ax+b$ is not one of these factors. Algebraically it is evident that constants A and B exist such that

(1) $$\frac{ax+b}{(x-\alpha)(x-\beta)} \equiv \frac{A}{x-\alpha} + \frac{B}{x-\beta},$$

because if the right-hand members be reduced to a common denominator, (1) becomes

(2) $$\frac{ax+b}{(x-\alpha)(x-\beta)} \equiv \frac{A}{x-\alpha} + \frac{B}{x-\beta} \equiv \frac{A(x-\beta)+B(x-\alpha)}{(x-\alpha)(x-\beta)}$$
$$\equiv \frac{(A+B)x+(-A\beta-B\alpha)}{(x-\alpha)(x-\beta)}$$

and A and B can be determined so that $A+B = a$, and $A\beta + B\alpha = -b$.   (In solving these simultaneous equations by determinants we find

$$A = \frac{\begin{vmatrix} a & 1 \\ -b & \alpha \end{vmatrix}}{\begin{vmatrix} 1 & 1 \\ \beta & \alpha \end{vmatrix}}, \quad B = \frac{\begin{vmatrix} 1 & a \\ \beta & -b \end{vmatrix}}{\begin{vmatrix} 1 & 1 \\ \beta & \alpha \end{vmatrix}}, \quad \text{and} \quad \begin{vmatrix} 1 & 1 \\ \beta & \alpha \end{vmatrix} = \alpha - \beta \neq 0,$$

since we suppose that α is distinct from β.)   Hence

(3) $$\int \frac{(ax+b)\,dx}{(x-\alpha)(x-\beta)} = \int \frac{A\,dx}{x-\alpha} + \int \frac{B\,dx}{x-\beta}$$
$$= A \log(x-\alpha) + B \log(x-\beta) + c.$$

Illustration 1. $\int \frac{(2x-3)\,dx}{x^2-x-42}$

Solution. $\frac{2x-3}{x^2-x-42} = \frac{A}{x-7} + \frac{B}{x+6}$

$$2x-3 = A(x+6) + B(x-7)$$

Hence $A = \frac{11}{13}$, $B = \frac{15}{13}$ and

$$\int \frac{(2x-3)\,dx}{x^2-x-42} = \frac{11}{13}\int \frac{dx}{x-7} + \frac{15}{13}\int \frac{dx}{x+6}$$

$$= \tfrac{11}{13}\log(x-7) + \tfrac{15}{13}\log(x+6) + c.$$

Sometimes it is convenient to write the arbitrary constant of integration as a logarithm, i.e., write $c = \log k$. Our answer then becomes

$$\log(x-7)^{\frac{11}{13}} + \log(x+6)^{\frac{15}{13}} + \log k = \log k(x-7)^{\frac{11}{13}}(x+6)^{\frac{15}{13}}.$$

Illustration 2. $\int \frac{6x^3 + 17x^2 + 13x - 6}{3x^3 + 2x^2 - x}\,dx$

Solution. In case the numerator is of the same degree as the denominator (or of higher degree), the first thing to do is to divide out until the numerator is of lower degree. Upon dividing we find

$$\frac{6x^3 + 17x^2 + 13x - 6}{3x^3 + 2x^2 - x} = 2 + \frac{13x^2 + 15x - 6}{3x^3 + 2x^2 - x}.$$

We now factor the denominator and write

$$\frac{13x^2 + 15x - 6}{x(3x-1)(x+1)} = \frac{A}{x} + \frac{B}{3x-1} + \frac{C}{x+1}.$$

$$13x^2 + 15x - 6 = A(3x-1)(x+1) + Bx(x+1) + Cx(3x-1)$$

Setting $x = 0$, $x = \frac{1}{3}$, $x = -1$ respectively we compute $A = 6$, $B = 1$, $C = -2$. Hence

$$\int \frac{6x^3 + 17x^2 + 13x - 6}{3x^3 + 2x^2 - x}\,dx = \int \left(2 + \frac{6}{x} + \frac{1}{3x-1} - \frac{2}{x+1}\right)dx$$

$$= 2x + 6\log x + \tfrac{1}{3}\log(3x-1)$$
$$- 2\log(x+1) + \log c$$

$$= 2x + \log \frac{cx^6(3x-1)^{\frac{1}{3}}}{(x+1)^2}.$$

In the case of a repeated root there is a slight modification of the process. It is evident that $\dfrac{ax+b}{(x-\alpha)(x-\alpha)(x-\alpha)}$ could not be written as the sum of three fractions each with constant numerator and linear denominator. That is

$$\frac{ax+b}{(x-\alpha)(x-\alpha)(x-\alpha)} \neq \frac{A}{x-\alpha} + \frac{B}{x-\alpha} + \frac{C}{x-\alpha}$$

since each of the right-hand members is of the same type. In this case we write

$$\frac{ax + b}{(x - \alpha)(x - \alpha)(x - \alpha)} = \frac{A}{x - \alpha} + \frac{B}{(x - \alpha)^2} + \frac{C}{(x - \alpha)^3}$$

from which

$$ax + b \equiv A(x - \alpha)^2 + B(x - \alpha) + C.$$

The numbers A, B, C can now be determined in the usual way and the integration reduces to the types $\int \frac{du}{u}$ and $\int u^n \, du$.

Illustration 3. Find $\int \frac{(x^2 - 5) \, dx}{x(x - 1)^2}$.

Solution. Write

$$\frac{x^2 - 5}{x(x - 1)^2} = \frac{A}{x} + \frac{B}{x - 1} + \frac{C}{(x - 1)^2}$$

$$x^2 - 5 = A(x - 1)^2 + Bx(x - 1) + Cx$$

$$A = -5, \quad B = 6, \quad C = -4$$

Hence

$$\int \frac{(x^2 - 5) \, dx}{x(x - 1)^2} = -5 \int \frac{dx}{x} + 6 \int \frac{dx}{x - 1} - 4 \int \frac{dx}{(x - 1)^2}$$

$$= -5 \log x + 6 \log (x - 1) + \frac{4}{x - 1} + \log c$$

$$= \log \frac{c(x - 1)^6}{x^5} + \frac{4}{x - 1}.$$

In case the denominator cannot be broken up wholly into real linear factors then another algebraic modification is necessary. For each non-repeated irreducible quadratic factor appearing in the denominator we must have a partial fraction of the form $\frac{Ax + B}{x^2 + px + q}$ the numerator of which is a linear function. An example will make it clear why this is so.

Illustration 4. Find $\int \frac{(3 x^2 - x - 3) \, dx}{(x + 1)(x^2 + x + 1)}$.

Solution. $\dfrac{3 x^2 - x - 3}{(x + 1)(x^2 + x + 1)} = \dfrac{A}{x + 1} + \dfrac{Bx + C}{x^2 + x + 1}$

(a) $3 x^2 - x - 3 = A(x^2 + x + 1) + (Bx + C)(x + 1)$

We note that if the second partial fraction did not have a linear numerator $Bx + C$ but instead had just a constant D, then we should in general be unable to determine the two constants A and D satisfying the three conditions implied in (a).

$[3 x^2 - x - 3 = A(x^2 + x + 1) + D(x + 1)$, or (1) $3 = A$, (2) $-1 = A + D$, and (3) $-3 = A + D$; it is obvious that conditions (2) and (3) are inconsistent.]

Returning to (a) we compute $A = 1, B = 2, C = -4$ and our integral becomes

(b) $\displaystyle \int \frac{(3 x^2 - x - 3)\, dx}{(x + 1)(x^2 + x + 1)} = \int \frac{dx}{x + 1} + \int \frac{(2 x - 4)\, dx}{x^2 + x + 1}$

$\displaystyle \qquad\qquad = \log (x + 1) + \int \frac{(2 x + 1)\, dx}{x^2 + x + 1} - 5 \int \frac{dx}{x^2 + x + 1}$

$\displaystyle \qquad\qquad = \log (x + 1) + \log (x^2 + x + 1)$

$\displaystyle \qquad\qquad\qquad - \frac{10}{\sqrt{3}} \tan^{-1} \frac{2 x + 1}{\sqrt{3}} + c$

The last integral in (b) is treated in the manner of Illustration 7, § 36.

If repeated quadratic factors are present, the situation is still more complex arithmetically; but the problem presents no theoretical difficulties.

Illustration 5.   Find $\displaystyle \int \frac{(x^3 + x - 3)\, dx}{(x^2 + 2 x + 2)^2}$.

Solution.   We write

$$\frac{x^3 + x - 3}{(x^2 + 2 x + 2)^2} = \frac{Ax + B}{(x^2 + 2 x + 2)} + \frac{Cx + D}{(x^2 + 2 x + 2)^2}.$$

Here $A = 1, B = -2, C = 3, D = 1$.   Hence

(a) $\displaystyle \int \frac{(x^3 + x - 3)\, dx}{(x^2 + 2 x + 2)^2} = \int \frac{(x - 2)\, dx}{x^2 + 2 x + 2} + \int \frac{(3 x + 1)\, dx}{(x^2 + 2 x + 2)^2}$.

The first integral on the right reduces, by methods previously used in Illustration 7, § 36, to $\frac{1}{2} \log (x^2 + 2 x + 2) - 3 \tan^{-1} (x + 1)$.   We break the second integral up into two pieces as follows:

$$\int \frac{(3 x + 1)\, dx}{(x^2 + 2 x + 2)^2} = \frac{3}{2} \int \frac{(2 x + 2)\, dx}{(x^2 + 2 x + 2)^2} - 2 \int \frac{dx}{(x^2 + 2 x + 2)^2}$$

$$= -\tfrac{3}{2}(x^2 + 2 x + 2)^{-1} - 2 \int \frac{dx}{(x^2 + 2 x + 2)^2}$$

This last integral is best handled by the reduction formula 33 in the table of integrals (Appendix B).   Using this with $a = 1, n = 2$ we get

$$-2 \int \frac{dx}{(x^2 + 2 x + 2)^2} = -2 \int \frac{dx}{[(x + 1)^2 + 1]^2}$$

$$= -2 \left[\frac{1}{2} \frac{x + 1}{(x + 1)^2 + 1} + \frac{1}{2} \int \frac{dx}{(x + 1)^2 + 1} \right]$$

$$= -\frac{x + 1}{(x + 1)^2 + 1} - \tan^{-1} (x + 1).$$

Combining these partial results, we get as the solution to our problem:

$$\int \frac{(x^3 + x - 3)\,dx}{(x^2 + 2\,x + 2)^2} = \frac{1}{2} \log (x^2 + 2\,x + 2) - \frac{x + \frac{5}{2}}{x^2 + 2\,x + 2}$$
$$- 4 \tan^{-1} (x + 1) + c.$$

We summarize the general principles of integration by partial fractions.

First divide out until the numerator is of lower degree than the denominator. There are then four cases. Where the denominator has:

Case I. Non-repeated Linear Factors.

For each such factor write a term $\dfrac{A}{x - \alpha}$. Each such partial fraction integrates into a logarithm.

Case II. Repeated Linear Factors.
For each r-fold linear factor write the sum

$$\frac{A_1}{x - \alpha} + \frac{A_2}{(x - \alpha)^2} + \cdots + \frac{A_r}{(x - \alpha)^r}.$$

The first of these will integrate into a logarithm; all of the others are of type $\int u^n\,du$.

Case III. Non-repeated Quadratic Factors.

For each such factor write $\dfrac{Ax + B}{x^2 + px + q}$. The integral of each such fraction is accomplished after the methods of Illustrations 7 and 8 in § 36 (by formulae V, XVI, XXII, XXIII).

Case IV. Repeated Quadratic Factors.
For each r-fold quadratic factor write the sum

$$\frac{A_1x + B_1}{x^2 + px + q} + \frac{A_2x + B_2}{(x^2 + px + q)^2} + \cdots + \frac{A_rx + B_r}{(x^2 + px + q)^r}.$$

The first of these is integrated as in Case III. Each of the others is integrated as follows. Write

$$\int \frac{(A_kx + B_k)\,dx}{(x^2 + px + q)^k} = \frac{A_k}{2} \int \frac{(2\,x + p)\,dx}{(x^2 + px + q)^k} + \left(B_k - \frac{pA_k}{2}\right)\int \frac{dx}{(x^2 + px + q)^k}.$$

The first integral on the right is of the type $\int u^n \, du$. The second integral yields (after completing the square) to repeated applications of the reduction formula 33 in the Table of Integrals.

Since every polynomial is factorable into linear and quadratic factors, the method of partial fractions will integrate any rational function (quotient of two polynomials).

38. Integration by Tables. Many integrals have been computed and catalogued in so-called Tables of Integrals. When a given integral does not readily yield to any of the three standard methods

Method A.   Integration by Parts,
Method B.   Integration by Transformations or Substitutions,
Method C.   Integration by Partial Fractions,

then it may be possible, by the use of these methods, to throw the given integral into a form that can be found in a Table of Integrals. Therefore, we list a fourth method of integration, if it can be called such,

Method D.   Integration by Use of Tables.

A short Table of Integrals is added in Appendix B.

EXERCISES

1. $\int \sin^3 2 x \cos 2 x \, dx = \frac{1}{8} \sin^4 2 x + c$

2. $\int \dfrac{e^x - e^{-x}}{e^x + e^{-x}} \, dx = \log (e^x + e^{-x}) + c$

3. $\int 4 \, x e^{2x^2} \, dx = e^{2x^2} + c$

4. $\int \sec^2 (3 \, x - 1) \, dx = \frac{1}{3} \tan (3 \, x - 1) + c$

5. $\int \csc 2 \, x \cot 2 \, x \, dx = - \frac{1}{2} \csc 2 \, x + c$

6. $\int \dfrac{dx}{x^2 + 4 \, x + 9} = \dfrac{\sqrt{5}}{5} \tan^{-1} \dfrac{x + 2}{\sqrt{5}} + c$

7. $\int \dfrac{dx}{\sqrt{1 - x - x^2}} = \sin^{-1} \dfrac{2 \, x + 1}{\sqrt{5}} + c$

8. $\int 3\, x^2 e^{2x}\, dx = \frac{3}{2}\, e^{2x}(x^2 - x + \frac{1}{2}) + c$

9. $\int \dfrac{dx}{x + \sqrt{x}} = 2 \log (1 + \sqrt{x}) + c$

10. $\int \dfrac{dx}{1 + e^x} = x - \log (1 + e^x) + c$

11. $\int \tan^{-1} x\, dx = x \tan^{-1} x - \frac{1}{2} \log (1 + x^2) + c$

12. $\int \dfrac{(x - 2)\, dx}{x^2 + 4\, x - 5} = ?$

CHAPTER X

DEFINITE INTEGRALS

39. Definite Integrals. So far we have added to each integral an arbitrary constant of integration and so the answer has been indefinite to that extent. This is proper since two functions differing only by a constant have the same derivative. All of the integrals discussed have been therefore indefinite integrals. We now wish to discuss integrals known as definite integrals.

Suppose we wish to find that function y of x whose derivative is $f(x)$ and whose value is y_0 when $x = x_0$. We seek $y = \int f(x) \, dx$ satisfying the condition $y = y_0$ when $x = x_0$. Let the indefinite integral of $f(x)$ be $F(x) + c$; that is

$$(1) \qquad y = \int f(x) \, dx = F(x) + c.$$

To impose the condition $y = y_0$ when $x = x_0$ means that

$$(2) \qquad y_0 = F(x_0) + c$$

and hence that c is determined:

$$(3) \qquad c = y_0 - F(x_0).$$

Thus the solution to the problem is

$$(4) \qquad y = F(x) + y_0 - F(x_0),$$

which reduces to y_0 when $x = x_0$. The function y in (4) is therefore definite (there is no longer any arbitrary constant in y) and satisfies the initial or boundary condition $y = y_0$ when $x = x_0$ as it is called. Of course y still depends upon x.

Write (4) in the form

$$(5) \qquad y - y_0 = F(x) - F(x_0)$$

and call $y = y_1$ when $x = x_1$. Then (5) becomes

$$(6) \qquad y_1 - y_0 = F(x_1) - F(x_0)$$

$$= \int f(x) \, dx]_{x=x_1} - \int f(x) \, dx]_{x=x_0}.$$

This difference is called the definite integral of $f(x)$; it is a constant and does not depend upon x at all.   Hence the

DEFINITION.   *The definite integral of $f(x)$ is the difference between two values of the integral of $f(x)$ for two distinct values of the variable x.*   This difference is usually represented by the notation $\int_{x_0}^{x_1} f(x)\, dx$.   Thus

$$(7) \qquad \int_{x_0}^{x_1} f(x)\, dx = F(x_1) + c - [F(x_0) + c]$$
$$= F(x_1) - F(x_0).$$

This is read "the integral from x_0 to x_1 of $f(x)$"; x_1 is called the upper limit, x_0 the lower limit.   Or again x_0 and x_1 are called the limits of integration and the function $f(x)$ is integrated between the limits x_0 and x_1.

Illustration 1.   Find $\int_0^1 (x^2 + e^x)\, dx$.

Solution. $\qquad \int_0^1 (x^2 + e^x)\, dx = \left[\dfrac{x^3}{3} + e^x\right]_0^1$
$$= (\tfrac{1}{3} + e) - (1)$$
$$= e - \tfrac{2}{3}.$$

Illustration 2.   Find $\int_0^{\pi} \sin x\, dx$.

Solution. $\quad \int_0^{\pi} \sin x\, dx = -\cos x\Big]_0^{\pi} = 1 + 1 = 2.$

EXERCISES

1. $\int_1^2 (1 - x + x^2)\, dx = \tfrac{11}{6}$

2. $\int_0^1 \cos 2\pi x\, dx = 0$

3. $\int_0^3 \sqrt{9 - x^2}\, dx = \dfrac{9\pi}{4}$

4. $\int_1^b \dfrac{dx}{x} = \log b$

5. $\int_0^t (5x^4 - 2)\, dx = t^5 - 2t$

6. $\int_a^b \dfrac{dx}{x^2 - 9} = \dfrac{1}{6} \log \dfrac{(b-3)(a+3)}{(b+3)(a-3)}$

7. $\int_0^{\frac{\pi}{3}} \tan x\, dx = \log 2$

8. $\int_{-1}^{1} (x^2 + x^3)\, dx = \frac{2}{3}$

9. $\int_{-1}^{0} (2 - x^3)^3\, dx = \frac{837}{70}$

10. $\int_{0}^{\frac{\pi}{2}} \sin^2 x\, dx = ?$

40. Improper Integrals. The question arises as to what meaning is to be attached to a definite integral when one (or both) of the limits of integration is infinite or when the integrand itself becomes infinite at or between the limits of integration. When either of these two things happens the integral is called an *improper integral*.

Case I. Infinite Limits of Integration.

Consider $\int_{a}^{\infty} f(x)\, dx$. The value of this integral is defined to be $\lim_{b \to \infty} \int_{a}^{b} f(x)\, dx$ provided this limit exists.

Illustration 1. Find $\int_{0}^{\infty} e^{-3x}\, dx$.

Solution.
$$\lim_{b \to \infty} \int_{0}^{b} e^{-3x}\, dx = \lim_{b \to \infty} \left[-\tfrac{1}{3} e^{-3x} \right]_{0}^{b}$$
$$= \lim_{b \to \infty} \left[-\tfrac{1}{3} e^{-3b} + \tfrac{1}{3} \right]$$
$$= \tfrac{1}{3}.$$

Therefore $\int_{0}^{\infty} e^{-3x}\, dx = \tfrac{1}{3}$.

Illustration 2. Find $\int_{1}^{\infty} \frac{dx}{x}$.

Solution.
$$\lim_{b \to \infty} \int_{1}^{b} \frac{dx}{x} = \lim_{b \to \infty} (\log b)$$
$$= \infty$$

Hence we may say that $\int_{1}^{\infty} \frac{dx}{x}$ has no value or is infinite. We write

$$\int_{1}^{\infty} \frac{dx}{x} = \infty.$$

Illustration 3. Find $\int_{0}^{\infty} \cos x\, dx$.

Solution.
$$\lim_{b \to \infty} \int_{0}^{b} \cos x\, dx = \lim_{b \to \infty} (\sin b)$$

Since $\sin b$ approaches no limit at all as $b \to \infty$, the original problem has no answer. $\int_{0}^{\infty} \cos x\, dx$ does not exist, has no meaning.

Case II. Integrand Discontinuous.

Let $f(x)$ be continuous in (a, b) except at x_1 and consider

$$\int_a^b f(x)\, dx, \quad f(x_1) = \infty, \quad a \le x_1 \le b.$$

The value of this integral depends upon the behavior of $f(x)$ in the neighborhood of x_1 and is defined to be

$$\int_a^b f(x)\, dx = \lim_{\epsilon_1 \to 0} \int_a^{x_1-\epsilon_1} f(x)\, dx + \lim_{\epsilon_2 \to 0} \int_{x_1+\epsilon_2}^b f(x)\, dx$$

provided the right-hand member exists (and is itself not an indeterminate form of the type $\infty - \infty$). If $x_1 = b$, say, there would be the obvious modification

$$\int_a^b f(x)\, dx = \lim_{\epsilon \to 0} \int_a^{b-\epsilon} f(x)\, dx.$$

Illustration 4. Find $\int_{-1}^1 \dfrac{dx}{x^{\frac{2}{3}}}$.

Solution. The function becomes infinite at the origin. Hence

$$\int_{-1}^1 \frac{dx}{x^{\frac{2}{3}}} = \lim_{\epsilon_1 \to 0} \int_{-1}^{-\epsilon_1} \frac{dx}{x^{\frac{2}{3}}} + \lim_{\epsilon_2 \to 0} \int_{\epsilon_2}^1 \frac{dx}{x^{\frac{2}{3}}}.$$

$$= \lim_{\epsilon_1 \to 0} 3\, x^{\frac{1}{3}} \Big]_{-1}^{-\epsilon_1} + \lim_{\epsilon_2 \to 0} 3\, x^{\frac{1}{3}} \Big]_{\epsilon_2}^{1}$$

$$= \lim_{\epsilon_1 \to 0} 3\left[(-\epsilon_1)^{\frac{1}{3}} - (-1)^{\frac{1}{3}}\right] + \lim_{\epsilon_2 \to 0} 3\left[1 - \epsilon_2^{\frac{1}{3}}\right]$$

$$= 3 + 3$$

$$= 6.$$

Illustration 5. Find $\int_1^2 \dfrac{dx}{(x-1)^2}$.

Solution. The integrand becomes infinite at $x = 1$. Here we define the value of the integral to be

$$\lim_{\epsilon \to 0} \int_{1+\epsilon}^2 \frac{dx}{(x-1)^2} = \lim_{\epsilon \to 0} \left[-\frac{1}{(x-1)}\right]_{1+\epsilon}^2$$

$$= \lim_{\epsilon \to 0} \left[-1 + \frac{1}{\epsilon}\right]$$

$$= \infty.$$

Illustration 6.   Find $\int_{-\frac{\pi}{2}}^{\frac{\pi}{2}} \tan x \, dx$.

Solution.   Here the integrand becomes infinite at both limits of integration. We write

$$\int_{-\frac{\pi}{2}}^{\frac{\pi}{2}} \tan x \, dx = \lim_{\substack{\epsilon_1 \to 0 \\ \epsilon_2 \to 0}} \int_{-\frac{\pi}{2}+\epsilon_1}^{\frac{\pi}{2}-\epsilon_2} \tan x \, dx$$

where these two limits are to be taken quite independently of each other.

$$= \lim_{\substack{\epsilon_1 \to 0 \\ \epsilon_2 \to 0}} \left[\log \sec \left(\frac{\pi}{2} - \epsilon_2 \right) - \log \sec \left(-\frac{\pi}{2} + \epsilon_1 \right) \right]$$

$$= \infty - \infty.$$

This is indeterminate and the original integral has no meaning.

EXERCISES

1. $\int_{-\infty}^{0} e^x \, dx = 1$

2. $\int_{1}^{\infty} x e^{-x^2} \, dx = \dfrac{1}{2e}$

3. $\int_{0}^{\infty} 2 e^{-x} \sin x \, dx = 1$

4. $\int_{-2}^{2} \dfrac{dx}{\sqrt{4 - x^2}} = \pi$

5. $\int_{0}^{2} \dfrac{dx}{(1 - x)^3} = $ meaningless $(\infty - \infty)$

6. $\int_{0}^{1} \dfrac{dx}{(1 - x)^2} = ?$

CHAPTER XI

APPLICATIONS OF INTEGRATION

41. Areas. Consider the curve $y = f(x)$, and the area A between it, the X-axis and the two ordinates at $x = a$, $x = b$. If it were possible to find an expression for $\frac{dA}{dx}$, then, by integration, the area A could be found. Examine Fig. 93 and let A, for the moment, be the variable area between the fixed ordinate at $x = a$ and the variable ordinate at $x = x$. Let ΔA be the increment of area between x and $x + \Delta x$. Define $\bar{y}$, called the mean ordinate, as that quantity such that

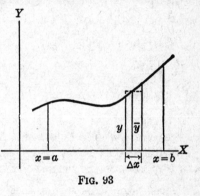

$$\Delta A = \bar{y}\,\Delta x.$$

Then

(1) $$\frac{\Delta A}{\Delta x} = \bar{y}$$

FIG. 93

and it is geometrically evident that $\bar{y} \rightarrow y$ as $\Delta x \rightarrow 0$. Hence in the limit

(2) $$\frac{dA}{dx} = y$$

which says that the rate of change of area per unit change in x is, at any point x, equal to the ordinate y at that point. Integrating (2) we get

(3) $$A = \int y\,dx.$$

As yet this is an indefinite integral and consequently does not represent any particular area. If we wish the area under the curve and between the ordinates at $x = a$ and $x = b$, then the area A must be counted as zero at $x = a$ since that is the start-ing point.   Hence the boundary condition $A = 0$ when $x = a$. Performing the integration in (3) we get, say

(4) $A = \int y \, dx = \int f(x) \, dx = F(x) + c.$

If $A = 0$ when $x = a$ this becomes $0 = F(a) + c$ which deter-mines the arbitrary constant $c = - F(a)$.   Therefore

(5) $A = F(x) - F(a).$

This gives the area under the curve and between $y(a)$ and any other ordinate $y(x)$.   The area from $x = a$ to $x = b$ would there-fore be

(6) $A = F(b) - F(a).$

But (6) is the form of the definite integral $\int_a^b f(x) \, dx$, hence the

THEOREM.   *The area between the curve $y = f(x)$, the X-axis and the ordinates erected at $x = a$ and at $x = b$ is given by*

(7) $A = \int_a^b y \, dx.$

This area will be positive if wholly above the X-axis, will be negative if wholly below the X-axis.   If part of the area is above and part below the X-axis, (7) gives the algebraic sum of the positive and negative pieces.

Illustration 1.   Find the area under the curve $y = x^2$ from $x = 0$ to $x = 2$

Solution.

$$A = \int_0^2 x^2 \, dx$$
$$= \frac{x^3}{3}\Big]_0^2$$
$$= \tfrac{8}{3} \text{ sq. units.}$$

Illustration 2.   Find the area between the X-axis and the curve $y = x^2 - x - 12$ bounded by the lines $x = 0$ and $x = 4$.

Solution.   The curve lies below the X-axis between $x = 0$ and $x = 4$.

$$A = \int_0^4 (x^2 - x - 12) \, dx$$
$$= \left[\frac{x^3}{3} - \frac{x^2}{2} - 12 \, x \right]_0^4$$
$$= - \tfrac{104}{3} \text{ sq. units.}$$

Although the area turns out to be negative in the problem of Illustration 2 because it lies below the Y-axis, yet in most cases we shall not be interested in the sign of the area. Hence we would take the absolute value of the area and give $\frac{104}{3}$ sq. units as the answer. This procedure will cause no trouble unless, in a given problem, some of the area is above the X-axis and some below, in which case the definite integral representing the area when evaluated over the whole interval will add algebraically the two areas. This would not give the sum of the absolute values of the areas. Therefore such an integral must be broken up into separate integrals for the positive and negative areas.

Illustration 3. Find the total area, regardless of sign, contained between the X-axis and the curve $y = x(x + 1)(x - 2)$ (Fig. 94).

Solution. The curve crosses the X-axis at $x = -1, 0, 2$. The total area, regardless of sign is therefore:

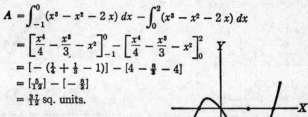

$$A = \int_{-1}^{0} (x^3 - x^2 - 2x)\,dx - \int_{0}^{2} (x^3 - x^2 - 2x)\,dx$$

$$= \left[\frac{x^4}{4} - \frac{x^3}{3} - x^2 \right]_{-1}^{0} - \left[\frac{x^4}{4} - \frac{x^3}{3} - x^2 \right]_{0}^{2}$$

$$= [- (\tfrac{1}{4} + \tfrac{1}{3} - 1)] - [4 - \tfrac{8}{3} - 4]$$

$$= [\tfrac{5}{12}] - [- \tfrac{8}{3}]$$

$$= \tfrac{37}{12} \text{ sq. units.}$$

Conditions of symmetry should be made use of, where they exist, to shorten computations. If the area is symmetric with respect to the X-axis, set up the integral for the part above

FIG. 94

the X-axis and multiply by two; etc. The student should be sure that symmetry is present before he applies this principle.

Illustration 4. Find the area of a circle of radius r.

Solution. Let the equation of the circle be

$$x^2 + y^2 = r^2$$

$$A = 4 \int_{0}^{r} \sqrt{r^2 - x^2}\,dx$$

$$= 4 \left[\frac{x}{2} \sqrt{r^2 - x^2} + \frac{r^2}{2} \sin^{-1} \frac{x}{r} \right]_{0}^{r}$$

$$= \pi r^2 \text{ sq. units.}$$

Illustration 5.   Find the area common to the two curves $y = x^2$, $y^2 = x$.

Solution.   These parabolas intersect in the points $(0, 0)$, $(1, 1)$.   Hence the area included by them is the difference of the areas under the curves; that is

$$A = \int_0^1 \sqrt{x}\, dx - \int_0^1 x^2\, dx$$

$$= \left[\frac{2}{3} x^{\frac{3}{2}} - \frac{x^3}{3} \right]_0^1$$

$$= \tfrac{1}{3} \text{ sq. unit.}$$

Generalizing the example of Illustration 5 we get (see Fig. 95) the area common to two curves:

(8)
$$A = \int_a^b y_1\, dx - \int_a^b y_2\, dx$$

$$= \int_a^b (y_1 - y_2)\, dx.$$

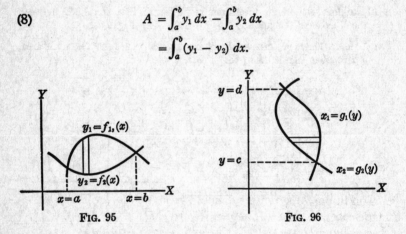

FIG. 95   FIG. 96

If the curves are situated as in Fig. 96 then it is not convenient to perform the integration with respect to x.   Instead we transform the integrals (8) into the following

(9)
$$A = \int_c^d x_1\, dy - \int_c^d x_2\, dy$$

where $x_1 = g_1(y)$, $x_2 = g_2(y)$ result from solving $y_1 = f_1(x)$ and $y_2 = f_2(x)$ for x in terms of y.

Illustration 6.   Find the area common to the curves $2(y - 1)^2 = x$ and $(y - 1)^2 = x - 1$.

Solution.   These curves intersect in the points $(2, 0)$, $(2, 2)$.   The area is given by

$$A = \int_0^2 [1 + (y-1)^2]\, dy - \int_0^2 2(y-1)^2\, dy$$

$$= \int_0^2 [1 - (y-1)^2]\, dy$$

$$= \left[y - \tfrac{1}{3}(y-1)^3 \right]_0^2$$

$$= (2 - \tfrac{1}{3}) - (\tfrac{1}{3})$$

$$= \tfrac{4}{3} \text{ sq. units.}$$

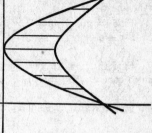

If the equation of the curve is given in parametric form $x = f(t),\ y = g(t)$, then the area formula (7) becomes

$$(10)\quad A = \int_a^b y\, dx = \int_c^d g(t)f'(t)\, dt,$$

FIG. 97

where $x = a$ when $t = c$, $x = b$ when $t = d$.

In polar coordinates the area formula is

$$(11)\qquad\qquad A = \tfrac{1}{2}\int_{\theta_0}^{\theta_1} \rho^2\, d\theta.$$

Illustration 7. Find the area under one arch of the cycloid $x = a(t - \sin t)$, $y = a(1 - \cos t)$. (Fig. 47.)

Solution.
$$A = \int y\, dx$$

$$= \int a^2(1 - \cos t)(1 - \cos t)\, dt$$

For one arch t runs from 0 to 2π. Hence

$$A = a^2\int_0^{2\pi} (1 - \cos t)^2\, dt$$

$$= a^2\int_0^{2\pi} [1 - 2\cos t + \cos^2 t]\, dt$$

$$= a^2\left[t - 2\sin t + \tfrac{1}{2}t + \tfrac{1}{4}\sin 2t \right]_0^{2\pi}$$

$$= 3\pi a^2 \text{ sq. units.}$$

This is three times the area of the generating circle.

Illustration 8. Find the area enclosed by the cardioid $\rho = a(1 - \cos\theta)$.

Solution.
$$A = \tfrac{1}{2}\int \rho^2\, d\theta$$

$$= \tfrac{1}{2}\int_0^{2\pi} a^2(1 - \cos\theta)^2\, d\theta.$$

By the methods of Illustration 7 this equals $\tfrac{3}{2}\pi a^2$ sq. units.

EXERCISES

1. Find the area of the ellipse $b^2x^2 + a^2y^2 = a^2b^2$. (Fig. 9.)   *Ans.* πab.

2. Find the area under one arch of $y = \sin x$.   *Ans.* 2.

3. Find the area cut off from the semicubical parabola (Fig. 45) $y^2 = x^3$ by the line $x = 4$.   *Ans.* $25\frac{3}{5}$.

4. Find the area bounded by the parabola $x^{\frac{1}{2}} + y^{\frac{1}{2}} = a^{\frac{1}{2}}$ and the coordinate axes (Fig. 43).

Ans. $\dfrac{a^2}{6}$.

5. Find the area of one loop of the lemniscate $x = a \cos \theta \sqrt{\cos 2\theta}$, $y = a \sin \theta \sqrt{\cos 2\theta}$.   (Fig. 65.)

Ans. $\dfrac{a^2}{2}$.

6. Find the area of one loop of $\rho = a \sin 2\theta$ (Fig. 63).

Ans. $\dfrac{\pi a^2}{8}$.

7. Find the area inside the circle $\rho = a \cos \theta$ and outside the cardioid $\rho = a(1 - \cos \theta)$.

Ans. $\dfrac{a^2}{3}(3\sqrt{3} - \pi)$.

42. Length of a Curve. In rectangular coordinates the differential of arc length is (see (3) § 26).

(1) $$ds = \sqrt{dx^2 + dy^2}$$

(2) $$= \sqrt{1 + \left(\frac{dy}{dx}\right)^2}\, dx$$

(3) $$= \sqrt{1 + \left(\frac{dx}{dy}\right)^2}\, dy.$$

Therefore, using (2) or (3) the length of a curve is given by

(4) $$s = \int ds = \int_a^b \sqrt{1 + y'^2}\, dx$$
$$= \int_c^d \sqrt{1 + x'^2}\, dy.$$

Illustration 1. Find the total length of the circumference of a circle of radius r.

Solution. Let $x^2 + y^2 = r^2$.

Then $$x\, dx + y\, dy = 0$$

or $$\frac{dy}{dx} = y' = -\frac{x}{y}$$

$$y'^2 = \frac{x^2}{y^2}$$

$$1 + y'^2 = 1 + \frac{x^2}{y^2} = \frac{x^2 + y^2}{y^2} = \frac{r^2}{y^2}$$

$$\sqrt{1 + y'^2} = \frac{r}{y} = \frac{r}{\sqrt{r^2 - x^2}}$$

The circumference C is therefore given by

$$C = 4 \int_0^r \frac{r \, dx}{\sqrt{r^2 - x^2}}$$

$$= 4 \, r \left[\sin^{-1} \frac{x}{r} \right]_0^r$$

$$= 2 \, \pi r.$$

In polar coordinates the differential of arc length is (see **(4)** § 26)

$$(5) \qquad ds = \sqrt{d\rho^2 + \rho^2 \, d\theta^2}$$

$$(6) \qquad = \sqrt{\rho^2 + \left(\frac{d\rho}{d\theta}\right)^2} \, d\theta$$

$$(7) \qquad = \sqrt{1 + \rho^2 \left(\frac{d\theta}{d\rho}\right)^2} \, d\rho.$$

Length of curve is, therefore,

$$(8) \qquad s = \int ds = \int_{\theta_1}^{\theta_2} \sqrt{\rho^2 + \rho'^2} \, d\theta$$

$$= \int_{\rho_1}^{\rho_2} \sqrt{1 + \rho^2 \theta'^2} \, d\rho.$$

Illustration 2. Find the length of the cardioid $\rho = a(1 - \cos \theta)$.

Solution.

$$\rho' = a \sin \theta$$

$$\rho'^2 = a^2 \sin^2 \theta$$

$$\rho^2 + \rho'^2 = a^2(1 - \cos \theta)^2 + a^2 \sin^2 \theta$$

$$= 2 \, a^2 (1 - \cos \theta)$$

$$s = \int_0^{2\pi} \sqrt{2 \, a^2 (1 - \cos \theta)} \, d\theta$$

$$= 2 \, a \int_0^{2\pi} \sqrt{\frac{1 - \cos \theta}{2}} \, d\theta$$

$$= 2 \, a \int_0^{2\pi} \sin \tfrac{1}{2} \theta \, d\theta$$

$$= 2 \, a \left[-2 \cos \tfrac{1}{2} \theta \right]_0^{2\pi}$$

$$= 8 \, a.$$

EXERCISES

1. Find the total length of the hypocycloid of four cusps $x^{\frac{2}{3}} + y^{\frac{2}{3}} = a^{\frac{2}{3}}$ (Fig. 50.)   Ans. $6 \, a$

2. Find the length of one arch of the cycloid $x = a(\theta - \sin \theta)$, $y = a(1 - \cos \theta)$. (Fig. 47.)   Ans. $8 \, a$.

3. Find the length of one revolution of the spiral of Archimedes, $\rho = a\theta$.
(Fig. 54.)   Ans. $\frac{a}{2} \left[2\pi \sqrt{1 + 4\pi^2} + \log \left(2\pi + \sqrt{1 + 4\pi^2} \right) \right]$ $21 \, a$.

43. First Fundamental Theorem of Integral Calculus. Consider the curve $y = f(x)$ in the interval (a, b) and suppose the interval subdivided by the $n + 1$ points $x_1 = a$, x_2, $\cdots$, x_i, x_{i+1}, $\cdots$, $x_{n+1} = b$. (Fig. 98.) Erect the corresponding ordinates y_i and write $\Delta x_i = x_{i+1} - x_i$ for the width of the ith interval.

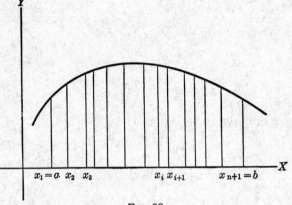

FIG. 98

Now form the sum

(1) $$f(x_1)\,\Delta x_1 + f(x_2)\,\Delta x_2 + \cdots + f(x_n)\,\Delta x_n.$$

This sum is usually denoted by the symbol

(2) $$\sum_{i=1}^{n} f(x_i)\,\Delta x_i.$$

It seems geometrically evident that this sum approximates the area under the curve between y_1 and y_{n+1} and that in the limit, as the number of points of division becomes infinite and the width of each interval approaches zero, it will be equal to the area.

A *fundamental theorem* of the *integral calculus* states that

(3) $$\lim_{\substack{n \to \infty \\ \Delta x_i \to 0}} \sum_{i=1}^{n} f(x_i)\,\Delta x_i = \int_a^b f(x)\,dx.$$

This process of summation, as it is called, affords a quick and easy way of setting up definite integrals representing areas, lengths of curves, etc. For areas in rectangular coordinates the reasoning runs something like this: To find the area under the curve $y = f(x)$ we consider a thin rectangular strip roughly y high and Δx wide. Its area is $y \, \Delta x$. The sum of all such strips would be $\Sigma y \, \Delta x$ and the limiting value of the sum of all such strips, $\lim \Sigma y \, \Delta x$, by the fundamental theorem would be equal to $\int_a^b y \, dx$. We shorten this process of reasoning as follows. The area of one strip would be $y \, dx$ and the sum of all such strips would be $\int_a^b y \, dx$. For the length of a curve we say that one little differential arc element is ds in length and the total length sought is the sum of all such elements, $\int ds$. (This we know to be equal to $s = \int ds = \int_a^b \sqrt{1 + y'^2} \, dx$.)

For the area under a curve whose equation is given in polar coordinates we reason as follows (see Fig. 99). The differential (limit of increment) area is no longer a strip but approximately the sector of a circle of radius ρ and central angle $d\theta$. The area of such a sector is $\frac{1}{2} \rho^2 \, d\theta$ (see review formula 2 (b) page 2). The sum of all such sectors, $\int \frac{1}{2} \rho^2 \, d\theta$, would give the total area sought.

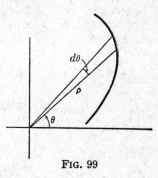

We now apply this method in finding volumes.

Fig. 99

44. Volumes of Revolution. Let the area under the curve $y = f(x)$, namely $\int_a^b f(x) \, dx$, be revolved about the X-axis thus generating a volume (Fig. 100). The area of a cross section of this solid by a plane perpendicular to the X-axis is πy^2. The volume of a little slice dx thick would be $\pi y^2 \, dx$. The total volume of the solid of revolution between two parallel planes $x = a$ and $x = b$ would therefore be the sum of all such slices or

(1) $$V = \pi \int_a^b y^2 \, dx.$$

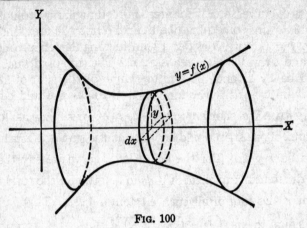

FIG. 100

Illustration 1. The area under the curve $y = x^3$ from $x = 0$ to $x = 1$ is revolved about the X-axis. Find the volume thus generated.

Solution.

$$V = \pi \int_0^1 y^2 \, dx = \pi \int_0^1 x^6 \, dx$$

$$= \frac{\pi x^7}{7} \Big]_0^1$$

$$= \frac{\pi}{7} \text{ cu. units.}$$

If the area $\int_c^d x \, dy$ is revolved about the Y-axis, the volume becomes

(2)

$$V = \pi \int_c^d x^2 \, dy.$$

Illustration 2. The area between the Y-axis, the curve $y = x^2$, and the lines $y = 1$, $y = 2$ is revolved about the Y-axis. Find the volume generated.

Solution.

$$V = \pi \int_1^2 x^2 \, dy = \pi \int_1^2 y \, dy$$

$$= \frac{\pi y^2}{2} \Big]_1^2$$

$$= \frac{3}{2} \pi \text{ cu. units.}$$

Illustration 3. The area common to the two parabolas $y = x^2$ and $y^2 = x$ is revolved about the Y-axis. Find the volume generated.

Solution. At any height y a slice will be washerlike: a disc with a hole in it. The area of this disc will be $\pi(x_1^2 - x_2^2)$ where x_1 refers to the x in $y = x^2$, and x_2 to the x in $y^2 = x$. Hence the volume of this elementary disc will be $\pi(x_1{}^2 - x_2{}^2) \, dy$ and the volume sought will be

$$V = \pi \int_0^1 (x_1{}^2 - x_2{}^2) \, dy$$

$$= \pi \int_0^1 (y - y^4) \, dy$$

$$= \pi \left[\frac{y^2}{2} - \frac{y^5}{5}\right]_0^1$$

$$= \tfrac{3}{10}\, \pi \text{ cu. units.}$$

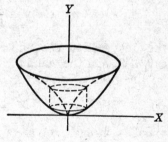

Fig. 101

Or we could make use of a cylindrical element of volume in examples such as that of Illustration 3. When an elementary area strip (as in Fig. 102) is revolved about the Y-axis, the volume element generated is a thin cylindrical shell with area $2\,\pi x(y_2 - y_1)$. The volume element is $2\,\pi x(y_2 - y_1)\, dx$; summing these, we get for the volume

$$(3) \qquad\qquad V = 2\,\pi \int_a^b x(y_2 - y_1)\, dx.$$

The student should not try to memorize these formulae — there are these and many others similar to them — but should master the technique of setting them up.

Illustration 4. Solve the problem in Illustration 3 by the use of cylindrical elements.

Solution. We have already set this up in (3) above

$$V = 2\,\pi \int_0^1 x(\sqrt{x} - x^2)\, dx$$

$$= 2\,\pi \left[\frac{2}{5}\, x^{\frac{5}{2}} - \frac{x^4}{4}\right]_0^1$$

$$= \tfrac{3}{10}\, \pi \text{ cu. units.}$$

Fig. 102

EXERCISES

Find the volume formed by revolving the area

1. Of a semicircle of radius r about a diameter.

Ans. $\tfrac{4}{3}\, \pi r^3$ (volume of a sphere).

2. Of the triangle formed by the lines $x = 0$, $y = h$, $y = \dfrac{h}{r}\, x$ about the Y-axis.

Ans. $\tfrac{1}{3}\, \pi r^2 h$ (volume of a cone).

3. Under one arch of $y = \sin x$ about the X-axis. Ans. $\dfrac{\pi^2}{2}$.

4. In the 2nd quadrant under $y = e^x$ about the X-axis.

$$\text{Ans. } \pi \int_{-\infty}^{0} e^{2x}\, dx = \frac{\pi}{2}.$$

5. Under one arch of $y = \sin x$ about the Y-axis.

$$\text{Ans. } 2\pi \int_{0}^{\pi} x \sin x\, dx = 2\pi^2.$$

45. Volumes of Known Cross Section. Consider the sections of a solid made by parallel planes. For purposes of illustration let these planes be perpendicular to the X-axis. If it is possible to write down the area of each section in terms of its distance from some fixed point on OX, say the origin O, then the volume of the solid can be determined. For, as in Fig. 103, the area of

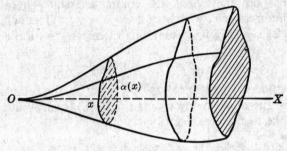

FIG. 103

the cross section at distance x is known to be a function of x, say $\alpha(x)$, and the volume element then is $\alpha(x)\, dx$. Hence the volume from $x = a$ to $x = b$ would be

$$(1) \qquad\qquad V = \int_{a}^{b} \alpha(x)\, dx.$$

Solids of revolution are a special case of this.

Illustration 1. A solid has a circular base (radius r) and every section perpendicular to a diameter is an equilateral triangle. Find the volume of the solid. (Fig. 104.)

Solution. At a distance x from the center along the diameter shown the cross section is an equilateral triangle whose base is, say, $2w$ and whose altitude is then $w\sqrt{3}$. The area of this triangle is $w^2\sqrt{3}$. But this can be expressed in terms of x since $w^2 + x^2 = r^2$. The area is

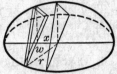

FIG. 104

then $\sqrt{3}(r^2 - x^2)$. The volume element becomes $\sqrt{3}(r^2 - x^2)\,dx$. The solid is symmetric and so we write

$$V = 2\int_0^r \sqrt{3}(r^2 - x^2)\,dx$$

$$= 2\sqrt{3}\left[r^2 x - \frac{x^3}{3}\right]_0^r$$

$$= \tfrac{4}{3}\sqrt{3}\,r^3 \text{ cu. units.}$$

Illustration 2. A newel post cap has a square base 6″ on a side. Each section parallel to the base is a square whose side is proportional to $(4 - x)$, where x is the distance (in inches) above the base. Find the volume of the cap. (Fig. 105.)

Solution. $w = k(4 - x)$
                        $w = 6$ when $x = 0$; $\therefore\ k = \tfrac{3}{2}$
                        $w = \tfrac{3}{2}(4 - x)$

A slice dx thick parallel to the base and x inches above it will therefore have a volume element $w^2\,dx$ or $\tfrac{9}{4}(4 - x)^2\,dx$. The volume of the cap is

$$V = \tfrac{9}{4}\int_0^4 (4 - x)^2\,dx$$

$$= \tfrac{9}{4}(-\tfrac{1}{3})(4 - x)^3\Big]_0^4$$

$$= 48 \text{ cu. inches.}$$

FIG. 105

EXERCISES

By the method of cross sections find the volume of the solid described.

1. The ellipsoid $\dfrac{x^2}{a^2} + \dfrac{y^2}{b^2} + \dfrac{z^2}{c^2} = 1$. (Fig. 16.)   *Ans.* $\tfrac{4}{3}\pi abc$.

2. The wedge cut from a cylinder of radius r by a plane passing through a diameter of the base and making with the base an angle $\theta = \tan^{-1}\dfrac{h}{r}$.

                                          Ans. $\tfrac{2}{3}\,hr^2$.

3. The solid whose base is the segment of the parabola $y^2 = x$, cut off by the chord $x = 5$ and whose section by a plane perpendicular to the axis of the parabola and at distance x from the vertex is a rectangle whose height equals $\tfrac{1}{2}(5 - x)$.   *Ans.* $\tfrac{4}{3}\sqrt{125}$ cu. units.

46. Areas of Surfaces of Revolution.

When the curve $y = f(x)$ is revolved about the X-axis, a surface is generated (Fig. 106). To find the area of this surface we consider the area generated by an element of arc ds. This area is roughly that of a cylinder of radius y and we write $dS = 2 \pi y \, ds$.   Summing all such elements of surface area we get

(1)
$$S = 2 \pi \int y \, ds,$$
$$= 2 \pi \int_a^b y \sqrt{1 + y'^2} \, dx.$$

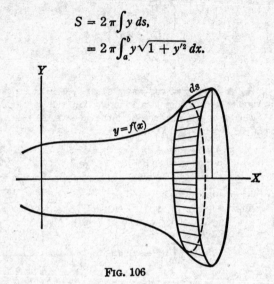

FIG. 106

Appropriate modifications of this formula will be necessary if the curve is revolved about some other line or if polar coordinates are used, etc.   (See Chap. XV, § 65, for the method of finding areas of more general surfaces.)

Illustration 1.   Find the surface area of a sphere of radius r.

Solution.   This area could be generated by revolving the upper half of the circle $x^2 + y^2 = r^2$ about the X-axis.

$$S = 2 \pi \int_{-r}^{r} y \sqrt{1 + y'^2} \, dx$$
$$= 4 \pi \int_0^r (\sqrt{r^2 - x^2}) \left(\frac{r}{y} \right) dx$$
$$= 4 \pi r \int_0^r dx$$
$$= 4 \pi r \Big[x \Big]_0^r$$
$$= 4 \pi r^2.$$

Illustration 2.   Revolve that arch of the cycloid $x = a(\theta - \sin \theta)$, $y = a(1 - \cos \theta)$ which passes through the origin about the Y-axis and compute the surface area generated.   (Fig. 47.)

Solution. Here

$$S = 2\pi \int x \, ds$$

$$= 2\pi \int x \sqrt{1 + y'^2} \, dx$$

Now

$$dx = a(1 - \cos\theta) \, d\theta$$

$$dy = a \sin\theta \, d\theta$$

And

$$y' = \frac{\sin\theta}{1 - \cos\theta}$$

$$y'^2 = \frac{\sin^2\theta}{(1 - \cos\theta)^2}$$

$$1 + y'^2 = \frac{2}{1 - \cos\theta} = \frac{1}{\sin^2 \frac{1}{2}\theta}$$

$$\sqrt{1 + y'^2} = \frac{1}{\sin \frac{1}{2}\theta}$$

$$S = 2\pi a^2 \int_0^{2\pi} (\theta - \sin\theta) \frac{1}{\sin \frac{1}{2}\theta} (1 - \cos\theta) \, d\theta$$

$$= 4\pi a^2 \int_0^{2\pi} (\theta - \sin\theta) \sin \frac{1}{2}\theta \, d\theta$$

$$= 4\pi a^2 \int_0^{2\pi} (\theta \sin \frac{1}{2}\theta - \sin\theta \sin \frac{1}{2}\theta) \, d\theta$$

$$= 4\pi a^2 \int_0^{2\pi} (\theta \sin \frac{1}{2}\theta - 2 \sin^2 \frac{1}{2}\theta \cos \frac{1}{2}\theta) \, d\theta$$

Integrating the first of these by parts we get

$$4\pi a^2 \int_0^{2\pi} \theta \sin \frac{1}{2}\theta \, d\theta$$

$$= 4\pi a^2 \left[-2\theta \cos \frac{1}{2}\theta \Big|_0^{2\pi} + 2\int_0^{2\pi} \cos \frac{1}{2}\theta \, d\theta \right]$$

$$= 4\pi a^2 \left[4\pi + 4 \sin \frac{1}{2}\theta \Big|_0^{2\pi} \right]$$

$$= 16\pi^2 a^2.$$

This is the answer since

$$4\pi a^2 \int_0^{2\pi} (-2 \sin^2 \frac{1}{2}\theta \cos \frac{1}{2}\theta) \, d\theta$$

$$= 4\pi a^2 \left[-\frac{4}{3} \sin^3 \frac{1}{2}\theta \right]_0^{2\pi}$$

$$= 0.$$

Illustration 3. Find the surface area generated by revolving the upper half of the cardioid $\rho = a(1 - \cos\theta)$ about the initial line. (Fig. 52.)

Solution. The radius of the circle through which the element ds swings is $\rho \sin \theta$. The surface element is therefore $2 \pi \rho \sin \theta \, ds$.

$$S = 2\pi \int_0^\pi \rho \sin \theta \sqrt{\rho^2 + \rho'^2} \, d\theta$$

$$= 2\pi a \int_0^\pi (1 - \cos \theta) \sin \theta \sqrt{2 \, a^2 (1 - \cos \theta)} \, d\theta$$

$$= 4\pi a^2 \int_0^\pi (1 - \cos \theta) \sin \theta \sin \tfrac{1}{2} \theta \, d\theta$$

$$= 8\pi a^2 \int_0^\pi \sin^3 \tfrac{1}{2} \theta \sin \theta \, d\theta$$

$$= 16\pi a^2 \int_0^\pi \sin^4 \tfrac{1}{2} \theta \cos \tfrac{1}{2} \theta \, d\theta$$

$$= 16\pi a^2 \left[\tfrac{2}{5} \sin^5 \tfrac{1}{2} \theta \right]_0^\pi$$

$$= \tfrac{32}{5} \pi a^2.$$

EXERCISES

1. Find the surface area of a zone of altitude h of a sphere of radius r. (A zone is the portion of a sphere included between two parallel planes; the altitude of a zone is the distance between the parallel planes.)   *Ans.* $2\pi r h$.

2. Find the surface area generated by revolving one arch of $y = \cos x$ about the X-axis.   *Ans.* $2\pi[\sqrt{2} + \log (1 + \sqrt{2})]$.

3. Find the surface area generated by revolving the lemniscate $\rho^2 = a^2 \cos 2\theta$ (Fig. 65) about the initial line.   *Ans.* $2\pi a^2(2 - \sqrt{2})$.

4. Find the surface area generated by revolving about the X-axis the ellipse $x = a \cos \theta$, $y = b \sin \theta$.

Ans. $2\pi ab \left[\sqrt{1 - e^2} + \dfrac{1}{e} \sin^{-1} e \right]$, where eccentricity $e = \dfrac{\sqrt{a^2 - b^2}}{a}$.

5. Find the surface area generated by revolving one arch of the cycloid $x = a(\theta - \sin \theta)$, $y = a(1 - \cos \theta)$ about the X-axis. (Fig. 47.)
Ans. $\tfrac{64}{3} \pi a^2$.

47. Work. Let a body move along a straight line under the application of a constant force F lbs. acting in the direction of motion. If the particle is displaced x ft., the work done is $W = Fx$ ft.-lbs. Thus the work done in lifting a body weighing 100 lbs. a vertical distance of 2 ft. against the force of gravity is 200 ft.-lbs.

To generalize this notion of work we consider a variable force F acting in the direction of motion which takes place along a curve. The distance (or displacement) element along the curve is ds; if the force F is a function of s, then the element of work

done will be $dW = F(s)\ ds$.   Summing all such elements we get
the total work done:

(1) $$W = \int_{s_1}^{s_2} F(s)\ ds.$$

In the applications which will concern us the motion will take
place along a line which may be taken as one of the axes.   For
example, if the motion is along the X-axis (1) becomes

(2) $$W = \int_{x_1}^{x_2} F(x)\ dx.$$

Illustration 1.   A vertical cylindrical tank of radius r ft. and height h ft. is
full of water.   Find the work done in emptying it
by pumping the water out over the rim of the
top.   (Fig. 107.)

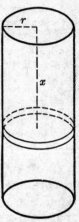

Solution.   Consider an element of water (a disc) at
depth x from the top.   The volume of this slice is
$\pi r^2\ dx$.   Its weight is therefore $w\pi r^2\ dx$ where the
weight of 1 cu. ft. of the liquid is w (density); here
$w = 62.5$ lbs. since the liquid is water.   In general
w will depend upon the liquid considered.   The work
done in lifting this weight (force) x feet is therefore
$dW = 62.5\ \pi r^2 x\ dx$ and the total work is

$$W = \int_0^h 62.5\ \pi r^2 x\ dx$$

$$= \frac{62.5\ \pi r^2 h^2}{2}\ \text{ft.-lbs.}$$

$$= \frac{w}{2}\ \pi r^2 h^2 \text{ in the case of a liquid of density } w.$$

FIG. 107

Illustration 2.   An anchor chain of a ship weighs 50 lbs./linear ft. while
the anchor itself weighs 2000 lbs.   What is the work done in pulling up
anchor if 100 ft. of chain are out, assuming that the lift is vertical?

Solution.   Let x be the number of feet of anchor chain out at any time and
consider an element dx.   This element weighs $50\ dx$ pounds and it must
be lifted x feet.   The work required is therefore

$$W = \int_0^{100} 50\ x\ dx + (2000)100$$

where $(2000)100$ represents the work of lifting the anchor itself.

$$W = 25\ x^2 \Big]_0^{100} + 200{,}000$$

$$= 250{,}000 + 200{,}000$$

$$= 450{,}000 \text{ ft.-lbs.}$$

Illustration 3. The force required to stretch a certain spring is proportional to the elongation. If a force of one pound stretches the spring half an inch, what is the work done in stretching the spring 2 inches?

Solution. Call L the natural length of the spring and x the elongation. Then $F = kx$, $1 = k \cdot \frac{1}{2}$, $k = 2$. Hence $F = 2x$ and the work is

$$W = \int_0^2 2\, x\, dx$$

$$= x^2 \Big]_0^2$$

$$= 4 \text{ in.-lbs.}$$

EXERCISES

1. A hemispherical tank of radius r is full of gasoline of density w. What is the work done in pumping the gasoline out over the rim of the tank?

Ans. $\frac{1}{4}\pi w r^4$.

2. The natural length of a spring is 4 inches and the force required to compress it is $F = 3x$, where x is the amount of compression in inches. Find the work done in compressing the spring until it is only 2.8″ long.

Ans. 2.16 in.-lbs.

3. A conical tank is full of water is 6 ft. deep (vertex down), and the top has a radius of 2 ft. Find the work required to empty the tank by pumping the water to a point 3 ft. above the top of the tank.

Ans. $12\,\pi w + 24\,\pi w = 36\,\pi w$ ft.-lbs.

48. Pressure.

When an area is submerged in a liquid, there is a pressure (force per unit area) on it due to the weight of the liquid above it. It is a fundamental principle of hydrostatics that the pressure $p = wh$, where w is the weight per unit volume of the liquid and h is the depth of submersion. It is also fundamental that the pressure is uniform in all directions. These principles and the calculus enable us to find the total force F due to liquid pressure on a submerged area of variable depth.

Think of a vertical area as being submerged and consider a horizontal strip of length l and depth h (Fig. 108). Let this

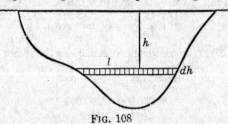

FIG. 108

element be of width dh.   Then the area of the strip is $l\,dh$ and the pressure on it is wh.   The force on this element is pressure $\times$ area or $dF = whl\,dh$.   Therefore the total force F will be given by

(1) $$F = \int_a^b whl\,dh.$$

This integral may be evaluated as soon as l is expressed as a function of h.

Illustration 1.   A plate in the form of an equilateral triangle, of side $2\,a$, is submerged vertically in water until one edge is just in the surface of the water.   Find the total force on one side of such a plate.   (Fig. 109.)

Solution.   If $2\,l$ is the length of an element submerged to a depth x then

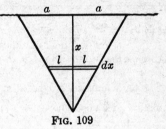

$$\frac{l}{\sqrt{3}\,a - x} = \frac{a}{\sqrt{3}\,a}$$

$$l = a - \frac{\sqrt{3}}{3}\,x$$

The total force is then given by

$$F = 2 \int_0^{\sqrt{3}a} wx\left(a - \frac{\sqrt{3}}{3}\,x\right)dx$$

$$= 2\,w\left[\frac{ax^2}{2} - \frac{\sqrt{3}\,x^3}{9}\right]_0^{\sqrt{3}a}$$

$$= wa^3 \text{ lbs.}$$

FIG. 109

Illustration 2.   The center of a circular floodgate of radius $2'$ in a reservoir is at a depth of $6'$.   Find the total force on the gate.   (Fig. 110.)

Solution.   Taking axes as shown, the equation of the circle is

$$x^2 + (y + 6)^2 = 4$$

At a depth y the width of an element is dy and the length is

$$2\,x = 2\sqrt{4 - (y + 6)^2}$$

The total force is then

$$F = 2\,w \int_{-4}^{-8} y\sqrt{4 - (y + 6)^2}\,dy$$

Set $y + 6 = z;\ dy = dz$

$$F = 2\,w \int_{2}^{-2} (z - 6)\sqrt{4 - z^2}\,dz$$

$$= 2\,w\left[-\tfrac{1}{3}(4 - z^2)^{\frac{3}{2}} - 3\,z\sqrt{4 - z^2} - 12\sin^{-1}\frac{z}{2}\right]_2^{-2}$$

$$= 24\,\pi w \text{ lbs.}$$

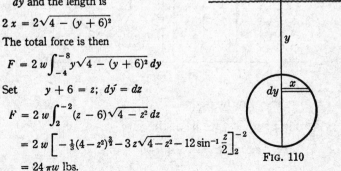

FIG. 110

Illustration 3.   A plate in the form of the parabola $y = x^2$ is lowered vertically into water to a depth of one foot, vertex downward.   Find the total force on one side.   (Fig. 111.)

Solution.   The length of an element submerged $(1 - y)$ ft. is $2x$.   The total force is then

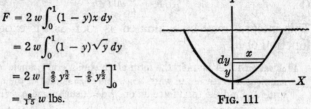

$$F = 2w \int_0^1 (1 - y)x \, dy$$

$$= 2w \int_0^1 (1 - y)\sqrt{y} \, dy$$

$$= 2w \left[\tfrac{2}{3} y^{\frac{3}{2}} - \tfrac{2}{5} y^{\frac{5}{2}} \right]_0^1$$

$$= \tfrac{8}{15} w \text{ lbs.}$$

FIG. 111

EXERCISES

1.   A $6' \times 8'$ rectangular floodgate is placed vertically in water with the $6'$ side in the surface of the water.   Find the force on one side.   *Ans.* $192 \, w$ lbs.

2.   A cylindrical tank of radius $5'$ is placed horizontally and is half full of gasoline that weighs w lbs./cu. ft.   Find the pressure exerted on one end of the tank.   *Ans.* $\tfrac{250}{3} w$ lbs.

3.   A hemispherical bowl $2'$ in radius is filled with water.   Find the total force exerted on the bowl.   *Ans.* $F = \int wx \, 2\pi\sqrt{4 - x^2} \, ds = 8\pi w$ lbs.

49.   Center of Mass.   For a point mass m_1 lying at a distance r_1 from a line L the first moment of the mass with respect to the line is defined as (Fig. 112)

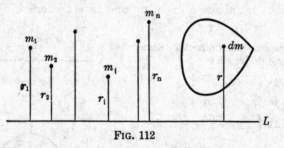

FIG. 112

(1)   1st moment $= r_1 m_1$

For n such particles, we have the sum

(2)   1st moment $= r_1 m_1 + r_2 m_2 + \cdots + r_n m_n$

$$= \Sigma r_i m_i$$

For a continuous mass distribution this sum becomes an integral.

(3)   1st moment $= \int r \, dm,$

where r represents the distance of the element of mass dm from the line L.

The center of mass, measured from L is

(4) $\bar{r} = $ center of mass $= \dfrac{\int r \, dm}{\int dm}$

From (4) we can readily compute the center of mass for a given mass measured from a given line (or from a given plane in the case where the mass is three-dimensional). Sometimes the center of mass is called the center of gravity or the c.g.; for masses that are pure geometrical figures the term *centroid* is often used. We shall use the abbreviation c.g. since its use rarely causes any confusion.

Case I. One-Dimensional Mass. Consider a wire in the shape of the curve $y = f(x)$. We modify (4) as follows in order to compute the coordinates of the c.g. Now mass equals density times volume but in this case the "volume" is the length of the curve. Hence

$$\text{mass} = \text{density} \times \text{length}$$
$$dm = \rho \, ds$$

and the coordinates of the c.g. are

(5) $\bar{x} = \dfrac{\int \rho x \, ds}{\int \rho \, ds}, \quad \bar{y} = \dfrac{\int \rho y \, ds}{\int \rho \, ds}$

Formulae (5) hold whether density ρ is a constant or not; in case ρ is a constant, it may be canceled.

Illustration 1. A wire of uniform density is in the form of a semicircle. Find its c.g.

Solution. Consider the wire as the upper half of the circle $x^2 + y^2 = r^2$. For reasons of symmetry $\bar{x} = 0$

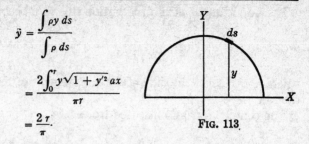

$$\bar{y} = \frac{\int \rho y \, ds}{\int \rho \, ds}$$

$$= \frac{2 \int_0^r y \sqrt{1 + y'^2} \, ax}{\pi r}$$

$$= \frac{2 r}{\pi}.$$

Fig. 113

Illustration 2. The density of a certain rod a foot long varies directly as the square of the distance from one end. Find the c.g.

Solution. Place the rod on the X-axis, one end at the origin so that

$$\rho = kx^2$$

$$\bar{x} = \frac{\int \rho x \, ds}{\int \rho \, ds}, \; \bar{y} = 0$$

$$\bar{x} = \frac{\int_0^a kx^3 \, dx}{\int_0^a kx^2 \, dx}$$

$$= \tfrac{3}{4} a.$$

Case II. Two-Dimensional Mass. Consider a plate as an area with a given contour and the mass as density × area (Fig. 114).

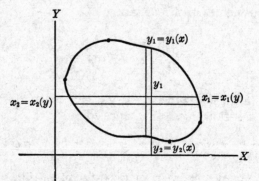

Fig. 114

Thus

$$dm = \rho \, dA = \rho(y_1 - y_2) \, dx = \rho(x_1 - x_2) \, dy$$

and the coordinates of the c.g. are given by

(6) $$\bar{x} = \frac{\int \rho x (y_1 - y_2) \, dx}{\int \rho (y_1 - y_2) \, dx}, \quad \bar{y} = \frac{\int \rho y (x_1 - x_2) \, dy}{\int \rho (x_1 - x_2) \, dy}$$

Note that for $\bar{x}$ the area element is taken as $(y_1 - y_2) \, dx$ since all parts of this strip are at the same distance x from the Y-axis; similarly for $\bar{y}$ all parts of the strip $(x_1 - x_2) \, dy$ are at the same distance y from the X-axis. In most problems commonly met ρ is a constant and in this case it is possible to use the area element $(y_1 - y_2) \, dx$ in computing $\bar{y}$ by considering all of the mass of the strip as concentrated at the middle point, i.e., at $\dfrac{y_1 + y_2}{2}$. When this is done

$$\bar{y} = \frac{\int \frac{1}{2}(y_1{}^2 - y_2{}^2) \, dx}{\int (y_1 - y_2) \, dx}$$

and this may be used instead of the expression for $\bar{y}$ in (6).

Illustration 3. Find the c.g. of a semicircular plate of radius r and of uniform density.

Solution. Write $x^2 + y^2 = r^2$

$$\bar{x} = 0, \bar{y} = \frac{\frac{1}{2} \int_{-r}^{r} y^2 \, dx}{\int_{-r}^{r} y \, dx}$$

$$\bar{y} = \frac{1}{\pi r^2} \int_{-r}^{r} (r^2 - x^2) \, dx$$

$$= \frac{1}{\pi r^2} \left[r^2 x - \frac{x^3}{3} \right]_{-r}^{r}$$

$$= \frac{4}{3} \frac{r}{\pi}.$$

FIG. 115

Illustration 4. Find the c.g. of that area cut from the parabola $y^2 = 4px$ by the latus rectum.

Solution. Because of symmetry
$$\bar{y} = 0.$$

$$\bar{x} = \frac{\displaystyle\int_0^p xy\, dx}{\displaystyle\int_0^p y\, dx} = \frac{\displaystyle\int_0^p x\, 2\sqrt{px}\, dx}{\displaystyle\int_0^p 2\sqrt{px}\, dx}$$

$$= \frac{\dfrac{2}{5} x^{\frac{5}{2}} \Big]_0^p}{\dfrac{2}{3} x^{\frac{3}{2}} \Big]_0^p}$$

$$= \tfrac{3}{5} p.$$

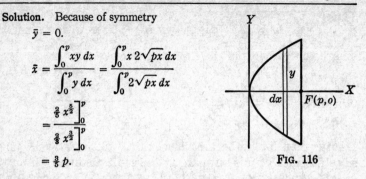

FIG. 116

Case III. Three-Dimensional Mass. Here $dm = \rho\, dv$ but thus far we have discussed only solids of revolution and solids with known cross sections. We shall take up more general cases in Chapter XIII. But for a three-dimensional mass (volume) we take moments with respect to a plane and so define the 1st moment with respect to that plane. Suppose the area between the curve $y = f(x)$, $x = 0$, $y = c$, $y = d$, is revolved about the Y-axis. Then taking slices perpendicular to the Y-axis as we did in computing the volume, we have $dm = \rho\pi x^2\, dy$. This mass is all at the same distance from the base plane perpendicular to the Y-axis. The first moment of this mass with respect to the base plane is (Fig. 117)

$$(7) \qquad \text{1st moment} = \pi \int \rho y x^2\, dy;$$

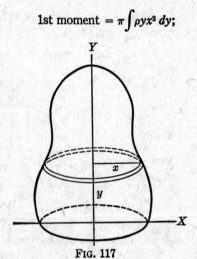

FIG. 117

and the $\bar{y}$ of the c.g. is given by

(8)
$$\bar{y} = \frac{\int \rho y x^2 \, dy}{\int \rho x^2 \, dy}$$

Since the solid is one of revolution, this will completely locate the c.g., provided the solid is homogeneous or provided the density is a function of the distance from the axis of rotation.

Illustration 5. Find the c.g. of a homogeneous hemisphere of radius r.

Solution. The c.g. will lie on the diameter perpendicular to the base at a distance $\bar{y}$ above the base.

$$\bar{y} = \frac{\int \pi y x^2 \, dy}{\int dv}$$

$$= \frac{\int_0^r \pi y (r^2 - y^2) \, dy}{\frac{2}{3} \pi r^3}$$

$$= \frac{3}{2 r^3} \left[\frac{r^2 y^2}{2} - \frac{y^4}{4} \right]_0^r$$

$$= \tfrac{3}{8} r.$$

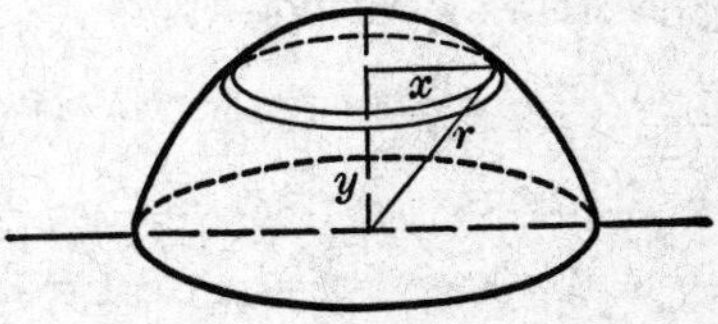

FIG. 118

Illustration 6. Find the c.g. of a cone of radius r and altitude h. (Measure from the vertex.)

Solution. $\bar{x} = 0,$

$$\bar{y} = \frac{\int_0^h \pi y x^2 \, dy}{\int dv}.$$

But $\dfrac{x}{y} = \dfrac{r}{h}, \; x = \dfrac{r}{h} y$; and the volume of the cone is $\frac{1}{3} \pi r^2 h$. Therefore

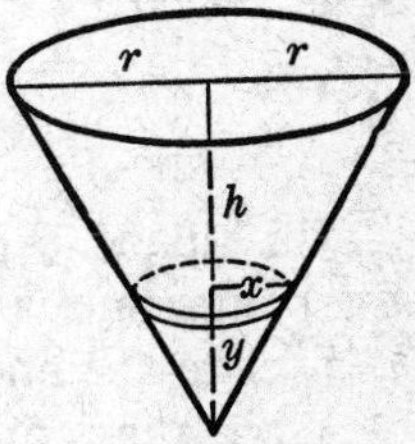

$$\bar{y} = \frac{\int_0^h \pi y \left(\frac{r}{h} y \right)^2 dy}{\frac{1}{3} \pi r^2 h}$$

$$= \frac{3}{h^3} \left[\frac{y^4}{4} \right]_0^h$$

$$= \tfrac{3}{4} h.$$

FIG. 119

EXERCISES

Find the c.g. of the following masses.

1. A wire bent in the form of a right triangle of legs a and b. Take the vertices at $(0, 0)$, $(a, 0)$, $(0, b)$. *Ans.* $\bar{x} = \frac{1}{3} a$, $\bar{y} = \frac{1}{3} b$. This point is at the center of the Spieker circle, which is the circle inscribed in the triangle whose vertices are the midpoints of the sides of the given triangle. (Prove that the center of the Spieker circle is the c.g. of a general triangle considered as a wire.)

2. A right-triangular area with legs a and b. Take the vertices at $(0, 0)$, $(a, 0)$, $(0, b)$. *Ans.* $\bar{x} = \frac{1}{3} a$, $\bar{y} = \frac{1}{3} b$. This is the point of intersection of the medians. (Prove that the median point is the c.g. of a general triangular area.)

3. The first arch of the cycloid $x = a(\theta - \sin \theta)$, $y = a(1 - \cos \theta)$. (Fig. 47.)   *Ans.* $\bar{x} = \pi a$, $\bar{y} = \frac{4}{3} a$.

4. The area under the first arch of the cycloid $x = a(\theta - \sin \theta)$, $y = a(1 - \cos \theta)$. (Fig. 47.)   *Ans.* $\bar{x} = \pi a$, $\bar{y} = \frac{5}{6} a$.

5. The area under $y = \cos x$ between $x = -\dfrac{\pi}{2}$ and $x = \dfrac{\pi}{2}$.

Ans. $\bar{x} = 0$, $\bar{y} = \dfrac{\pi}{8}$.

6. A rectangle whether considered as an arc or an area.

Ans. c.g. at the geometric center.

7. The volume formed by rotating the area in the first quadrant under the parabola $y^2 = 4px$ between the vertex and the latus rectum about the Y-axis.   *Ans.* $\bar{x} = 0$, $\bar{y} = \frac{5}{6} p$.

8. A hemisphere of radius r if density $\rho = ky$ where y is distance from the base plane.   *Ans.* $\bar{y} = \frac{8}{15} r$.

50. Moment of Inertia. Corresponding to (3) § 49 for the 1st moment we define the 2nd moment as

$$(1) \qquad\qquad \text{2nd moment} = I = \int r^2 \, dm.$$

This quantity plays an important part in the theory of rotating bodies and is called the moment of inertia of the body with respect to the line (called an axis) or to the plane.

Again there are several cases according to the character of the mass considered. But these are treated in precisely the same way they were treated in computing the 1st moments (§ 49), the only difference being that here the square of the distance is used instead of the first power of the distance.

Case I. One-Dimensional Mass. Let the curve $y = f(x)$ (a wire) be given. To find the moment of inertia I of this wire with respect to the X-axis we write, for (1)

(2) $$I_x = \int \rho y^2 \, ds$$

and evaluate in the usual way. I_y is defined similarly.

> **Illustration 1.** Find the moment of inertia of a circumference of a circle about a diameter.
>
> **Solution.** We consider $\rho = 1$ and write $x^2 + y^2 = r^2$. The moment of inertia of the whole circumference will be 4 times the moment of inertia of a quarter-circumference. Hence
>
> $$\begin{aligned} I_x &= \int y^2 \, ds \\ &= 4 \int_0^r y^2 \sqrt{1 + y'^2} \, dx \\ &= 4 \int_0^r ry \, dx \\ &= 4 r \int_0^r \sqrt{r^2 - x^2} \, dx \\ &= 4 r \left[\frac{x}{2} \sqrt{r^2 - x^2} + \frac{r^2}{2} \sin^{-1} \frac{x}{r} \right]_0^r \\ &= \pi r^3. \end{aligned}$$

This is the moment of inertia of the mathematical circumference. If this arc is replaced by a wire of density ρ and mass $M = \rho s$, where $s = 2 \pi r =$ length, then

$$I_x = \rho \pi r^3.$$

But $\rho = \dfrac{M}{2 \pi r}$; therefore, in terms of M we have

$$I_x = \frac{Mr^2}{2}.$$

Case II. Two-Dimensional Mass. Here the mass element is an area and the moments of inertia about the X- and Y-axes are respectively

(3) $$I_x = \int \rho y^2 \, dA$$

(4) $$I_y = \int \rho x^2 \, dA$$

where an area element is so taken that it all lies at the same distance from the given axis.

Illustration 2. Find I_x and I_y for the area common to the two curves $y = x^2$, $y^2 = x$.

Solution. These two parabolas intersect in the points $(0, 0)$, $(1, 1)$ and because of conditions of symmetry $I_x = I_y$.

$$I_x = \int_0^1 y^2 (\sqrt{y} - y^2)\, dy, \; \rho = 1$$

$$= \left[\frac{2}{7} y^{\frac{7}{2}} - \frac{y^5}{5} \right]_0^1$$

$$= \frac{3}{35}.$$

For a plate of density $\rho = \dfrac{M}{\frac{1}{3}}$ (see Illustration 5, § 41) this becomes

$$I_x = \tfrac{3}{35} \rho = \tfrac{9}{35} M.$$

Illustration 3. Find the moment of inertia of a circular area about (a) a diameter, (b) a tangent.

Solution. Write $(x - r)^2 + y^2 = r^2$. Since this circle is tangent to the Y-axis at the origin, the answers are (a) I_x and (b) I_y.

$$I_x = \int \rho y^2 (x - r)\, dy, \; \rho = 1$$

$$= 4 \int_0^r y^2 \sqrt{r^2 - y^2}\, dy$$

$$= 4 \left[\frac{y}{8} (2 y^2 - r^2) \sqrt{r^2 - y^2} + \frac{r^4}{8} \sin^{-1} \frac{y}{r} \right]_0^r$$

(Formula 49, Table of Integrals)

$$= \frac{\pi r^4}{4} \text{ (area)}$$

$$= \frac{\rho \pi r^4}{4} = \frac{M r^2}{4} \text{ (plate of mass } M\text{).}$$

$$I_y = \int x^2 y\, dx$$

$$= 2 \int_0^{2r} x^2 \sqrt{r^2 - (x - r)^2}\, dx.$$

Set $x - r = z$

$$I_y = 2 \int_{-r}^r (z + r)^2 \sqrt{r^2 - z^2}\, dz$$

$$= 2 \int_{-r}^r (z^2 + 2 rz + r^2) \sqrt{r^2 - z^2}\, dz$$

$$= 2 \left[\frac{z}{8} (2 z^2 - r^2) \sqrt{r^2 - z^2} + \frac{r^4}{8} \sin^{-1} \frac{z}{r} \right.$$

$$\left. - \tfrac{2}{3} r (r^2 - z^2)^{\frac{3}{2}} + \frac{r^2 z}{2} \sqrt{r^2 - z^2} + \frac{r^4}{2} \sin^{-1} \frac{z}{r} \right]_{-r}^r$$

(Formulae 44 and 49, Table of Integrals)

$$= \tfrac{5}{4} \pi r^4 \text{ (area)}$$

$$= \tfrac{5}{4} M r^2 \text{ (plate).}$$

Note that the methods used in Illustration 3 have some involved integrations. It is possible to compute the moment of inertia about a diameter with comparative ease after introducing the idea of the moment of inertia of a mass (one- or two-dimensional) about an axis perpendicular to the plane of the mass. This is called the *polar moment of inertia* I_0 and is defined, as before, as the mass times the square of the distance, or

$$(5) \qquad I_0 = \int (x^2 + y^2) \, dm.$$

But this can be broken up into the two parts

$$(6) \qquad I_0 = \int x^2 \, dm + \int y^2 \, dm,$$
$$= I_y + I_x.$$

Hence when the axis is taken through the origin and perpendicular to the XY-plane, then the moment of inertia about this axis is the sum of the regular moments about the X- and Y-axes. Let us return to the problem (a) in Illustration 3 by considering

Illustration 4. Find the polar moment of inertia of a circle about an axis through the center.

Solution. Write $x^2 + y^2 = r^2$ and consider the area element in the form of a ring of width dR, the area of which is $2\pi R \, dR$. All of this area is at distance R from the axis; hence

$$I_0 = \int_0^r R^2 \, 2\pi R \, dR$$

$$= \frac{\pi R^4}{2} \Big]_0^r = \frac{\pi r^4}{2} \text{ (area)}$$

$$= \frac{\rho \pi r^4}{2} = \frac{M r^2}{2} \text{ (plate)}.$$

Clearly

$$I_x = I_y = \tfrac{1}{2} I_0$$

$$= \frac{\pi r^4}{4} \text{ (area)}$$

$$= \frac{M r^2}{4} \text{ (plate)}.$$

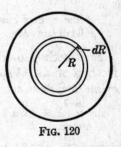

FIG. 120

This is the same result obtained in Illustration 3 (a), but is arrived at here with extreme ease.

It is also possible to get the moment of inertia about a tangent (Illustration 3 (b)) with ease. This we do in § 56, Illustration 4, after further theory on moments.

Case III. Three-Dimensional Mass. The general case of a solid is discussed later in Chapter XII. For the present if the mass considered is that of a solid of revolution about the Y-axis, we proceed to take disc elements perpendicular to the Y-axis. The mass of such an element will be $dm = \rho \pi x^2 \, dy$. The moment of inertia of this mass about the Y-axis is the polar moment of inertia of a circular plate about an axis through its center. By Illustration 4 above, this is equal to $\dfrac{Mr^2}{2}$ or $dI_y = \frac{1}{2}\rho\pi x^4 \, dy$. The total moment of inertia of the solid is the sum of the moments of inertia of all of the elementary discs; or

$$(7) \qquad I_y = \frac{1}{2}\rho\pi \int x^4 \, dy.$$

Illustration 5. The area of the ellipse $\dfrac{x^2}{a^2} + \dfrac{y^2}{b^2} = 1$ is revolved about the Y-axis. Find I_y for the solid thus generated. (Fig. 9.)

Solution.
$$I_y = \frac{1}{2}\rho\pi \int x^4 \, dy$$
$$= \rho\pi \frac{a^4}{b^4} \int_0^b (b^2 - y^2)^2 \, dy$$
$$= \rho\pi \frac{a^4}{b^4}\left[b^4 y - \frac{2}{3}b^2 y^3 + \frac{1}{5}y^5 \right]_0^b$$
$$= \tfrac{8}{15}\rho\pi a^4 b$$
$$= \tfrac{8}{15}\pi a^4 b \quad (\rho = 1; \text{ for volume}).$$

But the volume generated is $\frac{4}{3}\pi a^2 b$. Hence $M = \rho V$, $I_y = \frac{2}{5}Ma^2$ (for solid of mass M).

The method used in Illustration 5 is sometimes called the method of *disc elements*. Another useful method makes use of *cylindrical elements*. (Review page 117.)

Illustration 6. Work the problem in Illustration 5 by using cylindrical elements.

Solution. The mass element is $\rho\, 2\pi xy \, dx$ and all of this mass is at the distance x from the Y-axis. Therefore

$$I_y = 4\pi\rho \int_0^a x^3 y \, dx$$
$$= 4\pi\rho \frac{b}{a} \int_0^a x^3 \sqrt{a^2 - x^2} \, dx$$
$$= 4\pi\rho \frac{b}{a}\left[-\frac{x^2}{3}(a^2 - x^2)^{\frac{3}{2}} \Big|_0^a + \frac{2}{3}\int_0^a x(a^2 - x^2)^{\frac{3}{2}} \, dx \right]$$

(This integration was performed by parts with $u = x^2$ and $dv = x\sqrt{a^2 - x^2}$.)

$$= 4\pi\rho\frac{b}{a}\left[-\frac{x^2}{3}(a^2 - x^2)^{\frac{3}{2}} - \frac{2}{15}(a^2 - x^2)^{\frac{5}{2}}\right]_0^a$$

$$= \tfrac{8}{15}\rho\pi a^4 b$$

$$= \tfrac{8}{15}\pi a^4 b \text{ (for volume)}$$

$$= \tfrac{2}{5}Ma^2 \text{(for mass).}$$

Note that the integration by the method of discs was simpler than the integration in the second method where cylindrical elements were used. This is not always the case and the student should use the simpler method whichever it turns out to be.

Another important concept in mechanics is that of *radius of gyration k* defined as follows:

(8) $$k = \sqrt{\frac{I}{M}}.$$

This says that $I = Mk^2$ and so k can be interpreted as the fixed distance at which all of the mass M would have to be concentrated in order to yield the moment of inertia I. To calculate the radius of gyration first calculate I (in terms of M) and substitute in (8).

EXERCISES

1. Find I_y for the line segment joining $(0, 0)$ and $(L, 0)$.   *Ans.* $\frac{1}{3}L^3$.

2. A plate of density ρ is in the form of the ellipse $\frac{x^2}{a^2} + \frac{y^2}{b^2} = 1$. Find I_x and I_y for this plate.   *Ans.* $I_x = \frac{1}{4}Mb^2$, $I_y = \frac{1}{4}Ma^2$.

3. A plate is in the form of a triangle with vertices at $(0, 0)$, $(a, 0)$, $(0, b)$. Find I_x, I_y, I_0.   *Ans.* $I_x = \frac{1}{6}Mb^2$, $I_y = \frac{1}{6}Ma^2$, $I_0 = \frac{1}{6}M(a^2 + b^2)$.

4. Find the moment of inertia of a solid sphere of radius r about a diameter.   *Ans.* $\frac{2}{5}Mr^2$ (cf. Illustration 5).

5. Find the moment of inertia of a solid cylinder of radius r and height h about (a) the axis, (b) a generator.   *Ans.* (a) $\frac{1}{2}Mr^2$, (b) $\frac{3}{2}Mr^2$.

6. Find I_y for the solid formed by revolving the area common to the two parabolas $y^2 = x$, $y = x^2$ about the Y-axis. Fig. (102.)   *Ans.* $\frac{10}{27}M$.

CHAPTER XII

APPROXIMATE INTEGRATION

51. Trapezoidal Rule. It is impossible in some cases to express the indefinite integral, $\int f(x)\, dx$, in terms of the elementary functions. But it often happens, as in engineering problems, that only an approximation to the definite integral $\int_a^b f(x)\, dx$ is needed. Further it may happen that all that is known of the function $y = f(x)$ is a table of values obtained through experimentation. In either case it is possible to obtain an approximate value for $\int_a^b f(x)\, dx$.

Suppose this definite integral be interpreted as the area under $y = f(x)$ from $x = a$ to $x = b$ and suppose the interval $b - a$ be divided up into n equal parts each of width $\Delta x = \dfrac{b - a}{n}$ by points of division x_i. Erect ordinates y_i at these points and join the extremities by straight line segments. Then the

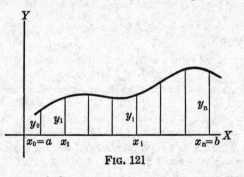

Fig. 121

sum of the areas of the trapezoids thus formed will be an approximation to the area under the curve. This sum is

$$\tfrac{1}{2}(y_0 + y_1)\, \Delta x + \tfrac{1}{2}(y_1 + y_2)\, \Delta x + \cdots + \tfrac{1}{2}(y_{n-1} + y_n)\, \Delta x$$
$$= \frac{\Delta x}{2}\,(y_0 + 2\,y_1 + 2\,y_2 + \cdots + 2\,y_{n-1} + y_n).$$

Hence the Trapezoidal Rule:

(1) $\quad \int_{x_0}^{x_n} f(x)\, dx \doteq \dfrac{\Delta x}{2}\,(y_0 + 2\,y_1 + 2\,y_2 + \cdots + 2\,y_{n-1} + y_n).$

If $f(x)$ is given as a table formula (1) may be applied if and only if the spacings between abscissa points are equal; if the spacings are unequal, the areas of the trapezoids can still be added together giving

$$\tfrac{1}{2}(y_0 + y_1)\,\Delta x_1 + \tfrac{1}{2}(y_1 + y_2)\,\Delta x_2 + \cdots + \tfrac{1}{2}(y_{n-1} + y_n)\,\Delta x_n$$

where

$$\Delta x_i = x_i - x_{i-1}.$$

This will give the approximation sought.

Illustration 1. Evaluate $\int_0^2 x^2\, dx$ by the Trapezoidal Rule, using $n = 4$.

Solution. We note that this can be integrated and so there would be no need to use a method of approximation. But as an exercise we take $n = 4$ and $\Delta x = .5$ and write

$$\int_0^2 x^2\, dx \sim \frac{.5}{2}\,(0 + \tfrac{1}{2} + 2 + \tfrac{9}{2} + 4)$$
$$= \tfrac{11}{4}.$$

The exact value is $\tfrac{8}{3}$ sq. units. The error is .08.

Illustration 2. Evaluate $\int_0^{\frac{\pi}{2}} \dfrac{\sin x}{x}\, dx$ by the Trapezoidal Rule, using $n = 3$.

Solution. The $\int \dfrac{\sin x}{x}\, dx$ cannot be expressed in terms of the elementary functions.

$$\int_0^{\frac{\pi}{2}} \frac{\sin x}{x}\, dx \sim \frac{\pi}{12}\left(1 + \frac{6}{\pi} + \frac{3\sqrt{3}}{\pi} + \frac{2}{\pi}\right)$$
$$= 1.361.$$

Illustration 3. In order to get an approximation to the area between a straight railroad track and a winding stream, measurements were made as in Fig. 122. Find approximately the area between the railroad and the stream.

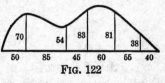

FIG. 122

Solution.
$$A \sim \tfrac{1}{2}(50)70 + \tfrac{1}{2}(70 + 54)(85)$$
$$+ \tfrac{1}{2}(54 + 83)45 + \tfrac{1}{2}(83 + 81)60$$
$$+ \tfrac{1}{2}(81 + 38)55 + \tfrac{1}{2}(38)40$$
$$= 19,055 \text{ sq. ft.}$$

52. Simpson's Rule. A definite integral may also be evaluated approximately by Simpson's Rule:

$$(2) \quad \int_a^b f(x)\, dx \sim \frac{\Delta x}{3} [y_0 + 4(y_1 + y_3 + y_5 + \cdots) + 2(y_2 + y_4 + y_6 + \cdots) + y_n].$$

In applying Simpson's Rule it is necessary that the number of intervals n be even. The way to remember this rule is to note that when the first ordinate is called y_0 and the last ordinate y_n, n even, then the operations are

1st. Add the first and last ordinates,

2nd. Add 4 times the sum of the ordinates with odd subscripts,

3rd. Add 2 times the sum of the ordinates with even subscripts (excluding, of course, y_n),

4th. Multiply the total sum by $\frac{1}{3}$ of the common distance between ordinates.

This rule is developed by using parabolic arcs (instead of straight lines as in the Trapezoidal Rule) with which to approximate the curve. The parabolas used are those with axes parallel to the Y-axis each one of them being passed through a consecutive set of three points on the curve of $y = f(x)$. Since each set of three points accounts for two intervals, the total number of intervals will be a multiple of 2 or an even number. In general Simpson's Rule gives a better approximation than the Trapezoidal Rule, where the number of intervals n is about the same.

Illustration 4. Apply Simpson's Rule to the problem in Illustration 1.

Solution.

$$\int_0^2 x^2\, dx = \frac{\Delta x}{3}[y_0 + 4(y_1 + y_3) + 2\,y_2 + y_0]$$

$$= \frac{0.5}{3}\left[0 + 4\left(\frac{1}{4} + \frac{9}{4}\right) + 2 + 4\right]$$

$$= \tfrac{8}{3} \text{ sq. units.}$$

Note that Simpson's Rule gives the exact answer in this case. (Simpson's Rule gives the exact answer in case $y = ax^3 + bx^2 + cx + d$ with $n = 2$.)

Illustration 5. Evaluate $\int_0^{1.2} e^{-x^2}\, dx$ by Simpson's Rule, using $n = 6$.

Solution. $\Delta x = .2$, $y_0 = 1$, $y_1 = .96079$

$\qquad\qquad y_2 = .85214$, $y_3 = .69768$

$\qquad\qquad y_4 = .52729$, $y_5 = .36788$

$\qquad\qquad y_6 = .23693$ (From numerical tables of e^{-t})

$$\int_0^{1.2} e^{-x^2}\,dx = .80675.$$

EXERCISES

1. Find the area under the curve $y = \dfrac{1}{2+x}$ from $x = 0$, $x = 2$, by (a) Trapezoidal Rule, $n = 4$; (b) Simpson's Rule, $n = 4$; (c) Integration.

$\qquad\qquad$ *Ans.* (a) .69702; (b) .69325; (c) $\log_e 2 = .69315$.

2. Evaluate $\displaystyle\int_0^4 e^{-\frac{x^2}{2}}\,dx$ by (a) Trapezoidal Rule, with $\Delta x = \frac{1}{10}$; and (b) Simpson's Rule, with $\Delta x = \frac{1}{5}$.$\qquad$ **·** *Ans.* (a) .3893; (b) .3896.

3. (a) Show that $4\displaystyle\int_0^1 \dfrac{dx}{1+x^2} = \pi$; (b) By applying Simpson's Rule with $n = 10$ to this integral show that, approximately, $\pi = 3.1416$.

4. A smooth curve is passed through the data of the following table:

x	0	1	2	3	4	5	6
y	0	1	1.2	1.6	2.3	2.4	0

Find the area under the curve by (a) Trapezoidal Rule; (b) Simpson's Rule.

$\qquad\qquad$ *Ans.* (a) 8.5 sq. units; (b) 9 sq. units.

CHAPTER XIII

MULTIPLE INTEGRATION

53. Repeated Integration. Since the integral of a function of x, $\int f(x)\,dx$, is itself a function of x, say $F(x) + c_1$, it may be integrated. We write

(1) $$\int f(x)\,dx = F(x) + c_1,$$

$$\int [F(x) + c_1]\,dx = G(x) + c_1 x + c_2.$$

(2) $$\int \left[\int f(x)\,dx \right] dx = \int \int f(x)\,dx\,dx$$

$$= \int \int f(x)\,dx^2.$$

Or the process of integration may be repeated any number of times.

(3) $$\int \left\{ \int \left[\int f(x)\,dx \right] dx \right\} dx = \int \int \int f(x)\,dx\,dx\,dx$$

$$= \int \int \int f(x)\,dx^3.$$

The integrals (2) and (3) are called repeated or iterated integrals; more often they are called double and triple integrals respectively. The n-fold iterated integral is written

(4) $$\int \int \cdots \int f(x)\,dx^n.$$

Illustration 1. Find $\int \int \sin 2\,x\,dx\,dx$.

Solution. $$\int \int \sin 2\,x\,dx\,dx$$

$$= \int (-\tfrac{1}{2}\cos 2\,x + c_1)\,dx$$

$$= -\tfrac{1}{4}\sin 2\,x + c_1 x + c_2.$$

Note the two constants of integration c_1 and c_2. Since the first constant of integration is to be integrated, we get the $c_1 x$ term.

Illustration 2. Find $\int\int\int (x^2 + e^{-3x})\, dx^3$.

Solution. $\int\int\int (x^2 + e^{-3x})\, dx^3$

$$= \int\int \left(\frac{x^3}{3} - \frac{1}{3} e^{-3x} + c_1\right) dx^2$$

$$= \int \left(\frac{x^4}{12} + \frac{1}{9} e^{-3x} + c_1 x + c_2\right) dx$$

$$= \frac{x^5}{60} - \frac{1}{27} e^{-3x} + \frac{c_1 x^2}{2} + c_2 x + c_3.$$

For iterated definite integrals the procedure is the same. The integration is performed from the inside out; that is to say, $\int_c^d \int_a^b f(x)\, dx^2$ means that $f(x)$ is to be integrated first between the limits a and b and then this constant is to be integrated between the limits c and d.

Illustration 3. Evaluate $\int_{-1}^2 \int_0^2 (x^2 - \sin x)\, dx\, dx$.

Solution. $\int_{-1}^2 \int_0^2 (x^2 - \sin x)\, dx\, dx$

$$= \int_{-1}^2 \left[\frac{x^3}{3} + \cos x\right]_0^2 dx$$

$$= \int_{-1}^2 (\tfrac{8}{3} + \cos 2 - 1)\, dx$$

$$= (\tfrac{5}{3} + \cos 2)x \Big]_{-1}^2$$

$$= 5 + 3 \cos 2.$$

The problem in Illustration 3 would have had the same answer even though we had written it in the form

$$\int_{-1}^2 \left[\int_0^2 (t^2 - \sin t)\, dt\right] dw$$

since t and w are only dummy variables anyway in this process of integrating and evaluating between definite limits. If x and y are independent variables, we can generalize the ideas of and notation used in (2) to the iterated integral of a function of x and y.

(5) $$\int\int f(x, y)\, dx\, dy,$$

(6) $$\int_c^d \int_a^b f(x, y)\, dx\, dy$$

In (5), (6) the integration is first performed with regard to x — the inside integration symbol going with the first differential symbol, in this case dx. (Some authors couple the first integration symbol with the first differential and the student, when referring to other works on the calculus, should determine which system the particular writer is using. Occasionally the notation $\int dx \int f(x, y) \, dy$ is used where integration takes place first with respect to y.)

Since, in (6), after the first integration with respect to x, there is to be a second integration with respect to y, a and b could be thought of as functions of y. Hence we are led to the consideration of such integrals as

$$(7) \qquad \int_c^d \int_{a(y)}^{b(y)} f(x, y) \, dx \, dy.$$

The triple integral corresponding to (7) can be written

$$(8) \qquad \int_c^d \int_{\alpha(z)}^{\beta(z)} \int_{a(y, z)}^{b(y, z)} f(x, y, z) \, dx \, dy \, dz.$$

Illustration 4. Evaluate $\int_0^1 \int_0^y (x + y^2) \, dx \, dy$.

Solution.
$$\int_0^1 \int_0^y (x + y^2) \, dx \, dy$$
$$= \int_0^1 \left[\frac{x^2}{2} + xy^2 \right]_0^y dy$$
$$= \int_0^1 \left(\frac{y^2}{2} + y^3 \right) dy$$
$$= \left[\frac{y^3}{6} + \frac{y^4}{4} \right]_0^1$$
$$= \tfrac{5}{12}.$$

Illustration 5. Evaluate $A = \int_0^\pi \int_{-z}^z \int_0^{yz} (x + \sin y - z^3) \, dx \, dy \, dz$.

Solution.
$$A = \int_0^\pi \int_{-z}^z \left[\frac{x^2}{2} + x \sin y - xz^3 \right]_0^{yz} dy \, dz$$
$$= \int_0^\pi \int_{-z}^z \left(\frac{y^2z^2}{2} + yz \sin y - yz^4 \right) dy \, dz$$
$$= \int_0^\pi \left[\frac{y^3z^2}{6} + z(\sin y - y \cos y) - \frac{y^2z^4}{2} \right]_{-z}^z dz$$
$$= \int_0^\pi \left[\frac{z^5}{3} + 2 z(\sin z - z \cos z) \right] dz$$
$$= \left[\frac{z^6}{18} + 2(\sin z - z \cos z) - 2\left\{ 2 z \cos z + (z^2 - 2) \sin z \right\} \right]_0^\pi$$
$$= \frac{\pi^6}{18} + 6 \pi.$$

EXERCISES

Evaluate the following integrals.

1. $4 \int_0^a \int_0^{\sqrt{a^2-y^2}} \dfrac{a}{\sqrt{a^2-y^2}} \, dz \, dy = 4 \, a^2.$

2. $\int_0^2 \int_0^{\sqrt{4-x^2}} dy \, dx = \pi.$

3. $\int_{-1}^1 \int_0^x \int_1^{x+y} dz \, dy \, dx = 1.$

54. Second Fundamental Theorem of Integral Calculus.
Consider the area A bounded by a closed curve and suppose
that the interval a, b (Fig. 123) is subdivided by the $n + 1$
points $x_1 = a, x_2, \cdots, x_i, x_{i+1}, \cdots x_{n+1} = b$ and the interval $c,$

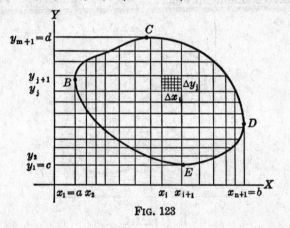

FIG. 123

d is subdivided by the $m + 1$ points $y_1 = c, y_2, \cdots, y_j,$
$y_{j+1}, \cdots, y_{m+1} = d.$ Erect ordinates at the x_i points and
abscissae at the y_j points thus covering the area A with a net
of lines forming small rectangular areas. Set $\Delta x_i = x_{i+1} - x_i$
and $\Delta y_j = y_{j+1} - y_j.$ Then the area of one of these rectangles is

$$\Delta A_{ij} = \Delta x_i \, \Delta y_j$$

and the sum of all of these areas as i and j independently take
on values from 1 to n and 1 to m respectively will be an approximation to the area $A.$ That is

(1) $A \doteq \sum_{i=1}^n \sum_{j=1}^m \Delta x_i \Delta y_j.$

Another *fundamental theorem* of the *integral calculus* (See § 43 for the first) states that

(2) $$A = \lim_{\substack{n, m \to \infty \\ \Delta x_i, \Delta v_j \to 0}} \sum_{i=1}^{n} \sum_{j=1}^{m} \Delta x_i \, \Delta y_j$$

(3) $$= \int_c^d \int_{\varphi_1(y)}^{\varphi_2(y)} dx \, dy$$

(4) $$= \int_a^b \int_{f_1(x)}^{f_2(x)} dy \, dx,$$

where $x = \varphi_1(y)$ is the equation of the curve CBE; $x = \varphi_2(y)$, the equation of CDE; $y = f_1(x)$, the equation of BED; and $y = f_2(x)$, the equation of BCD.

The corresponding formulae in polar coordinates are (Fig. 124)

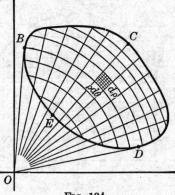

FIG. 124

(5) $$A = \int_\alpha^\beta \int_{\varphi_1(\theta)}^{\varphi_2(\theta)} \rho \, d\rho \, d\theta$$

(6) $$= \int_{\rho_1}^{\rho_2} \int_{f_1(\rho)}^{f_2(\rho)} \rho \, d\theta \, d\rho,$$

where $\rho = \varphi_1(\theta)$ is the equation of the curve DEB; $\rho = \varphi_2(\theta)$, the equation of BCD; $\theta = f_1(\rho)$, the equation of EDC; and $\theta = f_2(\rho)$, the equation of EBC.

In (3), where the integration is performed first with respect to x, a row of elementary rectangles is obtained. The second integration sums up all such rows. (Fig. 125.)

In (4), integrating first with respect to y, we obtain a column

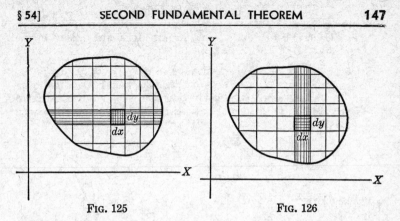

FIG. 125   FIG. 126

of elementary rectangular areas.   The second integration sums
up all such columns.   (Fig. 126.)

Similarly in polar coordinates (5) sums, first, elements lying
in one radial strip, then, second, all such strips (Fig. 127); and

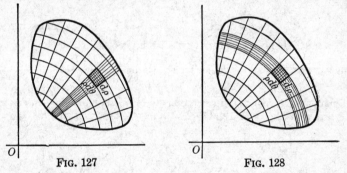

FIG. 127   FIG. 128

(6) sums, first, elements lying in one circular ring, then, second,
all such rings.   (Fig. 128.)

It is not possible to say offhand what order of integration will
be the simpler in a given problem of finding the area of a closed
region since so much depends upon the way in which the functions determining the boundary curves behave.   In all cases
the figures should be drawn in order that the geometry be made
clear.   The algebraic computation should agree with the geom
etry of the configuration.   After the geometry is understood,
the simpler order of integration can be determined.   The student will find it good practice to solve a few problems both ways,
this will give him more than just a check on his answers.

Illustration 6. Find by double integration the total area enclosed by the two curves $y = 2x$ and $y^3 = 2x$.

Solution. The points of intersection are $(-\frac{1}{2}, -1)$, $(0, 0)$, and $(\frac{1}{2}, 1)$. By symmetry the common area (not regarding sign) is twice that lying in the first quadrant. It should be clear that it will make no difference which order of integration we choose. Formulae (3) and (4) become respectively

$$A = 2 \int_0^1 \int_{\frac{1}{2} y^3}^{\frac{1}{2} y} dx \, dy$$

$$= 2 \int_0^{\frac{1}{2}} \int_{2x}^{(2x)^{\frac{1}{3}}} dy \, dx.$$

Evaluating the first, we get

$$A = 2 \int_0^1 (\tfrac{1}{2} y - \tfrac{1}{2} y^3) \, dy$$

$$= \tfrac{1}{4} \text{ sq. unit (total area).}$$

Evaluating the second, we get

$$A = 2 \int_0^{\frac{1}{2}} [(2x)^{\frac{1}{3}} - 2x] \, dx$$

$$= \tfrac{1}{4} \text{ sq. unit.}$$

The enclosed area lying in the first quadrant is $\frac{1}{8}$ sq. unit.

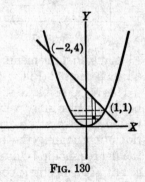

FIG. 129

Illustration 7. Find by double integration the area enclosed by $y = x^2$ and $x + y - 2 = 0$.

Solution. The points of intersection are $(-2, 4)$ and $(1, 1)$. Integrating first with respect to y and then with respect to x, we get

$$A = \int_{-2}^1 \int_{x^2}^{2-x} dy \, dx$$

$$= \int_{-2}^1 [2 - x - x^2] \, dx$$

$$= \tfrac{9}{2} \text{ sq. units.}$$

But if we take $dx \, dy$ as the element of area (where the integration is to be performed first with respect to x), we must write the area as the sum of two double integrals. Thus

$$A = \int_0^1 \int_{-\sqrt{y}}^{\sqrt{y}} dx \, dy + \int_1^4 \int_{-\sqrt{y}}^{2-y} dx \, dy.$$

FIG. 130

The reason is clear since a row element stretches first of all ($y = 0$ to $y = 1$) between the two branches of the same curve $y = x^2$ and only later ($y = 1$ to $y = 4$) stretches from $y = x^2$ to $x + y - 2 = 0$. But of course the answer is the same only the method is harder.

Illustration 8. Find by double integration the area inside the circle $\rho = a \cos \theta$ and outside the cardioid $\rho = a(1 - \cos \theta)$. (See Exercise 7, p. 112.)

Solution. It is better to integrate with respect to ρ first since ρ runs directly from the one curve to the other.

$$A = 2 \int_0^{\frac{\pi}{3}} \int_{a(1-\cos\theta)}^{a\cos\theta} \rho \, d\rho \, d\theta$$

$$= \int_0^{\frac{\pi}{3}} \left[\rho^2 \right]_{a(1-\cos\theta)}^{a\cos\theta} d\theta$$

$$= \int_0^{\frac{\pi}{3}} [a^2 \cos^2 \theta - a^2 (1 - \cos \theta)^2] \, d\theta$$

$$= a^2 \int_0^{\frac{\pi}{3}} (2 \cos \theta - 1) \, d\theta$$

$$= a^2 \left[2 \sin \theta - \theta \right]_0^{\frac{\pi}{3}}$$

$$= \frac{a^2}{3} (3\sqrt{3} - \pi) \text{ sq. units.}$$

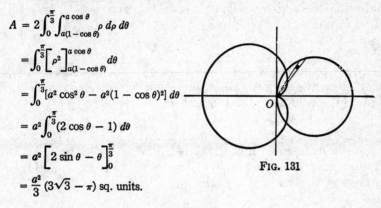

FIG. 131

EXERCISES

Set up the problems in the Exercises, p. 112, as double integrals and solve.

55. Volumes by Double and Triple Integration. If the element of area $dy \, dx$ in the XY-plane be projected vertically up-

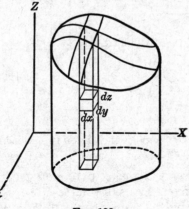

FIG. 132

ward to the surface $z = F(x, y)$, an elementary column (rectangular parallelepiped) is formed whose height is z and whose

volume is $F(x, y)\ dy\ dx$.   The sum of all such volume elements
(Fig. 132) over the region R bounded by the closed curve C in
the XY-plane will give the volume bounded above by the surface $z = F(x, y)$ and below by the XY-plane and which is contained in the vertical cylinder whose XY-trace is the curve C.
This sum is

(1) $$V = \int_a^b \int_{f_1(x)}^{f_2(x)} F(x, y)\ dy\ dx.$$

Or we could begin with an elementary "cube" $dz\ dy\ dx$ and
sum all such elements within the region considered in order to
obtain the volume.   This would give

(2) $$V = \int_a^b \int_{f_1(x)}^{f_2(x)} \int_0^{F(x, y)} dz\ dy\ dx \text{ (Rectangular Coordinates).}$$

In the first integration z travels from the XY-plane ($z = 0$)
up to the surface $z = F(x, y)$.   This reduces (2) to (1) and the
procedure thereafter is the same in both cases.

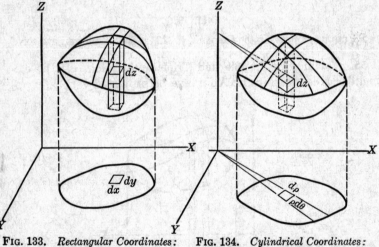

FIG. 133.   *Rectangular Coordinates:*   FIG. 134.   *Cylindrical Coordinates:*
$dv = dz\ dy\ dx.$ $dv = \rho\ dz\ d\rho\ d\theta.$

It will be necessary to make appropriate modifications in (1)
and (2) when different types of volumes are considered.   If the
volume enclosed by the two surfaces $z = F_1(x, y)$, $z = F_2(x, y)$
is desired. then (2) is modified to read (Fig. 133)

(3) $$V = \int_a^o \int_{f_1(x)}^{f_2(x)} \int_{F_1(x, y)}^{F_2(x, y)} dz\ dy\ dx \text{ (Rectangular Coordinates).}$$

The curve C, whose equations, by pieces, are $y = f_1(x)$ and $y = f_2(x)$, is the projection of the curve of intersection of the two surfaces in this case.

In cylindrical coordinates the volume element is $\rho \, dz \, d\rho \, d\theta$ and formula (3) becomes (Figs. 27 and 134)

(4) $V = \int_{\alpha}^{\beta} \int_{\varphi_1(\theta)}^{\varphi_2(\theta)} \int_{\Phi_1(\rho, \theta)}^{\Phi_2(\rho, \theta)} \rho \, dz \, d\rho \, d\theta$ (Cylindrical Coordinates).

The equations of the bounding surfaces are $z = \Phi_1(\rho, \theta)$ and $z = \Phi_2(\rho, \theta)$; $\rho = \varphi_1(\theta)$, $\rho = \varphi_2(\theta)$ are the equations of the projection of the curve of intersection of the surfaces onto the $\rho\theta$-plane.

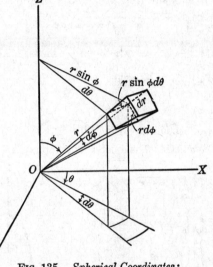

FIG. 135.   *Spherical Coordinates:*
$dv = r^2 \sin \varphi \, dr \, d\theta \, d\varphi.$

The volume element in spherical coordinates is (Figs. 28 and 135) $r^2 \sin \varphi \, dr \, d\theta \, d\varphi$ and the formula for the volume common to the two surfaces $r = \Psi_1(\theta, \varphi)$ and $r = \Psi_2(\theta, \varphi)$ is

(5) $V = \int_{\gamma}^{\delta} \int_{\theta_1(\varphi)}^{\theta_2(\varphi)} \int_{\Psi_1(\theta, \varphi)}^{\Psi_2(\theta, \varphi)} r^2 \sin \varphi \, dr \, d\theta \, d\varphi$ (Spherical Coordinates).

Here r travels from surface to surface while θ and φ sweep over the solid angle of the cone with vertex at the origin and passing through the curve of intersection of the two surfaces.

Some illustrations will help to show how these limits of integration are found in a given problem.

Illustration 1.   Find by triple integration the volume of a sphere of radius a.

Solution.   *Rectangular Coordinates.*   The equation of the sphere is

$$x^2 + y^2 + z^2 = a^2.$$

For reasons of symmetry we work only with the part lying in the first octant.

$$V = 8 \int_0^a \int_0^{\sqrt{a^2 - x^2}} \int_0^{\sqrt{a^2 - x^2 - y^2}} dz \, dy \, dx.$$

In the first integration z sweeps from surface ($z = 0$) to surface $z = \sqrt{a^2 - x^2 - y^2}$. In the second integration y travels from curve ($y = 0$) to curve $y = \sqrt{a^2 - x^2}$. This last is gotten by putting $z = 0$ in the equation of the surface since this gives the curve of intersection of the surface with the XY-plane. In the final integration x goes from 0 to a, the extent of the figure in the X-direction.

$$V = 8 \int_0^a \int_0^{\sqrt{a^2 - x^2}} \sqrt{a^2 - x^2 - y^2} \, dy \, dx$$

$$= 8 \int_0^a \left[\frac{y}{2} \sqrt{a^2 - x^2 - y^2} + \frac{a^2 - x^2}{2} \sin^{-1} \frac{y}{\sqrt{a^2 - x^2}} \right]_0^{\sqrt{a^2 - x^2}} dx$$

$$= 2\pi \int_0^a (a^2 - x^2) \, dx$$

$$= 2\pi \left[a^2 x - \frac{x^3}{3} \right]_0^a$$

$$= \tfrac{4}{3} \pi a^3 \text{ cu. units.}$$

Cylindrical Coordinates.   The equation of the sphere is

$$\rho^2 + z^2 = a^2$$

$$V = 8 \int_0^{\frac{\pi}{2}} \int_0^a \int_0^{\sqrt{a^2 - \rho^2}} \rho \, dz \, d\rho \, d\theta$$

$$= 8 \int_0^{\frac{\pi}{2}} \int_0^a \rho \sqrt{a^2 - \rho^2} \, d\rho \, d\theta$$

$$= 8 \int_0^{\frac{\pi}{2}} \left[-\tfrac{1}{3} (a^2 - \rho^2)^{\frac{3}{2}} \right]_0^a d\theta$$

$$= \tfrac{8}{3} \int_0^{\frac{\pi}{2}} a^3 \, d\theta$$

$$= \tfrac{4}{3} \pi a^3 \text{ cu. units.}$$

FIG. 136

Spherical Coordinates.   The equation of the sphere is $r = a$.

$$V = 8 \int_0^{\frac{\pi}{2}} \int_0^{\frac{\pi}{2}} \int_0^a r^2 \sin \varphi \, dr \, d\theta \, d\varphi$$

$$= \tfrac{8}{3} a^3 \int_0^{\frac{\pi}{2}} \int_0^{\frac{\pi}{2}} \sin \varphi \, d\theta \, d\varphi$$

$$= \tfrac{4}{3} \pi a^3 \int_0^{\frac{\pi}{2}} \sin \varphi \, d\varphi$$

$$= \tfrac{4}{3} \pi a^3 \text{ cu. units.}$$

Illustration 2. Find the volume common to the two cylinders $x^2 + y^2 = a^2$, $y^2 + z^2 = a^2$.

Solution. Again we work with the part of the volume lying in the first octant. Since the curve of intersection lies on the cylinders, it will project into $x^2 + y^2 = a^2$ in the XY-plane.

$$V = 8 \int_0^a \int_0^{\sqrt{a^2 - x^2}} \int_0^{\sqrt{a^2 - y^2}} dz \, dy \, dx$$

$$= 8 \int_0^a \int_0^{\sqrt{a^2 - x^2}} \sqrt{a^2 - y^2} \, dy \, dx.$$

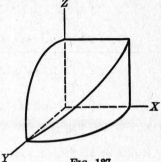

The integration can be performed in this order, but it is simpler to interchange the order of integration here and write

$$V = 8 \int_0^a \int_0^{\sqrt{a^2 - y^2}} \sqrt{a^2 - y^2} \, dx \, dy$$

$$= 8 \int_0^a \left[x \sqrt{a^2 - y^2} \right]_0^{\sqrt{a^2 - y^2}} dy$$

$$= 8 \int_0^a (a^2 - y^2) \, dy$$

$$= \tfrac{16}{3} a^3 \text{ cu. units.}$$

Fig. 137

Illustration 3. Find the volume cut from the elliptic paraboloid $z = x^2 + 4 y^2$ by the plane $z = 1$.

Solution.

$$V = 4 \int_0^1 \int_0^{\frac{\sqrt{1 - x^2}}{2}} \int_{x^2 + 4 y^2}^1 dz \, dy \, dx$$

$$= 4 \int_0^1 \int_0^{\frac{\sqrt{1 - x^2}}{2}} (1 - x^2 - 4 y^2) \, dy \, dx$$

$$= 4 \int_0^1 \left[y(1 - x^2) - \tfrac{4}{3} y^3 \right]_0^{\frac{\sqrt{1 - x^2}}{2}} dx$$

$$= 4 \int_0^1 \tfrac{1}{3} (1 - x^2)^{\frac{3}{2}} \, dx$$

$$= \tfrac{1}{3} \left[x(1 - x^2)^{\frac{3}{2}} + \tfrac{3}{2} x(1 - x^2)^{\frac{1}{2}} + \tfrac{3}{2} \sin^{-1} x \right]_0^1$$

(Formula 48, Table of Integrals)

$$= \frac{\pi}{4} \text{ cu. units.}$$

Fig. 138

Illustration 4. Find the volume bounded above by the cone $z = k\rho$, below by the XY-plane and which lies in the cylinder on one loop of $\rho = \cos 2\theta$.

Solution.

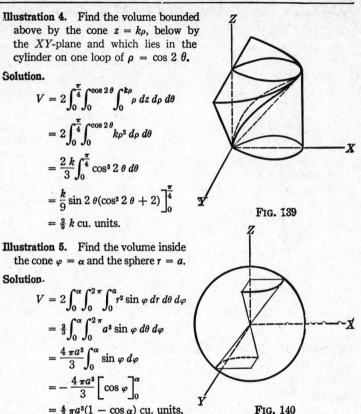

$$V = 2\int_0^{\frac{\pi}{4}} \int_0^{\cos 2\theta} \int_0^{k\rho} \rho\, dz\, d\rho\, d\theta$$

$$= 2\int_0^{\frac{\pi}{4}} \int_0^{\cos 2\theta} k\rho^2\, d\rho\, d\theta$$

$$= \frac{2\,k}{3} \int_0^{\frac{\pi}{4}} \cos^3 2\theta\, d\theta$$

$$= \frac{k}{9}\sin 2\theta(\cos^2 2\theta + 2)\Big]_0^{\frac{\pi}{4}}$$

$$= \tfrac{2}{9}\,k \text{ cu. units.}$$

FIG. 139

Illustration 5. Find the volume inside the cone $\varphi = \alpha$ and the sphere $r = a$.

Solution.

$$V = 2\int_0^{\alpha} \int_0^{2\pi} \int_0^{a} r^2 \sin\varphi\, dr\, d\theta\, d\varphi$$

$$= \tfrac{2}{3}\int_0^{\alpha} \int_0^{2\pi} a^3 \sin\varphi\, d\theta\, d\varphi$$

$$= \frac{4\,\pi a^3}{3} \int_0^{\alpha} \sin\varphi\, d\varphi$$

$$= -\frac{4\,\pi a^3}{3}\Big[\cos\varphi\Big]_0^{\alpha}$$

$$= \tfrac{4}{3}\,\pi a^3(1 - \cos\alpha) \text{ cu. units.}$$

FIG. 140

EXERCISES

Find by triple integration the volumes described.

1. Bounded by $x = 0,\ y = 0,\ z = 0,\ \dfrac{x}{a} + \dfrac{y}{b} + \dfrac{z}{c} = 1$ (Fig. 13).   *Ans.* $\tfrac{1}{6}\,abc$.

2. Inside the cylinder $\rho = a\cos\theta$ and the sphere $\rho^2 + z^2 = a^2$.

$$Ans. \quad \frac{4}{3}\,a^3\left(\frac{\pi}{2} - \frac{2}{3}\right).$$

3. The ellipsoid $\dfrac{x^2}{a^2} + \dfrac{y^2}{b^2} + \dfrac{z^2}{c^2} = 1$ (Fig. 16).   *Ans.* $\tfrac{4}{3}\,\pi abc$.

4. The spherical wedge made by cutting a slice from a sphere of radius a by two planes passing through a diameter and making an angle α with each other.   *Ans.* $\tfrac{2}{3}\,\alpha a^3$.

5. Cut off from the paraboloid $z = x^2 + y^2$ by the plane $z - y = 0$.

$$Ans. \quad \frac{\pi}{32}$$

56. Applications. The derivation and application of the following formulae should be wholly within the grasp of the student of the calculus at this stage in his study. They make use only of the definitions of center of mass and moment of inertia and of the ideas of multiple integration. Again the student is warned not to try to memorize these formulae but rather to spend the equivalent time on the fundamental principles involved in them. The notations used are self-explanatory.

FOR PLANE AREAS (DENSITY = σ)

Centroid, Rectangular and Polar Coordinates

(1)
$$\bar{x} = \frac{\int\int \sigma x \, dy \, dx}{\int\int \sigma \, dy \, dx},$$

(2)
$$\bar{y} = \frac{\int\int \sigma y \, dy \, dx}{\int\int \sigma \, dy \, dx},$$

(3)
$$\bar{x} = \frac{\int\int \sigma \rho^2 \cos\theta \, d\rho \, d\theta}{\int\int \sigma \rho \, d\rho \, d\theta},$$

(4)
$$\bar{y} = \frac{\int\int \sigma \rho^2 \sin\theta \, d\rho \, d\theta}{\int\int \sigma \rho \, d\rho \, d\theta}.$$

From (3) and (4), $\bar{\rho}$ and $\bar{\theta}$ can be determined: $\bar{\rho} = \sqrt{\bar{x}^2 + \bar{y}^2}$, $\bar{\theta} = \tan^{-1}\dfrac{\bar{y}}{\bar{x}}$.

Moment of Inertia, Rectangular and Polar Coordinates

(5)
$$I_x = \int\int \sigma y^2 \, dy \, dx,$$

(6)
$$I_y = \int\int \sigma x^2 \, dy \, dx,$$

(7)
$$I_0 = \int\int \sigma (x^2 + y^2) \, dy \, dx$$
$$= I_x + I_y.$$

(8) $$I_x = \int\int \sigma\rho^3 \sin^2 \theta \, d\rho \, d\theta,$$

(9) $$I_y = \int\int \sigma\rho^3 \cos^2 \theta \, d\rho \, d\theta,$$

(10) $$I_0 = \int\int \sigma\rho^3 \, d\rho \, d\theta.$$

For Volumes (Density $= \sigma$)

Centroid, Rectangular and Cylindrical Coordinates

(11) $$\bar{x} = \frac{\int\int\int \sigma x \, dz \, dy \, dx}{\int\int\int \sigma \, dz \, dy \, dx},$$

(12) $$\bar{y} = \frac{\int\int\int \sigma y \, dz \, dy \, dx}{\int\int\int \sigma \, dz \, dy \, dx},$$

(13) $$\bar{z} = \frac{\int\int\int \sigma z \, dz \, dy \, dx}{\int\int\int \sigma \, dz \, dy \, dx},$$

(14) $$\bar{x} = \frac{\int\int\int \sigma\rho^2 \cos \theta \, dz \, d\rho \, d\theta}{\int\int\int \sigma\rho \, dz \, d\rho \, d\theta},$$

(15) $$\bar{y} = \frac{\int\int\int \sigma\rho^2 \sin \theta \, dz \, d\rho \, d\theta}{\int\int\int \sigma\rho \, dz \, d\rho \, d\theta},$$

(16) $$\bar{z} = \frac{\int\int\int \sigma\rho z \, dz \, d\rho \, d\theta}{\int\int\int \sigma\rho \, dz \, d\rho \, d\theta}.$$

Moment of Inertia with Respect to the Coordinate Axes

(17) $$I_x = \int\int\int \sigma(y^2 + z^2) \, dz \, dy \, dx.$$

(18) $$I_y = \int\int\int \sigma(x^2 + z^2) \, dz \, dy \, dx,$$

(19) $$I_z = \int\int\int \sigma(x^2 + y^2) \, dz \, dy \, dx.$$

For geometric areas and volumes consider $\sigma = 1$. Where density is a constant (homogeneous masses), σ may be brought out from under the sign of integration.

Illustration 1. Find by triple integration the moment of inertia of a solid sphere of radius a about a diameter. (See Ex. 4, p. 137.)

Solution. We use spherical coordinates. Although we did not include such a formula in the above set, it should be clear that

$$I_d = 8 \int_0^{\frac{\pi}{2}} \int_0^{\frac{\pi}{2}} \int_0^a \sigma r^2 \sin^2 \varphi \cdot r^2 \sin \varphi \, dr \, d\theta \, d\varphi$$

$$= 8\, \sigma \frac{a^5}{5} \int_0^{\frac{\pi}{2}} \int_0^{\frac{\pi}{2}} \sin^3 \varphi \, d\theta \, d\varphi$$

$$= 8\, \sigma\pi \frac{a^5}{10} \int_0^{\frac{\pi}{2}} \sin^3 \varphi \, d\varphi$$

$$= \tfrac{8}{15}\, \pi\sigma a^5 \quad \text{(volume, } \sigma = 1\text{)}$$

$$= \tfrac{2}{5}\, Ma^2 \quad \text{(mass).}$$

Illustration 2. Find the c.g. of the tetrahedron formed by the coordinate planes and the plane $\dfrac{x}{a} + \dfrac{y}{b} + \dfrac{z}{c} = 1$.

Solution. The volume is (Ex. 1, p. 154) $\tfrac{1}{6} abc$.

$$\bar{x} = \frac{6}{abc} \int_0^a \int_0^{b\left(1 - \frac{x}{a}\right)} \int_0^{c\left(1 - \frac{x}{a} - \frac{y}{b}\right)} x \, dz \, dy \, dx$$

$$= \frac{6}{abc} \int_0^a \int_0^{b\left(1 - \frac{x}{a}\right)} cx\left(1 - \frac{x}{a} - \frac{y}{b}\right) dy \, dx$$

$$= \frac{6}{abc} \int_0^a \frac{bcx}{2} \left(1 - \frac{x}{a}\right)^2 dx$$

$$= \frac{3}{a} \int_0^a \left(x - \frac{2}{a} x^2 + \frac{x^3}{a^2}\right) dx$$

$$= \tfrac{1}{4}\, a.$$

By symmetry,

$$\bar{y} = \tfrac{1}{4} b.$$
$$\bar{z} = \tfrac{1}{4} c.$$

The c.g. of a composite body can be found from the formula

$$\bar{x} = \frac{m_1 \bar{x}_1 + m_2 \bar{x}_2 + \cdots + m_n \bar{x}_n}{m_1 + m_2 + \cdots + m_n},$$

where $\bar{x}_i$ is the c.g. of the ith part (m_i) of the total mass $(m_1 + m_2 + \cdots + m_n)$ considered.

Illustration 3. Find the c.g. of the plate shown in Fig. 141.

Solution. For the rectangle:

$$\bar{x} = 0, \bar{y} = \frac{a}{2}.$$

For the semicircular top:

$$\bar{x} = 0, \bar{y} = a + \frac{4}{3}\frac{b}{\pi}.$$

(See Illustration 3, p. 129.)
For the square cut out:

$$\bar{x} = \tfrac{1}{2}\,b, \bar{y} = \tfrac{1}{2}\,b.$$

The c.g. $(\bar{x}, \bar{y})$ of the composite body will be at

$$\bar{x} = \frac{(2\,ab)(0) + \tfrac{1}{2}\pi b^2(0) - b^2(\tfrac{1}{2}\,b)}{2\,ab + \tfrac{1}{2}\pi b^2 - b^2}$$

$$= \frac{-\,b^3}{4\,a + b(\pi - 2)}.$$

$$\bar{y} = \frac{(2\,ab)(\tfrac{1}{2}\,a) + \tfrac{1}{2}\pi b^2\!\left(a + \dfrac{4}{3}\dfrac{b}{\pi}\right) - b^2(\tfrac{1}{2}\,b)}{2\,ab + \tfrac{1}{2}\pi b^2 - b^2}$$

$$= \frac{2\,a^2 + b\!\left(\pi a + \dfrac{4\,b}{3}\right) - 1}{4\,a + b(\pi - 2)}.$$

FIG. 141

For determining the moment of inertia of a composite body we make use of the following *transfer* or

PARALLEL AXIS THEOREM. *The moment of inertia I_L of a mass M with respect to a line L equals the moment of inertia about the line parallel to L and passing through the c.g., plus the mass M times the square of the distance d between the two lines.* That is

(20) $$I_L = I_g + Md^2.$$

Illustration 4. Find the moment of inertia of a circular area about a tangent. (See Illustration 3, p. 134.)

Solution. $I_L = I_g + Md^2$

$$= \frac{\pi r^4}{4} + \pi r^2 \cdot r^2$$

$$= \tfrac{5}{4}\pi r^4 \text{ (area)}$$

$$= \frac{Mr^2}{4} + Mr^2$$

$$= \tfrac{5}{4}Mr^2 \text{(plate of mass } M\text{)}.$$

Illustration 5.   Find the moment of inertia of a solid cylinder of radius r and height h about a generator.

Solution. $I_g = \frac{1}{2} M r^2$.   (See Ex. 5 a, p. 137.)

$$I_L = \frac{1}{2} M r^2 + M r^2$$
$$= \frac{3}{2} M r^2.$$

Illustration 6.   Find the moment of inertia of a solid cylinder of radius r and height h about a diameter of the base.

Solution.   Take disc elements of mass $\rho \pi r^2 \, dy$.   The moment of inertia of this disc about a diameter is

$$\frac{M r^2}{4} \quad \text{or} \quad \frac{\rho \pi r^2 \, dy}{4} r^2.$$

Now we use the transfer theorem to get the moment about the diameter of the base of the cylinder.   This is, since the disc element is y units above the base,

$$I_{\text{disc}} = \frac{\rho \pi r^2 \, dy}{4} r^2 + \rho \pi r^2 \, dy \cdot y^2$$
$$= \frac{1}{4} \rho \pi r^2 (r^2 + 4 y^2) \, dy.$$

Hence

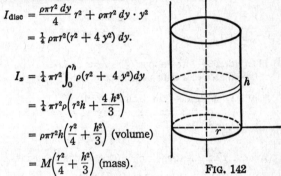

$$I_x = \frac{1}{4} \pi r^2 \int_0^h \rho (r^2 + 4 y^2) dy$$
$$= \frac{1}{4} \pi r^2 \rho \left(r^2 h + \frac{4 h^3}{3} \right)$$
$$= \rho \pi r^2 h \left(\frac{r^2}{4} + \frac{h^2}{3} \right) \text{ (volume)}$$
$$= M \left(\frac{r^2}{4} + \frac{h^2}{3} \right) \text{ (mass).}$$

Fig. 142

It should be emphasized that this parallel axis theorem applies only to parallel axes one of which passes through the center of gravity.

There are two theorems (known as the theorems of Pappus) which are of great use in the calculus.

PAPPUS' THEOREM I.   *When a plane area is revolved about a coplanar axis not cutting the area, the volume generated is equal to the product of the area and the length of the path described by the center of gravity of the area.*

PAPPUS' THEOREM II.   *When a plane curve is revolved about a coplanar axis not cutting the curve, the surface area generated is equal to the product of the length of the curve and the length of the path of the center of gravity of the curve.*

The reason for the condition that the line about which the revolution takes place shall not cut the area or curve is apparent since otherwise dual volumes and surface areas would be generated. (Algebraically the theorems would still be true and could be applied even in this exceptional case if appropriate use was made of signs.)

Illustration 7. A torus (doughnut) is generated by revolving the circle $(x - a)^2 + y^2 = b^2$, $(b < a)$, about the Y-axis. Find (a) the volume and (b) the surface area of this solid.

Solution. The c.g. of the area and also of the curve is at the center of the circle. Hence

(a)
$$V = \pi b^2 (2 \pi a)$$
$$= 2 \pi^2 a b^2 \text{ cu. units.}$$

(b)
$$S = 2 \pi b (2 \pi a)$$
$$= 4 \pi^2 b a \text{ sq. units.}$$

Illustration 8. Use Pappus' Theorems to find (a) the volume and (b) the lateral area of a right circular cone of height h and radius r.

Solution. Consider the triangle with vertices at $(0, 0)$, $(r, 0)$, $(0, h)$. The c.g. of this triangle, considered as an area (plate), is (see Exs. 1 and 2, p. 132):
$$\bar{x} = \tfrac{1}{3} r, \bar{y} = \tfrac{1}{3} h.$$

By revolving this triangle about the Y-axis the cone is generated.

(a)
$$V = \tfrac{1}{2} rh(\tfrac{2}{3} \pi r)$$
$$= \tfrac{1}{3} \pi r^2 h \text{ cu. units.}$$

(b) In order to get the surface area of the cone we merely revolve the hypotenuse of the triangle about the Y-axis. The c.g. of this curve is at $\bar{x} = \tfrac{1}{2} r, \bar{y} = \tfrac{1}{2} h.$ Hence
$$S = \sqrt{r^2 + h^2} \left(\frac{2 \pi r}{2} \right)$$
$$= \pi r \sqrt{r^2 + h^2} \text{ sq. units.}$$

Another useful theorem is the following.

LIQUID PRESSURE THEOREM. *When a plate of plane area A is submerged vertically, the total force on one side is equal to the product of the area of the plate, the depth of the center of gravity of the plate, and w the weight of the liquid per unit volume.*

Illustration 9.   The center of a circular floodgate of radius 2′ in a reservoir is at a depth of 6′.   Find the total force on the gate.   (See Illustration 2, p. 125.)

Solution. $F = 4\pi(6)w$
                    $= 24\pi w$ lbs.

EXERCISES

1. Find the c.g. of the solid bounded by the hyperboloid $z^2 = 1 + \rho^2$ and the upper half of the cone $z^2 = 2\rho^2$.   *Ans.* $\bar{x} = 0 = \bar{y}, \bar{z} = \frac{3}{8}(1 + \sqrt{2})$.

2. Find the moment of inertia of a rectangular bar of length L, width a, and thickness b, about an axis parallel to b and passing through the c.g.

$$\text{Ans. } \frac{M}{12}(a^2 + L^2).$$

3. Find the moment of inertia of a solid circular cylinder of radius r and height h about an axis perpendicular to the axis of the cylinder and passing through the c.g.   (See Illustration 6, p. 159.)

$$\text{Ans. } \frac{M}{12}(3r^2 + h^2).$$

4. Find the c.g. of the area of the ellipse $b^2x^2 + a^2y^2 = a^2b^2$ lying in the first quadrant.

$$\text{Ans. } \bar{x} = \frac{4a}{3\pi}, \bar{y} = \frac{4b}{3\pi}.$$

5. The triangular plate, with sides 3, 4, 5, is placed in the XY-plane so that its c.g. is at (2, 3).   Find the volume generated when this triangular plate is rotated about the X-axis.   *Ans.* 36π cu. units.

6. A semicircular plate of radius r feet is submerged vertically until its c.g. is at a depth of h feet.   Find the total pressure on one side.

$$\text{Ans. } \tfrac{1}{2}\pi w r^2 h \text{ lbs.}$$

7. Find the moment of inertia of a solid sphere about a tangent line. (See Ex. 4, p. 137.)   *Ans.* $\frac{7}{5}Mr^2$.

8. A cylindrical pencil $\frac{1}{8}$ inch in radius and 7 inches overall in length has a sharp conical point 1 inch long.   Find the c.g. measured from the point. (See Illustration 6, p. 131.)   *Ans.* $\frac{291}{76} = 3.83$ in.

9. Find the moment of inertia of the pencil in Ex. 8 about the axis.

$$\text{Ans. } \frac{3\rho\pi}{20,480}.$$

10. The total force on one side of a vertically submerged elliptical plate $\left(\frac{x^2}{9} + \frac{y^2}{4} = 1\right)$ is $120\pi w$ lbs.   At what depth is the c.g.?   *Ans.* 20 ft.

CHAPTER XIV

PARTIAL DIFFERENTIATION

57. Partial Derivatives. In $z = f(x, y)$ let one of the independent variables, say y, be held fixed. When an increment is given to the other independent variable, the function z itself will experience a change. We write

$$(1) \qquad\qquad z = f(x, y),$$

$$(2) \qquad z + \Delta z = f(x + \Delta x, y),$$

$$(3) \qquad\quad \Delta z = f(x + \Delta x, y) - f(x, y),$$

$$(4) \qquad\quad \frac{\Delta z}{\Delta x} = \frac{f(x + \Delta x, y) - f(x, y)}{\Delta x}.$$

This is the usual process of differentiation as applied to a function of a single variable; since y is held constant, z varies only with x. The *partial derivative* of z with respect to x is thus defined as

$$(5) \qquad\qquad \frac{\partial z}{\partial x} = \lim_{\Delta x \to 0} \frac{f(x + \Delta x, y) - f(x, y)}{\Delta x}.$$

Similarly

$$(6) \qquad\qquad \frac{\partial z}{\partial y} = \lim \frac{f(x, y + \Delta y) - f(x, y)}{\Delta y}.$$

The curled ∂ is used so that this will clearly distinguish this from ordinary differentiation. The symbols f_x and f_y are also in general use for $\frac{\partial z}{\partial x}$, $\frac{\partial z}{\partial y}$ respectively.

In the case of a function of a single independent variable, $y = f(x)$, the differential dy was defined to be $dy = \frac{df}{dx} dx$. Where $z = f(x, y)$, the *total differential dz* is defined as

$$(7) \qquad\qquad dz = \frac{\partial f}{\partial x} dx + \frac{\partial f}{\partial y} dy.$$

If $z = f(x, y)$ and $x = x(t)$, $y = y(t)$, then the *total derivative* of z with respect to t is

$$(8) \qquad \frac{dz}{dt} = \frac{\partial f}{\partial x}\frac{dx}{dt} + \frac{\partial f}{\partial y}\frac{dy}{dt}.$$

Straight d's are used here for $\frac{dz}{dt}, \frac{dx}{dt}, \frac{dy}{dt}$ since t is the only independent variable; the partial symbols $\frac{\partial f}{\partial x}, \frac{\partial f}{\partial y}$ are used to emphasize that, first of all, f is a function of two variables. In the event $z = f(x, y)$ and x and y are functions of two variables, $x = x(u, v)$, $y = y(u, v)$, then we write

$$(9) \qquad \frac{\partial z}{\partial u} = \frac{\partial f}{\partial x}\frac{\partial x}{\partial u} + \frac{\partial f}{\partial y}\frac{\partial y}{\partial u},$$

$$(10) \qquad \frac{\partial z}{\partial v} = \frac{\partial f}{\partial x}\frac{\partial x}{\partial v} + \frac{\partial f}{\partial y}\frac{\partial y}{\partial v}.$$

For a function u of n variables $u = f(x_1, x_2, \cdots, x_n)$ there are n first partial derivatives, $\frac{\partial u}{\partial x_1}, \frac{\partial u}{\partial x_2}, \cdots, \frac{\partial u}{\partial x_n}$. The differential du is

$$(11) \qquad du = \frac{\partial f}{\partial x_1} dx_1 + \frac{\partial f}{\partial x_2} dx_2 + \cdots + \frac{\partial f}{\partial x_n} dx_n,$$

and relations analogous to those in (8), (9), and (10) may be written down.

Geometrically $\frac{\partial z}{\partial x}$ represents the slope of the curve cut from the surface $z = f(x, y)$ by the plane $y = $ constant. (Fig. 143.) Evidently $\frac{\partial z}{\partial y}$ represents the slope of the plane curve $z = f(x, y)$, $x = $ const. As in Fig. 144 the total differential dz represents the increment of the Z-coordinate of the tangent plane to the surface $z = f(x, y)$ when x and y undergo independent changes (cf. the single variable case Fig. 86, p. 63).

Higher partial derivatives are obtained when the first partial derivatives are differentiated. Thus we have $\frac{\partial^2 f}{\partial x^2}, \frac{\partial^2 f}{\partial x\,\partial y}, \frac{\partial^2 f}{\partial y^2}$, $\frac{\partial^3 f}{\partial x^3}$, etc. The symbol $\frac{\partial^2 f}{\partial x\,\partial y}$ is read " the second partial derivative of f, first with respect to x, then with respect to y." Some authors write this $\dfrac{\partial^2 f}{\partial y \, \partial x}$, although usually this stands for the second partial derivative of f, first with respect to y, then with respect to x. But since, for most functions that are

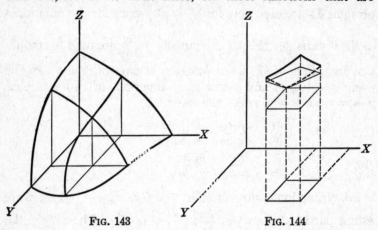

FIG. 143   FIG. 144

met with in the first course in the calculus the order of differentiation is immaterial, i.e., $\dfrac{\partial^2 f}{\partial x \, \partial y} = \dfrac{\partial^2 f}{\partial y \, \partial x}$, we shall pay little attention to the order in which the differentiation takes place. The symbols f_{xx}, f_{xy}, f_{yy}, f_{xxy}, etc., are frequently used.

Illustration 1. Given $z = e^x \sin y$. Find $\dfrac{\partial z}{\partial x}$, $\dfrac{\partial z}{\partial y}$, $\dfrac{\partial^2 z}{\partial x^2}$, $\dfrac{\partial^2 z}{\partial x \, \partial y} = \dfrac{\partial^2 z}{\partial y \, \partial x}$, $\dfrac{\partial^2 z}{\partial y^2}$.

Solution. $\quad \dfrac{\partial z}{\partial x} = e^x \sin y, \; \dfrac{\partial z}{\partial y} = e^x \cos y$

$$\frac{\partial^2 z}{\partial x^2} = e^x \sin y$$

$$\frac{\partial^2 z}{\partial x \, \partial y} = e^x \cos y = \frac{\partial^2 z}{\partial y \, \partial x}$$

$$\frac{\partial^2 z}{\partial y^2} = -\, e^x \sin y.$$

Illustration 2. Given $z = x^2 y + e^{xy}$, $x = t^2$, $y = \log t$. Find $\dfrac{dz}{dt}$.

Solution. $\quad \dfrac{dz}{dt} = \dfrac{\partial z}{\partial x} \dfrac{dx}{dt} + \dfrac{\partial z}{\partial y} \dfrac{dy}{dt}$

$$= (2\,xy + ye^{xy})2\,t + (x^2 + xe^{xy})\frac{1}{t}.$$

Illustration 3. Given $z = x^2 + y^2$, $x = \rho \cos \theta$, $y = \rho \sin \theta$. Find $\dfrac{\partial z}{\partial \rho}$, $\dfrac{\partial z}{\partial \theta}$.

Solution.

$$\frac{\partial z}{\partial \rho} = \frac{\partial z}{\partial x}\frac{\partial x}{\partial \rho} + \frac{\partial z}{\partial y}\frac{\partial y}{\partial \rho}$$

$$= 2\,x \cos \theta + 2\,y \sin \theta$$

$$= 2\,\rho \cos^2 \theta + 2\,\rho \sin^2 \theta$$

$$= 2\,\rho.$$

$$\frac{\partial z}{\partial \theta} = \frac{\partial z}{\partial x}\frac{\partial x}{\partial \theta} + \frac{\partial z}{\partial y}\frac{\partial y}{\partial \theta}$$

$$= -\,2\,x\,\rho \sin \theta + 2\,y\,\rho \cos \theta$$

$$= -\,2\,\rho^2 \sin \theta \cos \theta + 2\,\rho^2 \sin \theta \cos \theta$$

$$= 0.$$

EXERCISES

1. Given $z = x^2 y^3 + \tan^{-1}\dfrac{y}{x}$, find $\dfrac{\partial z}{\partial x}$, $\dfrac{\partial z}{\partial y}$.

$$\textit{Ans.}\ \ 2\,xy^3 - \frac{y}{x^2 + y^2},\ 3\,x^2 y^2 + \frac{x}{x^2 + y^2}.$$

2. Given $z = x \log y + x \sin y$, find dz.

$$\textit{Ans.}\ \ (\log y + \sin y)\,dx + \left(\frac{x}{y} + x \cos y\right) dy.$$

3. Given $u = xyz$, find $\dfrac{\partial u}{\partial x}$, $\dfrac{\partial^2 u}{\partial x\,\partial y}$, $\dfrac{\partial^2 u}{\partial z^2}$. $\textit{Ans.}\ \ yz,\ z,\ 0.$

4. Given $u = xyz$, $x = e^t$, $y = t$, $z = \dfrac{1}{t}$, find $\dfrac{du}{dt}$. $\textit{Ans.}\ \ e^t.$

5. Given $z = x^2 - y^2$, $x = \rho \cos \theta$, $y = \rho \sin \theta$, find $\dfrac{\partial z}{\partial \rho}$, $\dfrac{\partial z}{\partial \theta}$.

$$\textit{Ans.}\ \ 2\,\rho \cos 2\,\theta,\ -\,2\,\rho^2 \sin 2\,\theta.$$

58. Implicit Differentiation. Let $z = f(x, y) = 0$ so that in reality y is given implicitly as a function of x. Then

$$(1) \qquad\qquad dz = \frac{\partial f}{\partial x}\,dx + \frac{\partial f}{\partial y}\,dy = 0,$$

or

$$(2) \qquad\qquad \frac{dy}{dx} = -\,\frac{\dfrac{\partial f}{\partial x}}{\dfrac{\partial f}{\partial y}}.$$

Relation (2) affords a simple way of computing y' where $f(x, y) = 0$. This is essentially what was done in Chap. IV, § 14, although this notation was not used at the time.

Now consider a functional relation $F(x, y, z) = 0$, which defines implicitly z as a function of x and y. Since, in computing $\frac{\partial z}{\partial x}$, y is held constant so that z is considered a [function of x only, we may apply (2) in finding $\frac{\partial z}{\partial x}$. Thus modified for $F(x, y, z) = 0$, (2) becomes

$$(3) \qquad \frac{\partial z}{\partial x} = -\frac{\dfrac{\partial F}{\partial x}}{\dfrac{\partial F}{\partial z}}.$$

Similarly

$$(4) \qquad \frac{\partial z}{\partial y} = -\frac{\dfrac{\partial F}{\partial y}}{\dfrac{\partial F}{\partial z}}.$$

Illustration 1. Given $x^2 + y^2 \tan x + e^y = 0$. Find $\frac{dy}{dx}$.

Solution.
$$\frac{dy}{dx} = -\frac{f_x}{f_y}$$
$$= -\frac{2\,x + y^2 \sec^2 x}{2\,y \tan x + e^y}.$$

Illustration 2. Given $x^2 + y^2 \tan z - xe^z = 0$. Find $\frac{\partial z}{\partial x}, \frac{\partial z}{\partial y}$.

Solution.
$$\frac{\partial z}{\partial x} = -\frac{\dfrac{\partial F}{\partial x}}{\dfrac{\partial F}{\partial z}}$$
$$= -\frac{2\,x - e^z}{y^2 \sec^2 z - xe^z}.$$
$$\frac{\partial z}{\partial y} = -\frac{\dfrac{\partial F}{\partial y}}{\dfrac{\partial F}{\partial z}}$$
$$= -\frac{2\,y \tan z}{y^2 \sec^2 z - xe^z}.$$

EXERCISES

1. Given $\frac{x^2}{a^2} + \frac{y^2}{b^2} + \frac{z^2}{c^2} = 1$. Find $\frac{\partial z}{\partial x}, \frac{\partial z}{\partial y}$.   *Ans.* $-\frac{c^2 x}{a^2 z}, -\frac{c^2 y}{b^2 z}$.

2. Given $x \log y + y \log z + z \log x = 0$. Find $\frac{\partial z}{\partial x}, \frac{\partial z}{\partial y}$.

     Ans. $-\frac{z^2 + xz \log y}{xy + xz \log x}, -\frac{xz + yz \log z}{y^2 + yz \log x}$

CHAPTER XV

APPLICATION OF PARTIAL DIFFERENTIATION

59. Small Errors. The theory parallels that of the single variable case. (Chap. VI, § 25.) For small increments the differential dz is approximately equal to the increment Δz. That is

(1) $$\Delta z \sim dz = \frac{\partial z}{\partial x} dx + \frac{\partial z}{\partial y} dy.$$

Illustration 1. The sides of a rectangular plate $6' \times 9'$ are measured to be 6.01' and 8.98' respectively. Approximately what is the error made in the computed area?

Solution.
$$A = xy.$$
$$dA = y \, dx + x \, dy$$
$$= 6(-.02) + 9(.01)$$
$$= -.03 \text{ sq. ft.}$$

Illustration 2. In determining the acceleration due to gravity the formula $g = \dfrac{2 \cdot s}{t^2}$ is sometimes used. Find the approximate maximum percentage error in the computed value of g if s and t are measured only to within 1%.

Solution.
$$\log g = \log 2 + \log s - 2 \log t$$
$$\frac{dg}{g} = \frac{ds}{s} - \frac{2}{t} dt$$
$$= .01 - 2(.01).$$

Therefore the maximum percentage error in g is $(.01 + .02) = 3\%$ since the signs are to be taken so that $\dfrac{dg}{g}$ is largest.

EXERCISES

1. In order to determine the surface area of a conical filter the slant height s and the radius r are measured as $s = 3 \pm .02$ in. and $r = 2 \pm .01$ in. What is the approximate maximum error made in computing the surface area S from $S = \pi r s$? *Ans.* $.07 \pi$ sq. in.

2. The period of a pendulum is given by $t = \pi \sqrt{\dfrac{l}{g}}.$ (See Ex. 5, p. 66.) What is the maximum percentage error made in computing g from this formula if the percentage error in t and l are $\frac{1}{2}\%$ and 1% respectively? *Ans.* 2%.

3. The volume of a rectangular box is given by $V = xyz$. What is the error made in computing the volume where the measurements are $x = 10 \pm .03$, $y = 6 \pm .01$, $z = 8 \pm .02$?   *Ans.* Error ≤ 3.44 cu. units.

4. The acceleration of a particle down an inclined plane is given by $a = g \sin \alpha$, where α is the angle of inclination of the plane. Suppose that $g = 32 \pm .01$ and $\alpha = 30° \pm 1°$. What is the approximate maximum error in the computed value of a?   *Ans.* .49.

60. Tangent Plane, Normal Line to a Surface. Let the equation of the plane tangent to the surface $F(x, y, z) = 0$ at the point $P(x_0, y_0, z_0)$ be

(1) $$z - z_0 = A(x - x_0) + B(y - y_0).$$

This plane will be determined by the two tangent lines $z - z_0 = A(x - x_0)$, $y = y_0$ and $z - z_0 = B(y - y_0)$, $x = x_0$ gotten by cutting the plane (1) with the planes $y = y_0$ and $x = x_0$ respectively. But the slopes, A and B, of these two lines at P are $\dfrac{\partial z}{\partial x}$ and $\dfrac{\partial z}{\partial y}$ evaluated at (x_0, y_0, z_0). Further $\dfrac{\partial z}{\partial x} = -\dfrac{F_x}{F_z}$, and $\dfrac{\partial z}{\partial y} = -\dfrac{F_y}{F_z}$ (Chap. XIV, § 58). Therefore the *equation of the tangent plane* at P is

(2) $$z - z_0 = -\frac{(F_x)_0}{(F_z)_0}(x - x_0) - \frac{(F_y)_0}{(F_z)_0}(y - y_0),$$

or, more symmetrically,

(3) $$\left(\frac{\partial F}{\partial x}\right)_0 (x - x_0) + \left(\frac{\partial F}{\partial y}\right)_0 (y - y_0) + \left(\frac{\partial F}{\partial z}\right)_0 (z - z_0) = 0$$

(Tangent plane).

The symbol $\left(\dfrac{\partial F}{\partial x}\right)_0$ means that $\dfrac{\partial F}{\partial x}$ is first computed and then evaluated at $P(x_0, y_0, z_0)$.

If $F(x, y, z) = 0$ is solved for z, $z = f(x, y)$, then we have a special case of (3) which becomes

(4) $$z - z_0 = \left(\frac{\partial f}{\partial x}\right)_0 (x - x_0) + \left(\frac{\partial f}{\partial y}\right)_0 (y - y_0).$$

Since $\left(\dfrac{\partial F}{\partial x}\right)_0$, $\left(\dfrac{\partial F}{\partial y}\right)_0$, $\left(\dfrac{\partial F}{\partial z}\right)_0$ are the direction numbers of a line

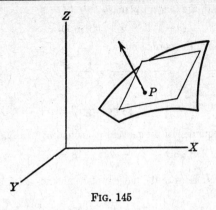

Fig. 145

perpendicular to the plane (3), the *equations of the line normal* to (3) and hence normal to the surface $F(x, y, z) = 0$ are

(5) $\qquad \dfrac{x - x_0}{\left(\dfrac{\partial F}{\partial x}\right)_0} = \dfrac{y - y_0}{\left(\dfrac{\partial F}{\partial y}\right)_0} = \dfrac{z - z_0}{\left(\dfrac{\partial F}{\partial z}\right)_0}$ (Normal line).

For the surface $z = f(x, y)$, the equations of the normal line (5) reduce as a special case to

(6) $\qquad \dfrac{x - x_0}{\left(\dfrac{\partial f}{\partial x}\right)_0} = \dfrac{y - y_0}{\left(\dfrac{\partial f}{\partial y}\right)_0} = \dfrac{z - z_0}{- 1}.$

Illustration 1. Find the equations of the tangent plane and normal line to $x^2 + 2 y^2 - 4 z^2 + 1 = 0$ at the point $(1, - 1, - 1)$.

Solution. $\qquad \dfrac{\partial F}{\partial x} = 2 x, \dfrac{\partial F}{\partial y} = 4 y, \dfrac{\partial F}{\partial z} = - 8 z.$

The equation of the tangent plane is

$$(x - 1) - 2 (y + 1) + 4(z + 1) = 0.$$

The equations of the normal line are

$$\frac{x - 1}{1} = \frac{y + 1}{- 2} = \frac{z + 1}{4}.$$

Illustration 2. Find the equation of the tangent plane and the normal line to $z = xy - x^3 + y^2$ at the point $(0, -1, 1)$.

Solution. $\qquad \dfrac{\partial z}{\partial x} = y - 3 x^2, \dfrac{\partial z}{\partial y} = x + 2 y.$

The equation of the tangent plane is

$$(z - 1) = - x - 2(y + 1).$$

The equations of the normal line are

$$\frac{x}{1} = \frac{y + 1}{2} = \frac{z - 1}{1}.$$

EXERCISES

1. Find the equation of the tangent plane and normal line to $xyz - 1 = 0$ at $(2, 3, \frac{1}{6})$. *Ans.* $3x + 2y + 36z - 18 = 0, \frac{x - 2}{3} = \frac{y - 3}{2} = \frac{z - \frac{1}{6}}{36}$.

2. Find the equations of the tangent plane and normal line to $z = x^{\frac{1}{2}} + y^{\frac{1}{2}}$ at the point $(4, 9, 5)$.

$$\text{*Ans.* } 3x + 2y - 12z + 30 = 0, \frac{x - 4}{3} = \frac{y - 9}{2} = \frac{z - 5}{-12}.$$

61. Tangent Line, Normal Plane to a Skew Curve. A space curve, not lying in a plane, is called a skew curve. The equations of such a curve C will be, in parametric form

(1) $$x = f(t), \quad y = g(t), \quad z = h(t).$$

Let the two points $P(x, y, z)$, $Q(x + \Delta x, y + \Delta y, z + \Delta z)$ lie on the curve (1). The direction cosines of PQ are proportional to Δx, Δy, and Δz. In the limit, as $Q \to P$, the secant line PQ becomes the tangent line at P with direction numbers dx, dy, dz, or $\frac{dx}{dt}, \frac{dy}{dt}, \frac{dz}{dt}$. Therefore the *equations of the line tangent* to the skew curve at (x_0, y_0, z_0) will be

(2) $$\frac{x - x_0}{\left(\frac{dx}{dt}\right)_0} = \frac{y - y_0}{\left(\frac{dy}{dt}\right)_0} = \frac{z - z_0}{\left(\frac{dz}{dt}\right)_0} \quad \text{(Tangent line)}.$$

The *equation of the plane normal* to the curve C at (x_0, y_0, z_0) will be

(3) $$\left(\frac{dx}{dt}\right)_0 (x - x_0) + \left(\frac{dy}{dt}\right)_0 (y - y_0) + \left(\frac{dz}{dt}\right)_0 (z - z_0) = 0$$
$$\text{(Normal plane)}.$$

If the skew curve C is given as the intersection of two surfaces $F(x, y, z) = 0$ and $G(x, y, z) = 0$, then the tangent line to C will lie in the two tangent planes to $F = 0$ and $G = 0$. At

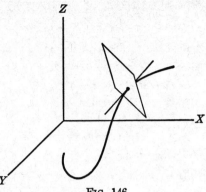

FIG. 146

$P(x_0, y_0, z_0)$ the equations of the tangent planes to $F = 0$, and $G = 0$ are respectively

(4) $\left(\dfrac{\partial F}{\partial x}\right)_0 (x - x_0) + \left(\dfrac{\partial F}{\partial y}\right)_0 (y - y_0) + \left(\dfrac{\partial F}{\partial z}\right)_0 (z - z_0) = 0,$ ⎫

(5) $\left(\dfrac{\partial G}{\partial x}\right)_0 (x - x_0) + \left(\dfrac{\partial G}{\partial y}\right)_0 (y - y_0) + \left(\dfrac{\partial G}{\partial z}\right)_0 (z - z_0) = 0$ ⎬ (Tangent line).

Together (4) and (5) are the equations of the tangent line. They may be written in symmetric form by computing the direction numbers

$$l : m : n = \begin{vmatrix} \left(\dfrac{\partial F}{\partial y}\right)_0 & \left(\dfrac{\partial F}{\partial z}\right)_0 \\ \left(\dfrac{\partial G}{\partial y}\right)_0 & \left(\dfrac{\partial G}{\partial z}\right)_0 \end{vmatrix} : - \begin{vmatrix} \left(\dfrac{\partial F}{\partial x}\right)_0 & \left(\dfrac{\partial F}{\partial z}\right)_0 \\ \left(\dfrac{\partial G}{\partial x}\right)_0 & \left(\dfrac{\partial G}{\partial z}\right)_0 \end{vmatrix} : \begin{vmatrix} \left(\dfrac{\partial F}{\partial x}\right)_0 & \left(\dfrac{\partial F}{\partial y}\right)_0 \\ \left(\dfrac{\partial G}{\partial x}\right)_0 & \left(\dfrac{\partial G}{\partial y}\right)_0 \end{vmatrix}$$

and writing

(6) $$\dfrac{x - x_0}{l} = \dfrac{y - y_0}{m} = \dfrac{z - z_0}{n}.$$

The equation of the normal plane would be

(7) $l(x - x_0) + m(y - y_0) + n(z - z_0) = 0$ (Normal plane).

Illustration 1.   Find the equations of the tangent line and normal plane to the space curve $x = t$, $y = 2t^2$, $z = t^3 - t$ at the point for which $t = 1$.

Solution. $\dfrac{dx}{dt} = 1, \quad \dfrac{dy}{dt} = 4t, \quad \dfrac{dz}{dt} = 3t^2 - 1.$

The equations of the tangent line are

$$\frac{x - 1}{1} = \frac{y - 2}{4} = \frac{z}{2}.$$

The equation of the normal plane is

$$(x - 1) + 4(y - 2) + 2z = 0.$$

Illustration 2. Find the equations of the line tangent to the curve of the intersection of $z = x^2 + y^2$ and $x^2 + y^2 = 2$ at the point (1,1,2).

Solution.
$$F \equiv x^2 + y^2 - z = 0$$
$$G \equiv x^2 + y^2 - 2 = 0$$
$$F_x = 2x, F_y = 2y, F_z = -1$$
$$G_x = 2x, G_y = 2y, G_z = 0.$$

The equations of the tangent line are

$$2(x - 1) + 2(y - 1) - (z - 2) = 0$$
$$(x - 1) + (y - 1) = 0.$$

Here $l : m : n = 1 : -1 : 0$ and the line is parallel to the XY-plane; hence the symmetric form would not be used.

EXERCISES

1. Find the equations of the tangent line and normal plane to the skew curve $x = t^2 + t$, $y = 2t - 8$, $z = t^4 - 6t^2$ at the point for which $t = 2$.

$$Ans. \quad \frac{x - 6}{5} = \frac{y + 4}{2} = \frac{z + 8}{8}, \quad 5x + 2y + 8z + 42 = 0.$$

2. Find the equations of the tangent line and normal plane to the skew curve $x = 2e^t$, $y = e^{-t}$, $z = 3e^t + e^{-t}$ at (2, 1, 4).

$$Ans. \quad \frac{x - 2}{2} = \frac{y - 1}{-1} = \frac{z - 4}{2}, \quad 2x - y + 2z - 11 = 0.$$

3. Find the equations of the tangent line and normal plane to the skew curve $z = x^2 + y^2$, $z^2 + x^2 = 5$ at (-1, 1, 2).

$$Ans. \quad \frac{x + 1}{4} = \frac{y - 1}{5} = \frac{z - 2}{2}, \quad 4(x + 1) + 5(y - 1) + 2(z - 2) = 0.$$

62. Related Rates. If, in a function of several variables, say $z = f(x, y)$, the variables x and y are themselves functions of another variable, say t, then z is a function of t and may be differentiated with respect to t (§ 57).

(1)
$$\frac{dz}{dt} = \frac{\partial f}{\partial x}\frac{dx}{dt} + \frac{\partial f}{\partial y}\frac{dy}{dt}.$$

This relation is useful in solving problems in related rates. (See Chap. V, § 22, for the one independent variable case.)

Illustration. The radius r of a cone is decreasing at the rate of 2 ft./sec. and the height h is increasing at the rate of 3 ft./sec. How fast is the volume changing when $r = 6$ ft. and $h = 10$ ft.?

Solution.
$$V = \tfrac{1}{3}\pi r^2 h$$
$$\frac{dV}{dt} = \frac{1}{3}\pi\left(2\,rh\frac{dr}{dt} + r^2\frac{dh}{dt}\right)$$
$$= \tfrac{1}{3}\pi[2\cdot 6\cdot 10(-2) + 36\cdot 3]$$
$$= -44\,\pi \text{ cu. ft./sec.}$$

EXERCISES

1. How fast is the area of a triangle increasing if the altitude increases at the rate of 3 in./sec. while the base increases at the rate of 4 in./sec.?
Ans. $\tfrac{3}{2}b + 2h$.

2. At any time t the dimensions of a rectangular box are x, y, z. If the volume remains constant and if y and z each increase at the rate of 2 ft./sec., how must x change? *Ans.* x must decrease at the rate of $\dfrac{2\,x(y+z)}{yz}$ ft./sec.

63. Directional Derivative. We have seen that $\dfrac{\partial z}{\partial x}$ and $\dfrac{\partial z}{\partial y}$ give the rate of change of z in the directions of the X- and Y-axes. The rate of change of z in any direction can be found as follows: Let P be a point on the surface $z = f(x, y)$ and pass a plane through P perpendicular to the XY-plane. This plane cuts out a curve on $z = f(x, y)$ (Fig. 147) the slope of

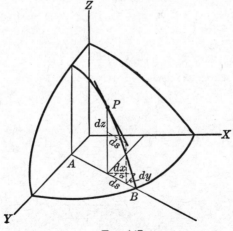

FIG. 147

which is the quantity sought. The trace AB of this plane in the XY-plane will specify the direction. Let the direction cosines of AB be $\cos \alpha$ and $\cos \beta = \sin \alpha$. Now

(1) $$\frac{dz}{ds} = \frac{\partial f}{\partial x}\frac{dx}{ds} + \frac{\partial f}{\partial y}\frac{dy}{ds},$$

where s is measured in the direction AB. But $\dfrac{dx}{ds} = \cos \alpha$, $\dfrac{dy}{ds} = \sin \alpha$. Therefore the rate of change of z in the direction AB is

(2) $$\frac{dz}{ds} = \frac{\partial f}{\partial x}\cos \alpha + \frac{\partial f}{\partial y}\sin \alpha.$$

This is called the *directional derivative* of z and represents the slope of the tangent line to the surface at any point P in the direction determined by α. When the point P is particularized, the partial derivatives $\dfrac{\partial f}{\partial x}$, $\dfrac{\partial f}{\partial y}$ can be evaluated.

Illustration. Find the rate of change of $z = x^2 - y^2$ in the direction $\alpha = 30°$ at the point $(2, 1, 3)$.

Solution.
$$\frac{\partial z}{\partial x} = 2x, \quad \frac{\partial z}{\partial y} = -2y$$
$$\frac{dz}{ds} = 2x\cos 30° - 2y\sin 30°$$
$$= 2\sqrt{3} - 1.$$

EXERCISES

1. Find the slope of the tangent line whose projection line in the XY-plane makes $45°$ with the X-axis, the surface being $z = x^2 + 2y^2$ and the point $(1, -1, 3)$. *Ans.* $-\sqrt{2}$.

2. Show that the angle α which produces a maximum value for $\dfrac{dz}{ds}$ is

$$\alpha = \tan^{-1}\frac{\dfrac{\partial z}{\partial y}}{\dfrac{\partial z}{\partial x}}.$$

Hence show that

$$\left|\frac{dz}{ds}\right|_{max} = \sqrt{\left(\frac{\partial z}{\partial x}\right)^2 + \left(\frac{\partial z}{\partial y}\right)^2}.$$

64. Maxima and Minima. A function of two independent variables, $z = f(x, y)$, is a maximum at a point (a, b) if $f(x, y) < f(a, b)$ for all values of x and y in the neighborhood of (a, b). Similarly the function is a minimum if $f(x, y) > f(a, b)$ for all values of x and y in the vicinity of (a, b).

For $z = f(x, y)$ to have an extreme (maximum or minimum) at a point (a, b), it is necessary that $\dfrac{\partial f}{\partial x} = 0$ and $\dfrac{\partial f}{\partial y} = 0$ at (a, b). But the condition is not sufficient.

In order to examine $z = f(x, y)$ for maxima and minima the procedure is as follows:

1st. Compute $\dfrac{\partial f}{\partial x}, \dfrac{\partial f}{\partial y}, \dfrac{\partial^2 f}{\partial x^2}, \dfrac{\partial^2 f}{\partial x \, \partial y}, \dfrac{\partial^2 f}{\partial y^2}.$

2nd. Solve simultaneously $\dfrac{\partial f}{\partial x} = 0, \dfrac{\partial f}{\partial y} = 0.$

Let a pair of (critical) values satisfying these equations be (x_0, y_0).

3rd. Evaluate $\Delta = \dfrac{\partial^2 f}{\partial x^2} \dfrac{\partial^2 f}{\partial y^2} - \left(\dfrac{\partial^2 f}{\partial x \, \partial y}\right)^2$ at (x_0, y_0).

4th. Then $z = f(x_0, y_0)$ will be a

Maximum if $\Delta > 0$ and $\dfrac{\partial^2 f}{\partial x^2} \left(\text{or } \dfrac{\partial^2 f}{\partial y^2}\right) < 0,$

Minimum if $\Delta > 0$ and $\dfrac{\partial^2 f}{\partial x^2} \left(\text{or } \dfrac{\partial^2 f}{\partial y^2}\right) > 0,$

Neither if $\Delta < 0$.

The test fails if $\Delta = 0$.

(Review discussion of maxima and minima for $y = f(x)$, § 19.)

Illustration 1. Examine $z = x^2 + xy + y^2 - y$ for maxima and minima.

Solution.
$$\frac{\partial z}{\partial x} = 2x + y, \quad \frac{\partial z}{\partial y} = x + 2y - 1$$

$$\frac{\partial^2 z}{\partial x^2} = 2, \quad \frac{\partial^2 z}{\partial x \, \partial y} = 1, \quad \frac{\partial^2 z}{\partial y^2} = 2$$

$$\left.\begin{array}{r} 2x + y = 0 \\ x + 2y = 1 \end{array}\right\} \quad x = -\tfrac{1}{3}, \, y = \tfrac{2}{3}.$$

This is the only critical point. At this point $\Delta > 0$ and $\dfrac{\partial^2 z}{\partial x^2} > 0$ and z is a minimum. The minimum value of z is $z = -\frac{1}{3}$.

Illustration 2.   Examine $z = x^2 - y^2$ for maxima and minima.

Solution.
$$\frac{\partial z}{\partial x} = 2\,x, \quad \frac{\partial z}{\partial y} = -2\,y,$$

$$\frac{\partial^2 z}{\partial x^2} = 2, \quad \frac{\partial^2 z}{\partial x\,\partial y} = 0, \quad \frac{\partial^2 z}{\partial y^2} = -2.$$

The critical point is the origin. But $\Delta = -4 < 0$. Therefore the point is neither a maximum nor a minimum. Such a point is called a saddle point (see Fig. 20) and corresponds to a point of inflection on a curve $y = f(x)$.

EXERCISES

1. Examine $z + xy + \dfrac{1}{x} + \dfrac{1}{y} = 0$ for maxima and minima.

Ans. Maximum, $(1, 1, -3)$.

2. Examine $4(x - 1)^2 + 4(y - 1)^2 + (z - 2)^2 - 4 = 0$.

Ans. Maximum, $(1, 1, 4)$; minimum, $(1, 1, 0)$.

3. Find the volume of the largest rectangular parallelepiped that can be inscribed in a sphere of radius r.

Ans. $\dfrac{8\,r^3}{3\sqrt{3}}$.

65. Surface Area. In Chapter XI, § 46, we treated areas of surfaces of revolution. For more general surfaces the following formula holds for the area of a curved surface $z = f(x, y)$:

(1) $$S = \iint \sqrt{\left(\frac{\partial z}{\partial x}\right)^2 + \left(\frac{\partial z}{\partial y}\right)^2 + 1}\; dy\, dx.$$

This integral is to be evaluated over the projected area in the XY-plane. If the surface area in question cannot be projected onto the XY-plane (as would be the case if the area were that of a cylinder, $f(x, y) = 0$, which is perpendicular to the XY-plane), the area should be projected onto another coordinate plane and formula (1) modified accordingly. Polar coordinates should be used if the integration in (1) is thus simplified.

Illustration 1. Find the surface area cut from the plane $x + 2\,y + z = 1$ by the coordinate planes.

Solution. $z = 1 - x - 2y.$

$$\frac{\partial z}{\partial x} = -1, \quad \frac{\partial z}{\partial y} = -2.$$

$$S = \int_0^1 \int_0^{\frac{1-x}{2}} \sqrt{6}\, dy\, dx$$

$$= \frac{\sqrt{6}}{2} \int_0^1 (1 - x)\, dx$$

$$= \frac{\sqrt{6}}{4} \text{ sq. units.}$$

Illustration 2.   Find the surface area cut from the surface $2z = x^2 + y^2$ by the two planes $z = 0$, $z = \frac{1}{2}$.

Solution. $\frac{\partial z}{\partial x} = x, \quad \frac{\partial z}{\partial y} = y.$

$$S = 4 \int_0^1 \int_0^{\sqrt{1-x^2}} \sqrt{x^2 + y^2 + 1}\, dy\, dx.$$

The integration will be simplified by using polar coordinates.

$$S = 4 \int_0^{\frac{\pi}{2}} \int_0^1 \sqrt{\rho^2 + 1}\, \rho\, d\rho\, d\theta$$

$$= \tfrac{4}{3} \int_0^{\frac{\pi}{2}} (2^{\frac{3}{2}} - 1)\, d\theta$$

$$= \frac{2\pi}{3} (2^{\frac{3}{2}} - 1) \text{ sq. units.}$$

EXERCISES

1. Find the surface area of a sphere of radius r.   *Ans.* $4\pi r^2$.

2. Find the surface area of a cylinder of radius r and height h (excluding the ends).   *Ans.* $2\pi rh$.

3. Find the surface area of the volume common to the two cylinders $x^2 + y^2 = a^2$, $x^2 + z^2 = a^2$.   *Ans.* $16\, a^2$.

CHAPTER XVI

INFINITE SERIES

66. Sequences and Series. An infinite sequence is an unending set of ordered elements, called terms, in which there is a first term, a second term, $\cdots$, an nth term, $\cdots$ etc. A sequence is written

$$(1) \qquad u_1, u_2, \cdots, u_n, \cdots.$$

A sequence is defined when the law of formation of the general term is known. An infinite series is an expression of the form

$$(2) \qquad u_1 + u_2 + \cdots + u_n + \cdots,$$

where the u's are the terms of an infinite sequence. For example, $\frac{1}{2}, \frac{1}{2^2}, \frac{1}{2^3}, \frac{1}{2^4}, \cdots$ are the first four terms of a sequence whose n^{th} term is evidently supposed to be $\frac{1}{2^n}$. To form an infinite series from these we write $\frac{1}{2} + \frac{1}{2^2} + \frac{1}{2^3} + \cdots + \frac{1}{2^n} + \cdots$. Again, if the general term of a series is $\log(n+1)$, then the series is $\log 2 + \log 3 + \log 4 + \cdots + \log(n+1) + \cdots$, where, in order to get the first term, we put $n = 1$; to get the second term we set $n = 2$; etc.

In most work involving infinite series it is desirable to have the nth term expressed as a function of n.

67. Convergence and Divergence. An infinite series may or may not have meaning. It is obvious that the sum $1 + 2 + 3 + \cdots + n + \cdots$ is infinite.

DEFINITION. *The sum of an infinite series is defined to be the limiting value of the sum of the first n terms as the number of terms increases indefinitely.* That is

$$(1) \qquad S = \lim_{n \to \infty} (u_1 + u_2 + \cdots + u_n).$$

When S_n is used to represent the sum of the first n terms, $S_n = u_1 + u_2 + \cdots + u_n$. (1) becomes

(2) $$S = \lim_{n \to \infty} S_n.$$

The series is written

$$S = u_1 + u_2 + \cdots + u_n + \cdots.$$

DEFINITION. *The series is said to converge, or to be convergent, when* $\lim_{n \to \infty} S_n$ *exists and is finite.*

DEFINITION. *The series is said to diverge, or to be divergent, when* $\lim_{n \to \infty} S_n$ *fails to exist or is infinite.*

68. Geometric Series. A geometric progression is a sequence in which the nth term is obtained by multiplying the $(n - 1)^{st}$ term by a constant ratio r. Thus, beginning with a first term a, a finite geometric progression of n terms would read

(1) $$a, \ ar, \ ar^2, \ \cdots, \ ar^{n-1}.$$

The sum $a + ar + \cdots + ar^{n-1}$ of such a progression is given by

(2) $$S_n = a \frac{1 - r^n}{1 - r}.$$

In the event (1) is an infinite progression, or sequence, S_n will represent the sum of the first n terms and the sum of the infinite geometric series $S = a + ar + \cdots + ar^{n-1} + \cdots$ will be

(3) $$S = \lim_{n \to \infty} S_n = \lim_{n \to \infty} a \frac{1 - r^n}{1 - r}.$$

Now if $|r| < 1$, $r^n \to 0$ as $n \to \infty$. Therefore

(4) $$S = \frac{a}{1 - r}$$

for an infinite geometric series of ratio r, with $|r| < 1$, and hence the series converges.

Since $|r|^n \to \infty$ as $n \to \infty$ if $|r| > 1$, the series will diverge in this case. It evidently diverges for $r = 1$.

We summarize: The geometric series

(5) $$S = a + ar + ar^2 + \cdots + ar^{n-1} + \cdots$$

converges when $|r| < 1$ and diverges when $|r| \geq 1$.

Illustration 1. Test for convergence the series $1 + \frac{1}{2} + \frac{1}{4} + \frac{1}{8} + \cdots$

Solution. The implication is that the general term is of the form $\frac{1}{2^n}$ (This is actually the $(n+1)^{st}$ term). With $r = \frac{1}{2}$, the series converges and converges to the value $S = \dfrac{1}{1 - \frac{1}{2}} = 2$. The sum of the series is said to be 2.

Illustration 2. Test for convergence the series for which the nth term is given by $(-1)^n \dfrac{1}{3^n}$.

Solution. The series is a geometric series with $r = -\frac{1}{3}$ and therefore converges. The series is

$$S = -\tfrac{1}{3} + \tfrac{1}{9} - \tfrac{1}{27} + \cdots + (-1)^n \frac{1}{3^n} + \cdots$$

and $\qquad S = \dfrac{-\frac{1}{3}}{1 + \frac{1}{3}} = -\dfrac{1}{4}.$

A series can converge in only one way: $\lim\limits_{n \to \infty} S_n$ must exist (and be finite). But series can diverge in two ways: (a) $\lim\limits_{n \to \infty} S_n = \infty$, and (b) $\lim\limits_{n \to \infty} S_n$ just simply fails to exist.

Illustration 3. The series $1 + 1 + 1 + \cdots$ diverges since

$$\lim_{n \to \infty} S_n = \lim_{n \to \infty} n = \infty.$$

This is type (a) divergence.

Illustration 4. Test for convergence the series $1 - 1 + 1 - 1 + \cdots$.

Solution. By inference the nth term is ± 1, according as n is odd or even. Since $S_n = 1$, for n odd, and $S_n = 0$, for n even, $S_n \to$ no limit as $n \to \infty$. The series is divergent and is said to oscillate. This is type (b) divergence.

69. Tests for Convergence. We list in the form of theorems and without proof the following tests for convergence and divergence. Illustrations will make their applications clear.

For Any Infinite Series

Theorem I. *In order that a series converge it is necessary that the general term approach zero as n approaches infinity.* That is, $\lim\limits_{n \to \infty} u_n = 0$ is a necessary condition for convergence.

This follows immediately from the definition of convergence: unless $\lim\limits_{n \to \infty} u_n = 0$, then $\lim\limits_{n \to \infty} S_n$ cannot exist and be finite. The condition is not sufficient; the series may diverge even though $\lim\limits_{n \to \infty} u_n = 0$. (See Illustration 1 below.)

FOR SERIES OF POSITIVE CONSTANT TERMS

Comparison Tests

THEOREM II. *If the terms of a positive series $u_1 + u_2 + \cdots + u_n + \cdots$ are not greater than the corresponding terms in a known convergent series, then the series converges.*

THEOREM III. *If the terms of a positive series $u_1 + u_2 + \cdots + u_n + \cdots$ are not less than the corresponding terms in a known divergent series, then the series diverges.*

These two theorems are self-explanatory.

Illustration 1. Test the series $1 + \dfrac{1}{2} + \dfrac{1}{3} + \cdots + \dfrac{1}{n} + \cdots$ for convergence.

Solution. Compare the given series

$$S = 1 + \tfrac{1}{2} + (\tfrac{1}{3} + \tfrac{1}{4}) + (\tfrac{1}{5} + \tfrac{1}{6} + \tfrac{1}{7} + \tfrac{1}{8}) + \cdots$$

with the series

$$T = 1 + \tfrac{1}{2} + (\tfrac{1}{4} + \tfrac{1}{4}) + (\tfrac{1}{8} + \tfrac{1}{8} + \tfrac{1}{8} + \tfrac{1}{8}) + \cdots.$$

It is evident that, from the first term, the terms in the given series S are not less than those in the test series T. That is to say, u_i in the given series is greater than or equal to the corresponding i^{th} term in the T series. But the T series evidently diverges since

$$T = 1 + \tfrac{1}{2} + \tfrac{1}{2} + \tfrac{1}{2} + \cdots.$$

Therefore the given series, known as the harmonic series, is divergent.

Illustration 2. Test the p-series, $1 + \dfrac{1}{2^p} + \dfrac{1}{3^p} + \cdots + \dfrac{1}{n^p} + \cdots$, for convergence.

Solution. This series is divergent when $p = 1$ since it then reduces to the harmonic series. For $p > 1$ write the series in the form

$$S = 1 + \left(\frac{1}{2^p} + \frac{1}{3^p}\right) + \left(\frac{1}{4^p} + \frac{1}{5^p} + \frac{1}{6^p} + \frac{1}{7^p}\right) + \cdots$$

and compare with

$$T = 1 + \left(\frac{1}{2^p} + \frac{1}{2^p}\right) + \left(\frac{1}{4^p} + \frac{1}{4^p} + \frac{1}{4^p} + \frac{1}{4^p}\right) + \cdots.$$

Each term in T is equal to or greater than the corresponding term in S. But T converges since

$$T = 1 + \frac{2}{2^p} + \frac{4}{4^p} + \cdots$$

$$= 1 + \frac{1}{2^{p-1}} + \frac{1}{(2^{p-1})^2} + \cdots,$$

which is a geometric series with ratio $\frac{1}{2^{p-1}}$ which is less than 1. Therefore S converges. For $p < 1$ the series S is termwise greater than the harmonic series (except for the first term). The S series therefore diverges. The p-series, therefore, is convergent for $p > 1$, divergent for $p \leq 1$.

Ratio Test

THEOREM IV. *Form the ratio of the $(n + 1)^{st}$ term to the nth term, namely, $\dfrac{u_{n+1}}{u_n}$ and take the limit as $n \to \infty$. Let $\lim\limits_{n \to \infty} \dfrac{u_{n+1}}{u_n} = r$. Then the series of positive terms $u_1 + u_2 + \cdots + u_n + \cdots$*

(a) *Converges if $r < 1$,*

(b) *Diverges if $r > 1$,*

(c) *Test fails if $r = 1$.*

Illustration 3. Test the series

$$\frac{1}{3} + \frac{1 \cdot 2}{3 \cdot 5} + \frac{1 \cdot 2 \cdot 3}{3 \cdot 5 \cdot 7} + \cdots + \frac{1 \cdot 2 \cdot 3 \cdots n}{3 \cdot 5 \cdot 7 \cdots (2n+1)} + \cdots$$

for convergence.

Solution. $\dfrac{u_{n+1}}{u_n} = \dfrac{\dfrac{1 \cdot 2 \cdot 3 \cdots n(n+1)}{3 \cdot 5 \cdot 7 \cdots (2n+1)(2n+3)}}{\dfrac{1 \cdot 2 \cdot 3 \cdots n}{3 \cdot 5 \cdot 7 \cdots (2n+1)}} = \dfrac{n+1}{2n+3}$

$$\lim_{n \to \infty} \frac{u_{n+1}}{u_n} = \lim_{n \to \infty} \frac{n+1}{2n+3} = \frac{1}{2}.$$

Hence the series converges.

Illustration 4. Test the series $\dfrac{1}{3} + \dfrac{1}{5} + \dfrac{1}{7} + \cdots + \dfrac{1}{2n+1} + \cdots$ for convergence.

Solution.

$$\lim_{n \to \infty} \frac{u_{n+1}}{u_n} = \lim_{n \to \infty} \frac{\dfrac{1}{2n+3}}{\dfrac{1}{2n+1}}$$

$$= \lim_{n \to \infty} \frac{2n+1}{2n+3}$$

$$= 1.$$

The test fails; this method does not tell us whether the series converges or diverges.

THEOREM V. *If, for a given series,* $\lim\limits_{n \to \infty} \dfrac{u_{n+1}}{u_n} = 1$ *and if then* $\dfrac{u_{n+1}}{u_n}$ *is reducible to the form* $\dfrac{u_{n+1}}{u_n} = \dfrac{n^k + an^{k-1} + \cdots}{n^k + bn^{k-1} + \cdots}$, *the series converges if* $b - a > 1$ *and diverges if* $b - a \leq 1$.

Illustration 5.   Test the series $\dfrac{1}{3} + \dfrac{1}{5} + \dfrac{1}{7} + \cdots + \dfrac{1}{2\,n+1} + \cdots$ in Illustration 4 for convergence.

Solution.   We saw that

$$\lim_{n \to \infty} \frac{u_{n+1}}{u_n} = \lim_{n \to \infty} \frac{2\,n+1}{2\,n+3} = 1$$

and the ratio test failed.

Here $\dfrac{u_{n+1}}{u_n} = \dfrac{n + \frac{1}{2}}{n + \frac{3}{2}}$ and $b - a = \frac{3}{2} - \frac{1}{2} = 1$.

Therefore, by Theorem V, the series diverges.

Cauchy's Integral Test

THEOREM VI.   *Let the general term of a series of positive terms* $u_1 + u_2 + \cdots$ *be* $u_n = f(n)$. *If* $f(x)$ *is a non-increasing function of the continuous variable* x *for* $x \geq a$, *then the series converges if* $\int_a^\infty f(x)\, dx$ *exists and diverges if this integral fails to exist.*

Illustration 6.   Test the p-series $1 + \dfrac{1}{2^p} + \dfrac{1}{3^p} + \cdots + \dfrac{1}{n^p} + \cdots$ for convergence.

Solution. $u_n = f(n) = \dfrac{1}{n^p}$

$$\int_a^\infty f(x)\, dx = \int_1^\infty \frac{1}{x^p}\, dx$$

$$= \lim_{n \to \infty} \int_1^n \frac{1}{x^p}\, dx$$

$$= \lim_{n \to \infty} \frac{1}{p-1} \left(1 - \frac{1}{n^{p-1}}\right).$$

If $p > 1$, this limit exists and equals $\dfrac{1}{p-1}$.   Therefore the series converges

If $p < 1$, this limit does not exist and the series diverges.   If $p = 1$,

$$\lim_{n \to \infty} \int_1^n \frac{1}{x}\, dx = \lim_{n \to \infty} \log n = \infty$$

and the series again diverges.

FOR SERIES WITH CONSTANT POSITIVE AND NEGATIVE TERMS

THEOREM VII. *A series containing positive and negative terms will converge if the corresponding series of the absolute values of the terms converges. That is to say* $u_1 + u_2 + \cdots + u_n + \cdots$ *converges if* $|u_1| + |u_2| + \cdots |u_n| + \cdots$ *converges.*

If the number of minus terms is finite, the theorem is obvious since the dropping of a finite number of terms in any series will not affect the convergence.

Illustration 7. Test the series

$$1 - \frac{1}{2} + \frac{1}{2^2} - \frac{1}{2^3} - \frac{1}{2^4} + \frac{1}{2^5} - \frac{1}{2^6} - \frac{1}{2^7} - \frac{1}{2^8} + \frac{1}{2^9} - \cdots$$

for convergence.

Solution. The series of absolute values $1 + \frac{1}{2} + \cdots + \frac{1}{2^n} + \cdots$ is a convergent series (geometric series with ratio $r = \frac{1}{2}$). Therefore the original series converges.

DEFINITION. *A series is said to converge absolutely if the corresponding series of absolute values converges.*

DEFINITION. *A series is said to converge conditionally if it converges but the corresponding series of absolute values diverges.*

DEFINITION. *An alternating series is one in which the signs of the terms alternate.*

THEOREM VIII. *An alternating series converges if* (a) $\lim\limits_{n \to \infty} u_n = 0$ *and if* (b) *from some point on,* $|u_i| > |u_{i+1}| > |u_{i+2}| > \cdots$.

Illustration 8. Test the series

$$\frac{1}{\sqrt{2}} - \frac{1}{\sqrt{3}} + \frac{1}{\sqrt{4}} - \cdots + (-1)^{n-1} \frac{1}{\sqrt{n+1}} + \cdots$$

for convergence.

Solution. This is an alternating series in which

(a) $$\lim_{n \to \infty} |u_n| = \lim_{n \to \infty} \left| \frac{1}{\sqrt{n+1}} \right| = 0$$

and (b) $$|u_i| > |u_{i+1}|$$

for all $i \geq 1$. Therefore the series converges. Moreover the series

$$\frac{1}{\sqrt{2}} + \frac{1}{\sqrt{3}} + \frac{1}{\sqrt{4}} + \cdots + \frac{1}{\sqrt{n}} + \cdots$$

is a p-series with $p = \frac{1}{2}$. This series diverges and therefore the original series converges conditionally.

Illustration 9.   Test the series $\frac{3}{4} - (\frac{3}{4})^2 + (\frac{3}{4})^3 - \cdots + (-1)^{n-1}(\frac{3}{4})^n + \cdots$ for convergence.

Solution.   Since the series of absolute values $\frac{3}{4} + (\frac{3}{4})^2 + \cdots + (\frac{3}{4})^n + \cdots$ is a geometric series with ratio $r = \frac{3}{4}$, it converges.   Therefore the original series converges absolutely.

EXERCISES

Test the following series for convergence.

1. $1 + \frac{1}{2} + \frac{1}{4} + \frac{1}{6} + \cdots + \frac{1}{2\,n} + \cdots$.   *Ans.* Divergent.

2. $1 - \frac{1}{2} + \frac{1}{4} - \frac{1}{6} + \cdots$.   *Ans.* Conditionally convergent.

3. $\frac{5}{3} + \frac{5}{5^2} + \frac{5}{7^3} + \cdots + \frac{5}{(2\,n+1)^n} \cdots$.   *Ans.* Convergent

4. $1 \cdot \frac{2}{3} + 2(\frac{2}{3})^2 + 3(\frac{2}{3})^3 + \cdots + n(\frac{2}{3})^n + \cdots$.   *Ans.* Convergent

5. $\frac{1}{10} + \frac{2!}{10^2} + \frac{3!}{10^3} + \cdots + \frac{n!}{10^n} + \cdots$.   *Ans.* Divergent

6. $\frac{2}{1} + \frac{2^2}{2^2} + \frac{2^3}{3^2} + \cdots + \frac{2^n}{n^2} + \cdots$.   *Ans.* Divergent.

7. The series for which $u_n = \dfrac{1}{n^4}$.   *Ans.* Convergent

8. $\dfrac{1}{\log 2} + \dfrac{1}{\log 3} + \cdots + \dfrac{1}{\log n} + \cdots$.   *Ans.* Divergent

9. $\dfrac{1}{2} - \dfrac{2}{3} + \dfrac{3}{4} - \dfrac{4}{5} + \cdots + (-1)^{n+1}\dfrac{n}{n+1} + \cdots$.   *Ans.* Divergent.

10. $1 - \dfrac{1}{3^3} + \dfrac{1}{3^6} - \cdots + (-1)^{n+1}\dfrac{1}{3^{3n-3}} + \cdots$.

Ans. Absolutely convergent.

70. Power Series.   A series of the form

(1) $a_0 + a_1 x + a_2 x^2 + \cdots + a_n x^n + \cdots,$

involving positive integral powers of a variable x and constant coefficients a_i is called a power series in x.   It is an immediate generalization of the polynomial $a_0 + a_1 x + \cdots + a_n x^n$.   A series of the form

(2) $a_0 + a_1(x - a) + a_2(x - a)^2 + \cdots + a_n(x - a)^n + \cdots$

is called a power series in $x - a$.

If in the power series (1) a particular value is assigned to x, the series is reduced to a series of constants which may or may not converge.   It is apparent that (1) converges for the value $x = 0$ but (1) might converge for no other value of x.   Or again a power series might converge for all values of x. If (1) converges for $x = b$, then it will converge for all values of x such that $|x| < b$. If (1) diverges for $x = b$, then it will diverge when $|x| > b$.

Let us apply the ratio test to the power series (1).

$$(3) \qquad \lim_{n \to \infty} \left| \frac{u_{n+1}}{u_n} \right| = \lim_{n \to \infty} \left| \frac{a_{n+1} x^{n+1}}{a_n x^n} \right| = \lim_{n \to \infty} |x| \left| \frac{a_{n+1}}{a_n} \right|.$$

If this limit is equal to a number L which is itself less than unity, $L < 1$, the series converges. This says that (1) will converge if $\lim_{n \to \infty} |x| \cdot \left| \frac{a_{n+1}}{a_n} \right| < 1$ or if $|x| < \lim_{n \to \infty} \left| \frac{a_n}{a_{n+1}} \right|$. Hence the

THEOREM. *The power series* $a_0 + a_1 x + \cdots + a_n x^n + \cdots$ converges when $|x| < \lim_{n \to \infty} \left| \frac{a_n}{a_{n+1}} \right|$ and diverges when $|x| > \lim_{n \to \infty} \left| \frac{a_n}{a_{n+1}} \right|$. The series may or may not converge when $|x| = \lim_{n \to \infty} \left| \frac{a_n}{a_{n+1}} \right|$.

The totality of points x at which the series converges makes up the interval of convergence, the end points of the interval being $\pm \lim_{n \to \infty} \left| \frac{a_n}{a_{n+1}} \right|$.

Illustration 1. Find the interval of convergence of the series

$$x - \frac{x^3}{3} + \frac{x^5}{5} - \cdots + (-1)^{n-1} \frac{x^{2n-1}}{2n-1} + \cdots.$$

Solution. $\lim_{n \to \infty} \left| \frac{a_n}{a_{n+1}} \right| = \lim_{n \to \infty} \left| \frac{2n+1}{2n-1} \right| = 1.$

Therefore the series converges for $|x| < 1$ and the interval of convergence is $-1 < x < 1$. At $x = -1$ the series is an alternating series and is convergent. At $x = 1$ the series is again a convergent alternating series. Therefore the series converges when $-1 \le x \le 1$.

Illustration 2. Find the interval of convergence for the series

$$1 + 2! \, x + 3! \, x^2 + \cdots + (n+1)! \, x^n + \cdots.$$

Solution.
$$\lim_{n \to \infty} \left| \frac{a_n}{a_{n+1}} \right| = \lim_{n \to \infty} \left| \frac{n!}{(n+1)!} \right|$$
$$= \lim_{n \to \infty} \left| \frac{1}{n+1} \right|$$
$$= 0.$$

Therefore the series converges only for $x = 0$.

Illustration 3. Find the interval of convergence of the series

$$1 + \frac{2\,x}{2!} + \frac{2^2 x^2}{3!} + \frac{2^3 x^3}{4!} + \cdots + \frac{2^n x^n}{(n+1)!} + \cdots.$$

Solution.
$$\lim_{n \to \infty} \left| \frac{a_n}{a_{n+1}} \right| = \lim_{n \to \infty} \left| \frac{2^n}{(n+1)!} \cdot \frac{(n+2)!}{2^{n+1}} \right|$$

$$= \lim_{n \to \infty} \left| \frac{n+2}{2} \right|$$

$$= \infty.$$

Therefore the series converges for all values of x and the interval of convergence is infinite.

EXERCISES

Find the interval of convergence for each of the following series.

1. $1 + 3\,x + (3\,x)^2 + (3\,x)^3 + \cdots + (3\,x)^n + \cdots.$ *Ans.* $-\frac{1}{3} < x < \frac{1}{3}.$

2. $x - \frac{3\,x^3}{1!} + \frac{5\,x^5}{2!} - \frac{7\,x^7}{3!} + \cdots + (-1)^{n-1}\frac{(2\,n-1)x^{2n-1}}{(n-1)!} + \cdots.$

$$\textit{Ans.}\ -\infty < x < \infty.$$

3. $1 + x + \frac{x^2}{\sqrt{2}} + \frac{x^3}{\sqrt[3]{2}} + \cdots + \frac{x^n}{\sqrt[n]{2}} + \cdots.$ *Ans.* $-1 < x < 1.$

4. $1 + x + \frac{x^2}{2} + \frac{x^3}{3} + \cdots + \frac{x^n}{n} + \cdots.$ *Ans.* $-1 \leq x < 1.$

5. $(x-2) - \frac{(x-2)^2}{2} + \frac{(x-2)^3}{3} - \cdots + (-1)^{n-1}\frac{(x-2)^n}{n} + \cdots.$

$$\textit{Ans.}\ 1 < x \leq 3.$$

71. Some Properties of Series. It is often desirable to make use of one or more of the following general properties of infinite series.

Property I. Regrouping of the terms of a convergent series by the insertion of parentheses will neither affect the convergence nor the value of the series. Regrouping by inserting parentheses may, however, change a conditionally convergent series into just a plain convergent series. In general parentheses may not be removed unless the series converges absolutely.

Property II. Rearrangement of the terms of an absolutely convergent series in any manner whatsoever will leave unaltered the sum of the series.

Property III. In an absolutely convergent series, the series of plus signs converges and also the series of minus signs converges. If the series of plus signs converges to P and if the series of minus signs converges to $-M$, then the whole series converges to $P - M$.

Property IV. In a conditionally convergent series, the series of plus signs diverges and also the series of minus signs diverges.

Property V. The terms of a conditionally convergent series may be rearranged so as to make the value of the series any desired quantity.

Property VI. The sum of a convergent alternating series will not differ numerically from the sum of the first n terms by more than the $(n + 1)^{st}$ term. That is, the error made in using the sum of the first few terms as an approximation to the sum of the whole series will not exceed the magnitude of the first term omitted.

Property VII. If the corresponding terms of two convergent series, $U = u_1 + u_2 + \cdots + u_n + \cdots$ and $V = v_1 + v_2 + \cdots + v_n + \cdots$, are added or subtracted, the sum of the new series thus formed will be $U \pm V = (u_1 \pm v_1) + (u_2 \pm v_2) + \cdots + (u_n + v_n) + \cdots$.

Property VIII. The interval of convergence of the power series $a_0 + a_1 x + \cdots + a_n x^n + \cdots$ is $-R$ to $+R$, where R is given by $R = \lim\limits_{n \to \infty} \left| \dfrac{a_n}{a_{n+1}} \right|$. The end points $-R$ and $+R$ may or may not be included. The series converges absolutely for all values of $|x| < R$.

Property IX. Let $f(x) = a_0 + a_1 x + \cdots + a_n x^n + \cdots$ and $g(x) = b_0 + b_1 x + \cdots + b_n x^n + \cdots$. Then

(a) Sum. $f(x) \pm g(x) = (a_0 \pm b_0) + (a_1 \pm b_1)x + \cdots + (a_n \pm b_n)x^n + \cdots$

for every value of x for which each series converges. That is, the sum or difference of two power series converges within the smaller interval of convergence.

(b) Product. $f(x) \cdot g(x) = a_0 b_0 + (a_0 b_1 + a_1 b_0)x + (a_0 b_2 + a_1 b_1 + a_2 b_0)x^2 + \cdots$

for every value of x for which each series converges absolutely. That is, the product of two power series converges within the smaller interval of absolute convergence. Note that since a power series always converges absolutely except, perhaps, at an end point, the condition of absolute convergence is not much more restrictive; the end points of the smaller series of convergence are the only points that may affect the validity of the product theorem.

(c)   Quotient. $\dfrac{f(x)}{g(x)} = \dfrac{a_0 + a_1 x + \cdots + a_n x^n + \cdots}{b_0 + b_1 x + \cdots + b_n x^n + \cdots}, \; b_0 \neq 0$

$$= q_1 + q_2 x + \cdots + q_n x^n + \cdots$$

for every value of x for which $a_0 + a_1 x + \cdots a_n x^n + \cdots$ converges and for which at the same time $|b_1 x| + |b_2 x^2| + \cdots < |b_0|$. The interval of convergence of the quotient series is seen to be complicated.

Property X. Within the interval of convergence a power series may be differentiated termwise in order to obtain the derivative of the function which the series represents. That is

$$\frac{df}{dx} = a_1 + 2\,a_2 x + \cdots + n a_n x^{n-1} + \cdots$$

and this is valid within the interval of convergence and may or may not be valid at the end points.

Property XI. Between any two limits within the interval of convergence a power series may be integrated termwise in order to obtain the definite integral of the function which the series represents. That is

$$\int_a^b f(x)\,dx = \int_a^b a_0\,dx + \int_a^b a_1 x\,dx + \cdots + \int_a^b a_n x^n\,dx + \cdots$$

and this is valid for all a and b such that $-R < a < b < R$. It may or may not be possible to extend the limits of integration to include the end points.

CHAPTER XVII

EXPANSION OF FUNCTIONS

72. Maclaurin's Series. When a known function $f(x)$ is written in the form of an infinite series, the function is said to be expanded in an infinite series and the infinite series is said to represent the function in the interval of convergence.

Illustration. Since $1 + x + x^2 + \cdots + x^n + \cdots$ is a geometric series, it will converge to $\dfrac{1}{1-x}$ for $|x| < 1$. Hence

$$\frac{1}{1-x} = 1 + x + x^2 + \cdots + x^n + \cdots, \; -1 \le x < 1$$

and the function $\dfrac{1}{1-x}$ is expanded in an infinite series. The series representation of the function is valid only when $-1 \le x < 1$ but the function exists and is continuous everywhere except at $x = 1$.

A given function $f(x)$ may be expanded in a power series as follows: Write

$$(1) \qquad f(x) = a_0 + a_1x + a_2x^2 + a_3x^3 + \cdots + a_nx^n + \cdots,$$

where the coefficients a_i are to be determined. Then by Property X, § 71, it is permissible to write

$$(2) \qquad f'(x) = a_1 + 2\,a_2x + 3\,a_3x^2 + \cdots + na_nx^{n-1} + \cdots,$$

$$(3) \qquad f''(x) = 2\,a_2 + 2 \cdot 3\,a_3x^2 + \cdots + n(n-1)a_nx^{n-2} + \cdots,$$

$$(4) \qquad f^{[n]}(x) = n!a_n + (n+1)!a_{n+1}x + \cdots.$$

From these equations the coefficients a_i can be determined. In (1) put $x = 0$; then

$$(5) \qquad a_0 = f(0).$$

In (2), (3), $\cdots$, (4) put $x = 0$ and compute the a's to be

$$(6) \qquad a_1 = f'(0), \quad a_2 = \frac{f''(0)}{2!}, \cdots,$$

$$(7) \qquad a_n = \frac{1}{n!}f^{[n]}(0).$$

We thus obtain the expansion of a known function $f(x)$ in Maclaurin's Series which is

(8) $$f(x) = f(0) + \frac{f'(0)}{1!}x + \frac{f''(0)}{2!}x^2 + \cdots + \frac{f^{[n]}(0)}{n!}x^n + \cdots.$$

The expansion is said to be about the origin or in the neighborhood of the origin.

Illustration 1. Expand e^x in a Maclaurin Series and determine the interval of convergence.

Solution. Here, for all n, $f^{[n]}(x) = e^x$. Therefore the expansion is

$$e^x = 1 + x + \frac{x^2}{2!} + \frac{x^3}{3!} + \cdots + \frac{x^n}{n!} + \cdots.$$

Since $\lim\limits_{n\to\infty} \left|\dfrac{a_n}{a_{n+1}}\right| = \infty$, the expansion is valid for all x.

Illustration 2. Expand $\sin x$ in a Maclaurin Series and determine the interval of convergence.

Solution. $f(x) = \sin x, f'(x) = \cos x$

$$f''(x) = -\sin x, f'''(x) = -\cos x, \cdots.$$

The $\sin 0 = 0$ and $\cos 0 = 1$; therefore the expansion is

$$\sin x = x - \frac{x^3}{3!} + \frac{x^5}{5!} - \frac{x^7}{7!} + \cdots.$$

It converges for all values of x since

$$\lim_{n\to\infty} \left|\frac{a_n}{a_{n+1}}\right| = \infty.$$

EXERCISES

Verify the Maclaurin expansions of the following important functions.

1. $\cos x = 1 - \dfrac{x^2}{2!} + \dfrac{x^4}{4!} - \cdots + (-1)^{n-1}\dfrac{x^{2n-2}}{(2n-2)!} + \cdots, \quad -\infty < x < \infty.$

2. $\tan x = x + \dfrac{x^3}{3} + \dfrac{2x^5}{15} + \cdots, \quad -\dfrac{\pi}{2} < x < \dfrac{\pi}{2}.$

(Do not try to get the general term as it is quite difficult to obtain.)

3. $\log(1 + x) = x - \dfrac{x^2}{2} + \dfrac{x^3}{3} - \cdots + (-1)^{n-1}\dfrac{x^n}{n} + \cdots, \quad -1 < x \leq 1.$

4. $\log\left(\dfrac{1+x}{1-x}\right) = 2\left(x + \dfrac{x^3}{3} + \dfrac{x^5}{5} + \cdots + \dfrac{x^{2n-1}}{2n-1} + \cdots\right), \quad -1 < x < 1.$

5. $\tan^{-1} x = x - \dfrac{x^3}{3} + \dfrac{x^5}{5} - \cdots + (-1)^{n-1}\dfrac{x^{2n-1}}{2n-1} + \cdots, \quad -1 \leq x \leq 1.$

6. $(1+x)^m = 1 + \dfrac{mx}{1!} + \dfrac{m(m-1)}{2!}x^2 + \cdots + \dfrac{m(m-1)\cdots(m-n+2)}{(n-1)!}x^{n-1} + \cdots.$

This is the binomial series and reduces to a polynomial when m is zero or a positive integer. When m is not a positive integer, the series converges for $-1 < x < 1$. The series will also converge at the left end point $x = -1$ if $m > 0$; it will converge at the right end point $x = 1$ if $m > -1$.

73. Taylor's Series. A function $f(x)$ may be expanded about a point a instead of about the origin. That is, $f(x)$ can be represented by a series of the form

(1) $f(x) = a_0 + a_1(x - a) + a_2(x - a)^2 + \cdots + a_n(x - a)^n + \cdots.$

The coefficients a_i are computed by repeated differentiations of this relation and subsequent evaluations at the point $x = a$. Thus we have

(2) $f'(x) = a_1 + 2\,a_2(x-a) + 3\,a_3(x-a)^2 + \cdots + na_n(x-a)^{n-1} + \cdots,$

(3) $f''(x) = 2\,a_2 + 2\cdot 3\,a_3(x-a) + \cdots + n(n-1)a_n(x-a)^{n-2} + \cdots,$

(4) $f^{[n]}(x) = n!a_n + (n + 1)!(x - a) + \cdots.$

From these we compute

(5) $a_i = \dfrac{f^{[i]}(a)}{i!}, \quad i = 0, 1, 2, \cdots,$

and the series expansion of $f(x)$ in the neighborhood of the point a becomes

(6) $f(x) = f(a) + \dfrac{f'(a)}{1!}(x-a) + \dfrac{f''(a)}{2!}(x-a)^2 + \cdots + \dfrac{f^{[n]}(a)}{n!}(x-a)^n + \cdots.$

This is known as Taylor's Series. When $a = 0$, it reduces, as a special case, to Maclaurin's Series. If we set $x = a + h$, another form of Taylor's Series is obtained, namely,

(7) $f(a+h) = f(a) + \dfrac{f'(a)}{1!}h + \dfrac{f''(a)}{2!}h^2 + \cdots + \dfrac{f^{[n]}(a)}{n!}h^n + \cdots.$

In (6) let $r_n(x)$ denote the remainder of the series after n terms, or, in symbols

(8) $f(x) = f(a) + \dfrac{f'(a)}{1!}(x - a) + \cdots + \dfrac{f^{[n-1]}(a)}{(n-1)!}(x - a)^{n-1} + r_n(x),$

$= S_n(x) + r_n(x).$

It can be shown that $r_n(x) = \dfrac{f^{[n]}(x_1)}{n!}(x - a)^n$ where $a < x_1 < x$. When (8) is written in the form

$$(9) \qquad f(x) = f(a) + f'(a)(x - a) + \cdots + \frac{f^{[n-1]}(a)}{(n-1)!}(x - a)^{n-1}$$
$$+ \frac{f^{[n]}(x_1)}{n!}(x - a)^n, \quad a < x_1 < x,$$

it is known as Taylor's formula with the remainder. For (7) Taylor's formula with the remainder takes on the form

$$(10) \; f(a+h) = f(a) + f'(a)h + \cdots + \frac{f^{[n-1]}(a)}{(n-1)!}h^{n-1} + \frac{f^{[n]}(a + \theta h)}{n!}h^n,$$
$$0 < \theta < 1.$$

THEOREM.   *The Taylor's Series expansion of a function $f(x)$ will be a valid representation of the function for those values of x and only for those values of x for which $\lim\limits_{n \to \infty} r_n(x) = 0$.*

If Taylor's Series in a given instance turns out to be an alternating series, the remainder $r_n(x)$ will not exceed numerically the first term in the remainder.   In general

$$r_n(x) = \frac{f^{[n]}(x_1)}{n!}(x - a)^n,$$

where x_1 is some point that lies between a and x; but it is impossible to calculate $r_n(x)$ with no detailed information about this point.   However, if x'_1 is arbitrarily chosen so as to make $f^{[n]}(x'_1)$ as large as possible, then

$$(11) \qquad |\, r_n(x)\,| \leq \left| \frac{f^{[n]}(x'_1)}{n!}(x - a)^n \right|.$$

The error made, therefore, in breaking off at the nth term will not exceed

$$\left| \frac{f^{[n]}(x'_1)}{n!}(x - a)^n \right|.$$

Illustration 1.   Expand $\sin x$ in a Taylor's Series about the point $\frac{\pi}{6}$.

Solution. $f(x) = \sin x, f'(x) = \cos x$, etc.   These, evaluated at $\frac{\pi}{6}$, become

$$f\left(\frac{\pi}{6}\right) = \frac{1}{2}, f'\left(\frac{\pi}{6}\right) = \frac{\sqrt{3}}{2}, \text{ etc.}$$

Therefore

$$\sin x = \frac{1}{2} + \frac{\sqrt{3}}{2}\left(x - \frac{\pi}{6}\right) - \frac{1}{2}\frac{\left(x - \frac{\pi}{6}\right)^2}{2!} - \frac{\sqrt{3}}{2}\frac{\left(x - \frac{\pi}{6}\right)^3}{3!} + \cdots, \; -\infty < x < \infty.$$

Illustration 2.   Expand e^x in powers of $(x - a)$.

Solution.

Since
$$f(x) = e^x,$$
$$f^{[i]}(x) = e^x,$$

and
$$f^{[i]}(a) = e^a,$$

the expansion becomes

$$e^x = e^a \left[1 + (x - a) + \frac{(x - a)^2}{2!} + \cdots + \frac{(x - a)^n}{n!} + \cdots \right] \quad -\infty < x < \infty.$$

EXERCISES

Verify the Taylor expansions of the following important functions.

1. $\sin x = \sin a + (x - a) \cos a - \dfrac{(x - a)^2}{2!} \sin a - \dfrac{(x - a)^3}{3!} \cos a + \cdots,$

$$-\infty < x < \infty.$$

2. $\cos x = \cos a - (x - a) \sin a - \dfrac{(x - a)^2}{2!} \cos a + \dfrac{(x - a)^3}{3!} \sin a + \cdots,$

$$-\infty < x < \infty.$$

3. $\log x = \log a + \dfrac{1}{a}(x-a) - \dfrac{1}{2}\dfrac{1}{a^2}(x-a)^2 + \cdots + \dfrac{(-1)^n}{(n-1)a^{n-1}}(x-a)^{n-1} + \cdots,$

$$a > 0, \quad 0 < x \leqq 2a.$$

74. Application of Series to Computation.

I. Increments.   We have seen before (Chap. VI, § 25) that, approximately, $\Delta y \doteqdot f'(x) \Delta x$.   A clearer picture of this is gotten by rewriting (7) § 73, setting $a = x$, $h = \Delta x$.   This gives

$$(1) \quad f(x + \Delta x) = f(x) + \frac{f'(x)}{1!} \Delta x + \frac{f''(x)}{2!} \overline{\Delta x}^2 + \cdots + \frac{f^{[n]}(x)}{n!} \overline{\Delta x}^n + \cdots.$$

Now transpose $f(x)$ and write $\Delta y = f(x + \Delta x) - f(x)$.   Formula 1 then reads

$$(2) \qquad \Delta y = f'(x) \Delta x + \frac{f''(x)}{2!} \overline{\Delta x}^2 + \cdots + \frac{f^{[n]}(x)}{n!} \overline{\Delta x}^n + \cdots.$$

From this, as a first approximation for small increments, we get

$$(3) \qquad dy \sim \Delta y \sim f'(x) \Delta x.$$

As a second approximation

$$(4) \qquad dy \sim \Delta y \sim f'(x) \Delta x + \frac{f''(x)}{2!} \overline{\Delta x}^2.$$

Still better approximation can be obtained by taking more terms in the expansion (2).

II. Computation by Series. Long before this point in his mathematical development the student may have wondered how the tables of the trigonometric, logarithmic, and exponential functions were obtained. The answer is they were largely made from computations by series.

Illustration 1. Compute, approximately, the value of e by series.

Solution. The Maclaurin expansion for e^x is

$$e^x = 1 + x + \frac{x^2}{2!} + \frac{x^3}{3!} + \cdots + \frac{x^n}{n!} + \cdots.$$

If $x = 1$, this becomes

$$e = 1 + 1 + \frac{1}{2!} + \frac{1}{3!} + \frac{1}{4!} + \cdots + \frac{1}{n!} + \cdots$$

$$= 1 + 1 + 0.5 + 0.166667 + 0.041667$$
$$+ 0.008333 + 0.001389 + 0.000198 + \cdots.$$

Hence approximately, $e = 2.718254$, which is correct to 4 decimals.

Illustration 2. Compute $\sin 10° = \sin \frac{\pi}{18}$ correct to 5 decimals.

Solution. $\sin x = x - \frac{x^3}{3!} + \frac{x^5}{5!} - \frac{x^7}{7!} + \cdots.$

$$\sin 10° = \frac{\pi}{18} - \frac{1}{3!}\left(\frac{\pi}{18}\right)^3 + \frac{1}{5!}\left(\frac{\pi}{18}\right)^5 - \cdots.$$

Now this is an alternating series and the error committed in using only a few terms will not exceed the numerical value of the first term omitted (cf. Property VI, § 71).

$$\sin 10° = 0.174532 - 0.000886 + 0.000001 - \cdots.$$

The third term does not affect the 5th decimal place. Therefore, taking only the first two terms in the expansion, we compute, correct to 5 places

$$\sin 10° = 0.17364.$$

(The sum of the first two terms is 0.173646 and a better approximation to $\sin 10°$ is 0.17365, the value listed in a five-place table of sines.)

Illustration 3. Find $\cos 44°$ correct to 5 decimals.

Solution. Maclaurin's Series for cosine is

$$\cos x = 1 - \frac{x^2}{2!} + \frac{x^4}{4!} - \cdots;$$

but for $x = 44° = \frac{11\pi}{45},$

this series will not converge very rapidly. We should use Taylor's Series instead and expand about the point $\frac{\pi}{4}$. Thus

$$\cos x = \frac{\sqrt{2}}{2}\left[1 - \left(x - \frac{\pi}{4}\right) - \frac{1}{2!}\left(x - \frac{\pi}{4}\right)^2 + \frac{1}{3!}\left(x - \frac{\pi}{4}\right)^3 + \cdots\right],$$

from which it follows that

$$\cos 44° = \frac{\sqrt{2}}{2}\left[1 + \frac{\pi}{180} - \frac{1}{2!}\left(\frac{\pi}{180}\right)^2 - \frac{1}{3!}\left(\frac{\pi}{180}\right)^3 + \cdots\right],$$

which converges rapidly.

$$\cos 44° = 0.707106\,[1 + 0.017453 - \tfrac{1}{2}(0.017453)^2 - \tfrac{1}{6}(0.017453)^3 + \cdots]$$
$$= 0.707106 + 0.012341 - 0.000107 - 0.0000006 + \cdots$$
$$= 0.71934.$$

But the error committed by using only 3 terms does not exceed the 4th term since the largest value of $f'''(x)$ in the interval is $\frac{\sqrt{2}}{2}$. (See formula 11, § 73.)

EXERCISES

1. Expand e^{-x} in a Maclaurin Series and compute e^{-2} correct to 5 decimals.
                                                            Ans. 0.13533.

2. By using a Maclaurin expansion show that $\log 2 = 0.6931$ correct to 4 places.

3. Show that for angles less than about 1° 46′, $\sin \theta = \theta$ with accuracy to 5 decimals.

4. Use the Maclaurin Series expansion of $\tan^{-1} x$ and the relation $\frac{\pi}{4} = \tan^{-1}\frac{1}{7} + 2\tan^{-1}\frac{1}{3}$ to compute $\pi = 3.1416$ which is correct to 3 places.

5. Expand $\sin x$ in a Taylor Series and compute $\sin 61° = 0.8746$ correct to 4 places.

6. Expand $\log x$ in a Taylor Series and use 4 terms to compute $\log 1.2$. Estimate the error.

   Ans. $\log 1.2 = 0.182667$ with an error not in excess of .0004; the correct value of $\log 1.2$, to 4 decimals is $\log 1.2 = 0.1823$ so that our answer, based on 4 terms, is correct to 3 places.

CHAPTER XVIII

HYPERBOLIC FUNCTIONS

75. Relation between Exponential and Trigonometric Functions. The following expansions were obtained in Chapter XVII.

(1) $$e^x = 1 + x + \frac{x^2}{2!} + \frac{x^3}{3!} + \cdots + \frac{x^n}{n!} + \cdots,$$

(2) $$\sin x = x - \frac{x^3}{3!} + \frac{x^5}{5!} - \cdots + (-1)^{n-1}\frac{x^{2n-1}}{(2n-1)!} + \cdots,$$

(3) $$\cos x = 1 - \frac{x^2}{2!} + \frac{x^4}{4!} - \cdots + (-1)^{n-1}\frac{x^{2n-2}}{(2n-2)!} + \cdots.$$

It can be shown that these series converge for all values of x, real or complex. Indeed when $x = \alpha + i\beta$, these series will serve as definitions of $e^{\alpha+i\beta}$, $\sin(\alpha + i\beta)$, $\cos(\alpha + i\beta)$ respectively. For $x = i\theta$, a pure imaginary number, (1) becomes

(4) $$e^{i\theta} = 1 + i\theta - \frac{\theta^2}{2!} - i\frac{\theta^3}{3!} + \frac{\theta^4}{4!} + \cdots,$$

since $i = \sqrt{-1}$, $i^2 = -1$, $i^3 = -i$, $i^4 = 1$, etc. Multiplying (2) by i and writing θ for x yields

(5) $$i\sin\theta = i\theta - \frac{i\theta^3}{3!} + \frac{i\theta^5}{5!} - \cdots.$$

For $x = \theta$ (3) becomes

(6) $$\cos\theta = 1 - \frac{\theta^2}{2!} + \frac{\theta^4}{4!} - \cdots.$$

By adding (5) and (6) we get (4). That is

(7) $$e^{i\theta} = \cos\theta + i\sin\theta.$$

This is a remarkable relation and is generally known as Euler's Identity. It exhibits a very simple connection between $\sin\theta$, $\cos\theta$, and $e^{i\theta}$. Evidently $e^{i(-\theta)} = \cos(-\theta) + i\sin(-\theta)$ or

(8) $$e^{-i\theta} = \cos\theta - i\sin\theta.$$

Solving (7) and (8) simultaneously for $\sin \theta$ and $\cos \theta$, we get

$$(9) \qquad\qquad \sin \theta = \frac{e^{i\theta} - e^{-i\theta}}{2\,i},$$

$$(10) \qquad\qquad \cos \theta = \frac{e^{i\theta} + e^{-i\theta}}{2}.$$

These relations are very important in advanced mathematics and (9) and (10) could be used as definitions of $\sin \theta$ and $\cos \theta$.

76. Hyperbolic Functions. In many branches of applied mathematics there are functions very similar to the right-hand members of (9) and (10) of § 75 that are of definite importance. These are $\dfrac{e^{\theta} - e^{-\theta}}{2}$ and $\dfrac{e^{\theta} + e^{-\theta}}{2}$, where the exponents are now real. Although these are just simple combinations of the exponential functions e^{θ} and $e^{-\theta}$, they are used so extensively that tables have been prepared for them and names given to them. For reasons that will shortly be made clear, they are called the "hyperbolic sine of the variable θ" and the "hyperbolic cosine of the variable θ" respectively. These are written "$\sinh \theta$" and "$\cosh \theta$." That is, by definition,

$$(1) \qquad\qquad \sinh \theta = \frac{e^{\theta} - e^{-\theta}}{2},$$

$$(2) \qquad\qquad \cosh \theta = \frac{e^{\theta} + e^{-\theta}}{2}.$$

In order to make clear the reference to a hyperbola in these definitions we first reconsider the trigonometric definition of $\sin \theta$ (Fig. 148). Let P$(x,\ y)$ be a point on the circle $x^2 + y^2 = a^2$. Now the area of the sector OAP is equal to $\frac{1}{2}\,a^2\theta$; the area of triangle OAB is $\frac{1}{2}\,a^2$. Thus the angle θ can be thought of as the ratio of the area of the sector to the area of the triangle. That is,

$$(3) \qquad\qquad \theta = \frac{\text{Sector } OAP}{\triangle OAB}$$

Moreover it turns out that

$$(4) \qquad\qquad \sin \theta = \frac{\triangle OAP}{\triangle OAB} = \frac{y}{a},$$

which is in agreement with the usual definition of sin θ where θ is the angle AOP.

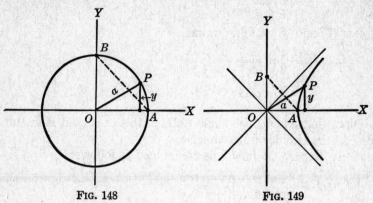

FIG. 148   FIG. 149

In an analogous manner, if the rectangular hyperbola $x^2 - y^2 = a^2$ is used (Fig. 149), it turns out that if

(5) $\theta = \dfrac{\text{Sector } OAP}{\triangle OAB},$

then

(6) $\sinh \theta = \dfrac{\triangle OAP}{\triangle OAB} = \dfrac{y}{a},$

where, now, P is a point on the hyperbola.   For

$$\theta = \frac{\frac{1}{2} xy - \int_a^x \sqrt{x^2 - a^2}\, dx}{\frac{1}{2} a^2},$$

or

$$a^2\theta = xy - 2\int_a^x \sqrt{x^2 - a^2}\, dx$$

$$= xy - \left[x\sqrt{x^2 - a^2} - a^2 \log (x + \sqrt{x^2 - a^2}) \right]_a^x$$

which, after reducing,

$$= a^2 \log \frac{x + y}{a}.$$

Therefore

(7) $e^\theta = \dfrac{x + y}{a};$

and similarly

(8) $e^{-\theta} = \dfrac{a}{x+y}.$

From (7) and (8) it follows that

$$\frac{e^{\theta} - e^{-\theta}}{2} = \frac{1}{2}\left(\frac{x+y}{a} - \frac{a}{x+y}\right)$$

$$= \frac{y}{a} = \sinh \theta.$$

Note that θ is *not* the angle AOP in this case as it is in the case of the circular function $\sin \theta$.

Other hyperbolic functions are defined as follows:

$$\tanh \theta = \frac{\sinh \theta}{\cosh \theta} = \frac{e^{\theta} - e^{-\theta}}{e^{\theta} + e^{-\theta}},$$

$$\coth \theta = \frac{1}{\tanh \theta}, \quad \text{sech } \theta = \frac{1}{\cosh \theta}, \quad \text{csch } \theta = \frac{1}{\sinh \theta}.$$

A trigonometry of hyperbolic functions can be developed comparable to that of the circular function.

Illustration 1. Show that $\cosh^2 \theta - \sinh^2 \theta = 1$.

Solution. $\cosh^2 \theta = \dfrac{(e^{\theta} + e^{-\theta})^2}{4}$

$$= \frac{e^{2\theta} + 2 + e^{-2\theta}}{4}.$$

$$\sinh^2 \theta = \frac{e^{2\theta} - 2 + e^{-2\theta}}{4}.$$

By subtraction the result follows.

Illustration 2. Sketch the graph of $y = \sinh x$.

Solution. $y = \sinh x = \dfrac{e^x - e^{-x}}{2}.$

Using the exponential definition of $\sinh x$ we develop the following table of values.

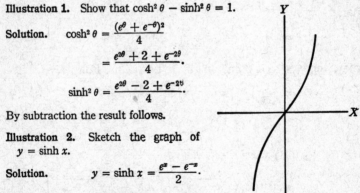

Fig. 150

x	0	1	2	3	∞
$\sinh x$	0	1.2	3.6	10.0	∞

Since $\sinh(-x) = -\sinh x$, the graph (Fig. 150) is symmetric with respect to the origin.

Whereas the direct hyperbolic functions are given in terms of exponentials, the inverse hyperbolic functions involve logarithms. For example, let

$$y = \sinh^{-1} x.$$

Then

$$x = \sinh y$$
$$= \frac{e^y - e^{-y}}{2},$$

which, on multiplying both sides by e^y, becomes a quadratic in e^y, namely,

$$e^{2y} - 2\, xe^y - 1 = 0.$$

Solving this we get

$$e^y = x \pm \sqrt{x^2 + 1},$$

where the minus sign must be discarded since e^y is always positive. Finally, therefore, we have

(9) $$y = \sinh^{-1} x = \log (x + \sqrt{x^2 + 1}),$$

which holds for all values of x.

EXERCISES

Prove the following identities.

1. $\operatorname{sech}^2 \theta = 1 - \tanh^2 \theta$.

2. $\operatorname{csch}^2 \theta = \coth^2 \theta - 1$.

3. $\sinh (x + y) = \sinh x \cosh y + \cosh x \sinh y$.

4. Sketch the graph of $y = \cosh x$.

5. Sketch the graph of $y = \tanh x$.

6. Show that $\sinh ix = i \sin x$.

7. Show that $\cosh ix = \cos x$.

8. Show that $\cosh^{-1} x = \log (x \pm \sqrt{x^2 - 1})$, $x \geq 1$.

9. Show that $\tanh^{-1} x = \frac{1}{2} \log \dfrac{1 + x}{1 - x}$, $-1 < x < 1$

77. Differentiation and Integration of Hyperbolic Functions. By making use of the exponential definitions of the hyperbolic functions the following rules of differentiation are easily verified.

(1) $$\frac{d}{dx} \sinh u = \frac{d}{dx}\left(\frac{e^u - e^{-u}}{2}\right)$$

$$= \frac{e^u + e^{-u}}{2}\frac{du}{dx}$$

$$= \cosh u \frac{du}{dx}.$$

(2) $$\frac{d}{dx} \cosh u = \sinh u \frac{du}{dx}.$$

(3) $$\frac{d}{dx} \tanh u = \operatorname{sech}^2 u \frac{du}{dx}.$$

(4) $$\frac{d}{dx} \coth u = -\operatorname{csch}^2 u \frac{du}{dx}.$$

(5) $$\frac{d}{dx} \operatorname{sech} u = -\operatorname{sech} u \tanh u \frac{du}{dx}.$$

(6) $$\frac{d}{dx} \operatorname{csch} u = -\operatorname{csch} u \coth u \frac{du}{dx}.$$

Further, from the relations given above (§ 76, formula (9) and Exercises 8 and 9) for the inverse hyperbolic functions, it follows that

(7) $$\frac{d}{dx} \sinh^{-1} u = \frac{1}{\sqrt{u^2 + 1}}\frac{du}{dx}, \quad \text{all } u.$$

(8) $$\frac{d}{dx} \cosh^{-1} u = \frac{\pm 1}{\sqrt{u^2 - 1}}\frac{du}{dx}, \quad u > 1.$$

(9) $$\frac{d}{dx} \tanh^{-1} u = \frac{1}{1 - u^2}\frac{du}{dx}, \quad -1 < u < 1.$$

To find the integrals of the elementary hyperbolic functions we may make use of the exponential forms of the functions and of course of the usual methods of integration.

(10) $$\int \sinh u \, du = \tfrac{1}{2}\int (e^u - e^{-u}) \, du$$

$$= \tfrac{1}{2}(e^u + e^{-u}) + c$$

$$= \cosh u + c.$$

(11) $$\int \cosh u \, du = \sinh u + c.$$

(12) $$\int \tanh u \, du = \log \cosh u + c.$$

(13) $$\int \coth u \, du = \log \sinh u + c.$$

Illustration 1. Find $\int \operatorname{sech} u \, du$.

Solution. Write

$$\operatorname{sech} u = \frac{1}{\cosh u}$$

$$= \frac{\cosh u}{\cosh^2 u}$$

$$= \frac{\cosh u}{1 + \sinh^2 u}.$$

Whence

$$\int \operatorname{sech} u \, du = \int \frac{\cosh u \, du}{1 + \sinh^2 u}$$

$$= \int \frac{d(\sinh u)}{1 + \sinh^2 u}$$

$$= \tan^{-1} (\sinh u) + c.$$

Illustration 2. Find $\int x \cosh x \, dx$.

Solution. Integrating by parts, we get

$$\int x \cosh x \, dx = x \sinh x - \int \sinh x \, dx$$

$$= x \sinh x - \cosh x + c.$$

Many of the integrals that we have already met can be expressed in terms of hyperbolic functions. For example, by a slight generalization of formulae (7), (8), and (9) above it follows that

$$(14) \qquad \int \frac{du}{\sqrt{u^2 + a^2}} = \sinh^{-1} \frac{u}{a} + c, \quad \text{all } u$$

$$= \log (u + \sqrt{u^2 + a^2}) + c.$$

$$(15) \qquad \int \frac{du}{\sqrt{u^2 - a^2}} = \cosh^{-1} \frac{u}{a} + c, \quad u \geq a$$

$$= \log (u + \sqrt{u^2 - a^2}) + c.$$

$$(16) \qquad \int \frac{du}{a^2 - u^2} = \frac{1}{a} \tanh^{-1} \frac{u}{a} + c, \quad -a < u < a$$

$$= \frac{1}{2a} \log \frac{a + u}{a - u} + c.$$

EXERCISES

1. Write the equation of the catenary $y = \dfrac{a}{2}\left(e^{\frac{x}{a}} + e^{-\frac{x}{a}}\right)$ in terms of a hyperbolic function.

$$Ans. \quad y = a \cosh \frac{x}{a}.$$

2. Show that $\dfrac{d}{dx} \coth^{-1} u = \dfrac{1}{1 - u^2}\dfrac{du}{dx}, \quad u^2 > 1.$

3. Show that $\displaystyle\int \operatorname{csch} u \, du = \log \tanh \dfrac{u}{2} + c.$

4. Show that $\displaystyle\int \sqrt{u^2 + a^2} \, du = \dfrac{u}{2}\sqrt{u^2 + a^2} + \dfrac{a^2}{2}\sinh^{-1}\dfrac{u}{a} + c$

APPENDIX A

SAMPLE EXAMINATIONS

DIFFERENTIAL CALCULUS

EXAMINATION I

1. Find $\dfrac{dy}{dx}$ in each case:

  (a) $x = e^{\tan y}$;

  (b) $y = \sqrt{\dfrac{x^2 + 2}{1 - 3x}}$;

  (c) $y = \sec (5 x^2 - 7)$;

  (d) $x = \theta + \sin \theta$, $y = 1 - \cos \theta$;

  (e) $y = 2^x + \text{Arc} \sin (1 - 2x)$.

2. A cistern is in the shape of an inverted cone (vertex down), with its diameter equal to its height, each being 10 ft. How fast is the water pouring in when it is 3 ft. deep and rising at the rate of 4 in. per minute? (Leave answer in terms of π.)

3. Find the maximum and minimum values of

$$y = \frac{1 + x + x^2}{1 - x + x^2}.$$

4. A particle is projected vertically upward with an initial velocity of 640 ft./sec. The height y after t sec. is given by $y = 640 t - 16 t^2$.

  (a) How high will the particle rise?
  (b) What will be its velocity when it strikes the ground?
  (c) How long will the particle remain in the air?

5. Find the angle at which the curve whose equation is $x^3 - 3 xy^2 - 2 y + 4 = 0$ cuts the Y-axis.

6. The height h of a tower is deduced from an observation of the angular elevation θ at a fixed distance b from the foot. Find:

(a) The error due to a small error in the observed value of θ;
(b) Find the relative error;
(c) If $b = 100$ ft., $\theta = 30°$, and the error in the angle θ is $1'(= 0.0003$ rad), find the error in calculated height.

7. Sketch the curve $\rho = \dfrac{1}{1 - \cos \theta}$ and find its slope at $\theta = \dfrac{\pi}{3}$.

8. Find, at the point $(1, 1)$, the value of the curvature of $x^{\frac{1}{2}} + y^{\frac{1}{2}} = 2$.

9. Compute:

(a) $\lim\limits_{x \to \infty} \dfrac{e^x}{x^n}$, n a positive integer;

(b) $\lim\limits_{x \to 0} \dfrac{\log x}{\log \sin x}$.

10. A particle moves along the parabola $y^2 = 4x$. At a particular point (x, y), the velocity component in the y direction is 1. Find the velocity component in the x direction and the tangential velocity.

EXAMINATION II

1. Find $\dfrac{dy}{dx}$:

(a) $y = (1 - x^2)^3$ (b) $y = \log (1 - x)$ (c) $y = \sin e^{-x}$
(d) $y = \csc^3 2x$ (e) $y = (1 - x)^2(x^3 + 1)$ (f) $xy^2 + \log (x + y) = 1$

2. Find the minimum value of $y = x^2 + \dfrac{1}{x^2}$.

3. (a) Find the slope of the curve $x = a(\theta - \sin \theta)$, $y = a(1 - \cos \theta)$ at $\theta = 60°$.

(b) For $\rho = a(1 - \cos \theta)$ find the slope at $\theta = \dfrac{\pi}{6}$.

4. The diameter of a circle is found by measurement to be 5.2 inches, with a maximum error of 0.05 in. Find the percentage error made in computing the area.

5. A rectangular storage space, to contain 7,200 sq. ft., is to be fenced off adjacent to a factory. If no fence is needed along the factory, what must be the dimensions requiring the least amount of fencing?

6. Evaluate

$$\text{(a)} \ \lim_{x \to \infty} \frac{\log x^n}{x^2},$$

$$\text{(b)} \ \lim_{x \to \frac{\pi}{2}} \left(x - \frac{\pi}{2} \right) \tan x.$$

7. Find the radius of curvature of $y = \sin x$ at $x = \frac{\pi}{3}$.

8. A point P moves in accord with the equations $x = a \cos t$, $y = b \sin t$.

(a) Find the least positive value of t for which the speed of P is a maximum.

(b) At that instant find the magnitude and direction of the acceleration vector.

9. Find the Cartesian equation of the evolute of the parabola $x^2 = 2 y$.

10. Find the equation of the line normal to the curve $y = x^3 + 6 x^2 - 2 x + 8$ at the point of inflection.

INTEGRAL CALCULUS

EXAMINATION III

1.

$$\text{(a)} \ \int x \tan x^2 \, dx;$$

$$\text{(b)} \ \int \frac{2 x + 1}{(x - 1)(x + 2)} \, dx;$$

$$\text{(c)} \ \int_0^{\frac{1}{2}} 3 \, x e^{2x} \, dx.$$

2. Find the area under one arch of the curve $x = a\theta$, $y = a(1 - \cos \theta)$.

3. A trough 10 ft. long and whose cross section is a triangle 4 ft. deep and 6 ft. across at the top is full of water. Find the total force on one end.

4. Find the value of $\bar{x}$ for the area bounded by the circles $\rho = 4 \cos \theta$ and $\rho = 8 \cos \theta$.

5. Find the moment of inertia about the x-axis of the solid formed by revolving about the y-axis that portion of the curve $2y - 4 + x^2 = 0$ lying in the first quadrant.

6. Expand $\cos x$ in a Taylor Series in powers of $\left(x - \frac{\pi}{4}\right)$.

7. Using Simpson's Rule and four strips, find the approximate area bounded by $y = \frac{1}{100} x^4$, $x = 1$, $y = 0$, and $x = 5$.

8. (a) Find the equation of the plane tangent to $x^2 + y^2 + z^2 = 14$ at $(1, 2, 3)$.

(b) Find the directional derivative of $z = xy^2$ at $(1, 2, 4)$ in the direction $\alpha = \tan^{-1} 2$.

9. (a) Find the sum of the series $1 - \frac{1}{2!} + \frac{1}{3!} - \frac{1}{4!} + \cdots$ correct to the first three decimal places.

(b) Find the interval of convergence of the series $x - \frac{x^2}{2} + \frac{x^3}{3} - \frac{x^4}{4} + \cdots$. Test the end points.

10. Use cylindrical coordinates and triple integration to find the volume which lies inside $x^2 + y^2 = z$ and outside $x^2 + y^2 = 4(z - 1)$.

EXAMINATION IV

1.

(a) $\int 3x\sqrt{1 - 2x^2}\, dx$;

(b) $\int \sin^2 (2x - 5)\, dx$;

(c) $\int_0^{2\sqrt{2}} (8x^2 - x^4)\, dx$.

2. Find the area, regardless of sign, enclosed between $y = \sin x$ and $y = \cos x$ between consecutive points of intersection.

3. Find the area of the surface of revolution generated by revolving about the y-axis the arc of $y = x^2$ from $(0, 0)$ to $(2, 4)$.

4. A vertical cylindrical cistern of radius 8 ft. and depth 10 ft. is full of an oil weighing w lbs./cu. ft. Calculate the work necessary to pump the water to a height of 15 ft. above the top of the cistern.

5. Find the length of that part of the curve $9\,y^2 = 4\,x^3$ joining $(0, 0)$ and $(3, 2\sqrt{3})$.

6. Find the value of $\bar{y}$ for the area of the segment of the ellipse $x^2 + 4\,y^2 = 4$ in the first quadrant cut off by the line $x + 2\,y - 2 = 0$.

7. The resistance R (ohms) of a circuit was found by using the formula $R = \dfrac{E}{i}$, where E = voltage (volts) and i = current (amperes). If there is an error of 0.1 amp. in reading $i(= 10)$ and 0.1 volt in reading $E(= 100)$, what is the approximate maximum error in the computed value of R?

8. The volume of a cylinder is increasing at the rate of $2\,\pi$ cu. ft./min. How is the radius changing, when $r = 4$ ft. and $h = 20$ ft. if the height is increasing at the rate of 6 ft./min.?

9. Expand $\tan x$ in the neighborhood of $x = \dfrac{\pi}{4}$, finding four terms.

10. (a) Set up the triple integral for the volume of the ellipsoid $\dfrac{x^2}{a^2} + \dfrac{y^2}{b^2} + \dfrac{z^2}{c^2} = 1$.

(b) A volume is generated by revolving the area of the ellipse $\dfrac{(x - h)^2}{a^2} + \dfrac{(y - k)^2}{b^2} = 1$ about the line $x = h - a$. Use Pappus' Theorem to find the volume, having given the area of the ellipse $A = \pi ab$.

ANSWERS TO EXAMINATIONS

Examination I

1. (a) $\dfrac{1}{x}\cos^2 y$ (d) $\dfrac{\sin \theta}{1 + \cos \theta}$

(b) $\dfrac{1}{2}\sqrt{\dfrac{1 - 3x}{x^2 + 2}}\left(\dfrac{6 + 2x - 3x^2}{(1 - 3x)^2}\right)$ (e) $2^x \log 2 - \dfrac{1}{\sqrt{x - x^2}}$

(c) $10x \sec (5x^2 - 7) \tan (5x^2 - 7)$

2. $\frac{3}{4}\pi$ cu. ft./min.

3. Max., 3; min., $\frac{1}{3}$.

4. (a) 6400 ft.; (b) -640 ft./sec.; (c) 40 sec.

5. Arc cot 6.

6. (a) $dh = b \sec^2 \theta \, d\theta$; (b) $\dfrac{dh}{h} = \sec \theta \csc \theta \, d\theta$; (c) .04 ft.

7. $\frac{1}{3}\sqrt{3}$.

8. $\frac{1}{4}\sqrt{2}$.

9. (a) ∞; (b) 1.

10. $\dfrac{y}{2}$, $\sqrt{x+1}$.

Examination II

1. (a) $-6x(1-x^2)^2$

   (b) $\dfrac{1}{x-1}$

   (c) $-e^{-x}\cos e^{-x}$

   (d) $-6\csc^3 2x \cot 2x$

   (e) $3x^2(1-x)^2 - 2(1-x)(x^3+1)$

   (f) $-\dfrac{1+y^2(x+y)}{1+2xy(x+y)}$

2. 2.

3. (a) $\sqrt{3}$; (b) 1.

4. 1.92%.

5. $60' \times 120'$ (long side along the factory).

6. (a) 0; (b) -1.

7. $\dfrac{\sqrt{3}}{12}$ $(5)^{\frac{3}{2}}$.

8. (a) $t = \dfrac{\pi}{2}$; (b) $|a| = b, \varphi = \dfrac{\pi}{2}$.

9. $8(y-1)^3 = 27x^2$.

10. $x - 14y + 394 = 0$.

Examination III

1. (a) $-\frac{1}{2}\log \cos x^2 + c$;

   (b) $\log (x-1)(x+2) + c$;

   (c) $\frac{3}{4}$.

2. $2\pi a^2$ sq. units.

3. $16w$.

4. $\frac{14}{3}$.

5. $\frac{16}{3}\pi$.

6. $\cos x = \dfrac{\sqrt{2}}{2}\left[1 - \dfrac{\left(x - \frac{\pi}{4}\right)}{1!} - \dfrac{\left(x - \frac{\pi}{4}\right)^2}{2!} + \dfrac{\left(x - \frac{\pi}{4}\right)^3}{3!} + \cdots \right]$.

7. 6.253 sq. units.

8. (a) $x + 2y + 3z - 14 = 0$; (b) $\frac{12}{5}\sqrt{5}$.

9. (a) 0.632.

   (b) $-1 < x \leqq 1$.

10. $\frac{2}{3}\pi$ cu. units.

Examination IV

1. (a) $-\frac{1}{2}(1-2x^2)^{\frac{3}{2}} + c$;

   (b) $\frac{1}{2}x - \frac{1}{8}\sin 2(2x-5) + c$;

   (c) $\frac{256}{15}\sqrt{2}$.

2. $2\sqrt{2}$ sq. units.

3. $\frac{\pi}{6}(17\sqrt{17} - 1)$ sq. units.

4. $12,800\ \pi w$ ft.-lbs.

5. $\frac{14}{3}$.

6. $\bar{y} = \dfrac{2}{3(\pi - 2)}$.

7. 0.11 ohm.

8. Decreasing at the rate of $\frac{47}{80}$ ft./min.

9. $\tan x = 1 + 2\left(x - \dfrac{\pi}{4}\right) + 2\left(x - \dfrac{\pi}{4}\right)^2 + \dfrac{8}{3}\left(x - \dfrac{\pi}{4}\right)^3 + \cdots$.

10. (a) $V = 8\displaystyle\int_0^a \int_0^{b\sqrt{1-\frac{x^2}{a^2}}} \int_0^{c\sqrt{1-\frac{x^2}{a^2}-\frac{y^2}{b^2}}} dz\,dy\,dx$;

    (b) $2\pi^2 a^2 b$ cu. units.

APPENDIX B

SHORT TABLE OF INTEGRALS

1. $\int u^n \, du = \dfrac{u^{n+1}}{n+1} + c, \quad n \neq -1$

2. $\int \dfrac{du}{u} = \log u + c$

3. $\int \dfrac{du}{u(a+bu)} = -\dfrac{1}{a} \log \left(\dfrac{a+bu}{u} \right) + c$

4. $\int \dfrac{du}{u(a+bu)^2} = \dfrac{1}{a(a+bu)} - \dfrac{1}{a^2} \log \left(\dfrac{a+bu}{u} \right) + c$

5. $\int \dfrac{du}{u^2(a+bu)} = -\dfrac{1}{au} + \dfrac{b}{a^2} \log \left(\dfrac{a+bu}{u} \right) + c$

6. $\int u\sqrt{a+bu} \, du = -\dfrac{2(2a-3bu)(a+bu)^{\frac{3}{2}}}{15\,b^2} + c$

7. $\int u^2\sqrt{a+bu} \, du = \dfrac{2(8a^2 - 12abu + 15b^2u^2)(a+bu)^{\frac{3}{2}}}{105\,b^3} + c$

8. $\int u^m\sqrt{a+bu} \, du = \dfrac{2\,u^m(a+bu)^{\frac{3}{2}}}{b(2m+3)} - \dfrac{2\,am}{b(2m+3)} \int u^{m-1}\sqrt{a+bu} \, du$

9. $\int \dfrac{u \, du}{\sqrt{a+bu}} = -\dfrac{2(2a-bu)\sqrt{a+bu}}{3\,b^2} + c$

10. $\int \dfrac{u^2 \, du}{\sqrt{a+bu}} = \dfrac{2(8a^2 - 4abu + 3b^2u^2)\sqrt{a+bu}}{15\,b^3} + c$

11. $\int \dfrac{u^m \, du}{\sqrt{a+bu}} = \dfrac{2\,u^m\sqrt{a+bu}}{b(2m+1)} - \dfrac{2\,am}{b(2m+1)} \int \dfrac{u^{m-1} \, du}{\sqrt{a+bu}}$

12. $\int \dfrac{du}{u\sqrt{a+bu}} = \dfrac{2}{\sqrt{-a}} \tan^{-1} \sqrt{\dfrac{a+bu}{-a}} + c, \text{ for } a < 0$

13. $\int \dfrac{du}{u\sqrt{a+bu}} = \dfrac{1}{\sqrt{a}} \log \dfrac{\sqrt{a+bu}-\sqrt{a}}{\sqrt{a+bu}+\sqrt{a}} + c, \text{ for } a > 0$

14. $\int \dfrac{du}{u^m\sqrt{a+bu}} = -\dfrac{\sqrt{a+bu}}{a(m-1)u^{m-1}} - \dfrac{b(2m-3)}{2\,a(m-1)} \int \dfrac{du}{u^{m-1}\sqrt{a+bu}}$

15. $\int \dfrac{\sqrt{a+bu} \, du}{u} = 2\sqrt{a+bu} + a \int \dfrac{du}{u\sqrt{a+bu}}$

16. $\displaystyle\int \frac{\sqrt{a+bu}\,du}{u^m} = -\frac{(a+bu)^{\frac{3}{2}}}{a(m-1)u^{m-1}} - \frac{b(2m-5)}{2\,a(m-1)}\int \frac{\sqrt{a+bu}\,du}{u^{m-1}}$

17. $\displaystyle\int \sqrt{2\,au-u^2}\,du = \frac{u-a}{2}\sqrt{2\,au-u^2} + \frac{a^2}{2}\cos^{-1}\frac{a-u}{a} + c$

18. $\displaystyle\int u\sqrt{2\,au-u^2}\,du = -\frac{3\,a^2+au-2\,u^2}{6}\sqrt{2\,au-u^2}$
$$+ \frac{a^3}{2}\cos^{-1}\frac{a-u}{a} + c$$

19. $\displaystyle\int u^m\sqrt{2\,au-u^2}\,du = -\frac{u^{m-1}(2\,au-u^2)^{\frac{3}{2}}}{m+2}$
$$+ \frac{a(2m+1)}{m+2}\int u^{m-1}\sqrt{2\,au-u^2}\,du$$

20. $\displaystyle\int \frac{\sqrt{2\,au-u^2}\,du}{u} = \sqrt{2\,au-u^2} + a\cos^{-1}\frac{a-u}{a} + c$

21. $\displaystyle\int \frac{\sqrt{2\,au-u^2}\,du}{u^m} = -\frac{(2\,au-u^2)^{\frac{3}{2}}}{a(2m-3)u^m} + \frac{m-3}{a(2m-3)}\int \frac{\sqrt{2\,au-u^2}\,du}{u^{m-1}}$

22. $\displaystyle\int \frac{du}{\sqrt{2\,au-u^2}} = \cos^{-1}\frac{a-u}{a} + c$

23. $\displaystyle\int \frac{du}{\sqrt{2\,au+u^2}} = \log\left(u+a+\sqrt{2\,au+u^2}\right) + c$

24. $\displaystyle\int \frac{u\,du}{\sqrt{2\,au-u^2}} = -\sqrt{2\,au-u^2} + a\cos^{-1}\frac{a-u}{a} + c$

25. $\displaystyle\int \frac{du}{u\sqrt{2\,au-u^2}} = -\frac{\sqrt{2\,au-u^2}}{au} + c$

26. $\displaystyle\int \sqrt{\frac{a+u}{b+u}}\,du = \sqrt{(a+u)(b+u)} + (a-b)\log\left(\sqrt{a+u}+\sqrt{b+u}\right) + c$

27. $\displaystyle\int \sqrt{\frac{a-u}{b+u}}\,du = \sqrt{(a-u)(b+u)} + (a+b)\sin^{-1}\sqrt{\frac{u+b}{a+b}} + c$

28. $\displaystyle\int \sqrt{\frac{a+u}{b-u}}\,du = -\sqrt{(a+u)(b-u)} - (a+b)\sin^{-1}\sqrt{\frac{b-u}{a+b}} + c$

29. $\displaystyle\int \frac{du}{\sqrt{(u-a)(b-u)}} = 2\sin^{-1}\sqrt{\frac{u-a}{b-a}} + c$

30. $\displaystyle\int \frac{du}{a^2+u^2} = \frac{1}{a}\tan^{-1}\frac{u}{a} + c$

31. $\displaystyle\int \frac{du}{a^2-u^2} = \frac{1}{2\,a}\log\frac{a+u}{a-u} + c, \quad u^2 < a^2$

32. $\int \dfrac{du}{u^2 - a^2} = \dfrac{1}{2a} \log \dfrac{u - a}{u + a} + c, \quad u^2 > a^2$

33. $\int \dfrac{du}{(u^2 + a^2)^n} = \dfrac{1}{2(n-1)a^2} \left[\dfrac{u}{(u^2 + a^2)^{n-1}} + (2n-3) \int \dfrac{du}{(u^2 + a^2)^{n-1}} \right]$

34. $\int (u^2 \pm a^2)^{\frac{1}{2}} \, du = \dfrac{u}{2} \sqrt{u^2 \pm a^2} \pm \dfrac{a^2}{2} \log (u + \sqrt{u^2 \pm a^2}) + c$

35. $\int \dfrac{du}{(u^2 \pm a^2)^{\frac{1}{2}}} = \log (u + \sqrt{u^2 \pm a^2}) + c$

36. $\int \dfrac{u^2 \, du}{(u^2 \pm a^2)^{\frac{1}{2}}} = \dfrac{u}{2} \sqrt{u^2 \pm a^2} - \dfrac{\pm a^2}{2} \log (u + \sqrt{u^2 \pm a^2}) + c$

37. $\int \dfrac{u^2 \, du}{(u^2 \pm a^2)^{\frac{3}{2}}} = - \dfrac{u}{\sqrt{u^2 \pm a^2}} + \log (u + \sqrt{u^2 \pm a^2}) + c$

38. $\int \dfrac{du}{u(u^2 + a^2)^{\frac{1}{2}}} = - \dfrac{1}{a} \log \left(\dfrac{a + \sqrt{u^2 + a^2}}{u} \right) + c$

39. $\int \dfrac{du}{u(u^2 - a^2)^{\frac{1}{2}}} = \dfrac{1}{a} \sec^{-1} \dfrac{u}{a} + c$

40. $\int \dfrac{du}{u^2(u^2 \pm a^2)^{\frac{1}{2}}} = - \dfrac{\sqrt{u^2 \pm a^2}}{\pm a^2 u} + c$

41. $\int \dfrac{(u^2 + a^2)^{\frac{1}{2}} \, du}{u} = \sqrt{u^2 + a^2} - a \log \left(\dfrac{a + \sqrt{u^2 + a^2}}{u} \right) + c$

42. $\int \dfrac{(u^2 - a^2)^{\frac{1}{2}} \, du}{u} = \sqrt{u^2 - a^2} - a \sec^{-1} \dfrac{u}{a} + c$

43. $\int \dfrac{(u^2 \pm a^2)^{\frac{1}{2}} \, du}{u^2} = - \dfrac{\sqrt{u^2 \pm a^2}}{u} + \log (u + \sqrt{u^2 \pm a^2}) + c$

44. $\int (a^2 - u^2)^{\frac{1}{2}} \, du = \dfrac{u}{2} \sqrt{a^2 - u^2} + \dfrac{a^2}{2} \sin^{-1} \dfrac{u}{a} + c$

45. $\int \dfrac{du}{(a^2 - u^2)^{\frac{1}{2}}} = \sin^{-1} \dfrac{u}{a} + c$

46. $\int \dfrac{du}{(a^2 - u^2)^{\frac{3}{2}}} = \dfrac{u}{a^2 \sqrt{a^2 - u^2}} + c$

47. $\int \dfrac{u^2 \, du}{(a^2 - u^2)^{\frac{1}{2}}} = - \dfrac{u}{2} \sqrt{a^2 - u^2} + \dfrac{a^2}{2} \sin^{-1} \dfrac{u}{a} + c$

48. $\int (a^2 - u^2)^{\frac{3}{2}} \, du = \dfrac{u}{4} (a^2 - u^2)^{\frac{3}{2}} + \dfrac{3 a^2 u}{8} \sqrt{a^2 - u^2} + \dfrac{3 a^4}{8} \sin^{-1} \dfrac{u}{a} + c$

49. $\int u^2(a^2 - u^2)^{\frac{1}{2}} \, du = \dfrac{u}{8} (2u^2 - a^2) \sqrt{a^2 - u^2} + \dfrac{a^4}{8} \sin^{-1} \dfrac{u}{a} + c$

50. $\displaystyle\int e^{au}\, du = \frac{e^{au}}{a} + c$

51. $\displaystyle\int b^{au}\, du = \frac{b^{au}}{a \log b} + c$

52. $\displaystyle\int u e^{au}\, du = \frac{e^{au}}{a^2} (au - 1) + c$

53. $\displaystyle\int u^n e^{au}\, du = \frac{u^n e^{au}}{a} - \frac{n}{a} \int u^{n-1} e^{au}\, du$

54. $\displaystyle\int \log u\, du = u \log u - u + c$

55. $\displaystyle\int u^n \log u\, du = u^{n+1} \left[\frac{\log u}{n+1} - \frac{1}{(n+1)^2} \right] + c$

56. $\displaystyle\int e^{au} \log u\, du = \frac{e^{au} \log u}{a} - \frac{1}{a} \int \frac{e^{au}}{u}\, du$

57. $\displaystyle\int \frac{du}{u \log u} = \log (\log u) + c$

58. $\displaystyle\int \sin u\, du = - \cos u + c$

59. $\displaystyle\int \cos u\, du = \sin u + c$

60. $\displaystyle\int \tan u\, du = \log \sec u + c$

61. $\displaystyle\int \cot u\, du = \log \sin u + c$

62. $\displaystyle\int \sec u\, du = \log (\sec u + \tan u) + c$
$$= \log \tan \left(\frac{u}{2} + \frac{\pi}{4} \right) + c'$$

63. $\displaystyle\int \csc u\, du = \log (\csc u - \cot u) + c$
$$= \log \tan \frac{u}{2} + c'$$

64. $\displaystyle\int \sin^2 u\, du = \frac{u}{2} - \frac{1}{4} \sin 2u + c$

65. $\displaystyle\int \sin^3 u\, du = - \frac{1}{3} \cos u\, (\sin^2 u + 2) + c$

66. $\displaystyle\int \sin^4 u\, du = \frac{3}{8} u - \frac{\sin 2u}{4} + \frac{\sin 4u}{32} + c$

67. $\displaystyle\int \sin^n u\, du = - \frac{\sin^{n-1} u \cos u}{n} + \frac{n-1}{n} \int \sin^{n-2} u\, du$

68. $\int \cos^2 u \, du = \dfrac{u}{2} + \dfrac{1}{4} \sin 2u + c$

69. $\int \cos^3 u \, du = \frac{1}{3} \sin u \, (\cos^2 u + 2) + c$

70. $\int \cos^4 u \, du = \dfrac{3}{8} u + \dfrac{\sin 2u}{4} + \dfrac{\sin 4u}{32} + e$

71. $\int \cos^n u \, du = \dfrac{\cos^{n-1} u \sin u}{n} + \dfrac{n-1}{n} \int \cos^{n-2} u \, du$

72. $\int \tan^n u \, du = \dfrac{\tan^{n-1} u}{n-1} - \int \tan^{n-2} u \, du$

73. $\int \cot^n u \, du = -\dfrac{\cot^{n-1} u}{n-1} - \int \cot^{n-2} u \, du$

74. $\int \sec^n u \, du = \dfrac{\sin u}{(n-1) \cos^{n-1} u} + \dfrac{n-2}{n-1} \int \sec^{n-2} u \, du$

75. $\int \csc^n u \, du = -\dfrac{\cos u}{(n-1) \sin^{n-1} u} + \dfrac{n-2}{n-1} \int \csc^{n-2} u \, du$

76. $\int \cos^m u \sin^n u \, du = \dfrac{\cos^{m-1} u \sin^{n+1} u}{m+n} + \dfrac{m-1}{m+n} \int \cos^{m-2} u \sin^n u \, du$

77. $\int \cos^m u \sin^n u \, du = -\dfrac{\sin^{n-1} u \cos^{m+1} u}{m+n} + \dfrac{n-1}{m+n} \int \cos^m u \sin^{n-2} u \, du$

78. $\int \sin mu \sin nu \, du = -\dfrac{\sin (m+n)u}{2(m+n)} + \dfrac{\sin (m-n)u}{2(m-n)} + c$

79. $\int \cos mu \cos nu \, du = \dfrac{\sin (m+n)u}{2(m+n)} + \dfrac{\sin (m-n)u}{2(m-n)} + c$

80. $\int \sin mu \cos nu \, du = -\dfrac{\cos (m+n)u}{2(m+n)} - \dfrac{\cos (m-n)u}{2(m-n)} + c$

81. $\int u \sin u \, du = \sin u - u \cos u + c$

82. $\int u^2 \sin u \, du = 2u \sin u - (u^2 - 2) \cos u + c$

83. $\int u^m \sin au \, du = \dfrac{u^{m-1}}{a^2} (m \sin au - au \cos au)$
$$- \dfrac{m(m-1)}{a^2} \int u^{m-2} \sin au \, du$$

84. $\int u \cos u \, du = \cos u + u \sin u + c$

85. $\int u^2 \cos u \, du = 2u \cos u + (u^2 - 2) \sin u + c$

86. $\int u^m \cos au \, du = \dfrac{u^{m-1}}{a^2} (au \sin au + m \cos au)$
$$- \dfrac{m(m-1)}{a^2} \int u^{m-2} \cos au \, du$$

87. $\displaystyle\int e^{au} \sin nu \, du = \frac{e^{au}(a \sin nu - n \cos nu)}{a^2 + n^2} + c$

88. $\displaystyle\int e^{au} \cos nu \, du = \frac{e^{au}(n \sin nu + a \cos nu)}{a^2 + n^2} + c$

89. $\displaystyle\int \sin^{-1} \frac{u}{a} \, du = u \sin^{-1} \frac{u}{a} + \sqrt{a^2 - u^2} + c$

90. $\displaystyle\int \cos^{-1} \frac{u}{a} \, du = u \cos^{-1} \frac{u}{a} - \sqrt{a^2 - u^2} + c$

91. $\displaystyle\int \tan^{-1} \frac{u}{a} \, du = u \tan^{-1} \frac{u}{a} - \frac{a}{2} \log (a^2 + u^2) + c$

92. $\displaystyle\int \cot^{-1} \frac{u}{a} \, du = u \cot^{-1} \frac{u}{a} + \frac{a}{2} \log (a^2 + u^2) + c$

93. $\displaystyle\int \sec^{-1} \frac{u}{a} \, du = u \sec^{-1} \frac{u}{a} - a \log (u + \sqrt{u^2 - a^2}) + c$

94. $\displaystyle\int \csc^{-1} \frac{u}{a} \, du = u \csc^{-1} \frac{u}{a} + a \log (u + \sqrt{u^2 - a^2}) + c$

95. $\displaystyle\int \sinh u \, du = \cosh u + c$

96. $\displaystyle\int \cosh u \, du = \sinh u + c$

97. $\displaystyle\int \tanh u \, du = \log \cosh u + c$

98. $\displaystyle\int \coth u \, du = \log \sinh u + c$

99. $\displaystyle\int \operatorname{sech} u \, du = 2 \tan^{-1} e^u + c = \tan^{-1} \sinh u + c'$

100. $\displaystyle\int \operatorname{csch} u \, du = \log \tanh \frac{u}{2} + c = \tan^{-1} \cosh u + c'$

INDEX